PARTICIPATION, ACHIEVEMENT, AND INVOLVEMENT ON THE JOB

PARTICIPATION, ACHIEVEMENT, AND INVOLVEMENT ON THE JOB

Martin Patchen

Purdue University
Lafayette, Indiana

PRENTICE-HALL, INC.

Englewood Cliffs, New Jersey

© 1970

by PRENTICE-HALL, Inc.
Englewood Cliffs, New Jersey

C- 13-651380-8
P- 13-651372-7
Library of Congress
Catalog Card Number 76-97903

Current Printing (Last Digit)
10 9 8 7 6 5 4 3 2 1

PRENTICE-HALL INTERNATIONAL, INC., *London*
PRENTICE-HALL OF AUSTRALIA PTY, LTD., *Sydney*
PRENTICE-HALL OF CANADA, LTD., *Toronto*
PRENTICE-HALL OF INDIA PRIVATE LTD., *New Delhi*
PRENTICE-HALL OF JAPAN, INC., *Tokyo*

Printed in the United States of America

To the men and women of TVA

PREFACE

As our society becomes more affluent and our people become more mobile, there is increasing attention being given to the job as more than just the source of a "living." Sheer economic survival is less pressing for most and traditional social ties of community, family, and church have been loosened. In this context, a man's job is increasingly recognized as a key both to his personal fulfillment and to his relation to society. On the one hand, a job may contribute heavily to his feelings of purposelessness and alienation from one's fellows which some observers see as common by-products of modern "mass society." On the other hand, the job may be his major source of accomplishment, of pride, and of social identification.

Whether people are alienated or involved on the job is of interest not only to those who are concerned with the psychological well-being of individuals or with the general social good. It is increasingly important also to those who are responsible for the efficient operation of business, government, and other organizations. For the growing complexity of jobs brought by advancing technology means that a high level of job involvement, rather than merely "putting in time," is increasingly needed in order for jobs to be done well.

The ideas and evidence presented in this volume are intended to further our understanding of the factors which lead to greater or lesser employee involvement in their jobs. It reports the results of a study conducted by the Survey Research Center, University of Michigan, in parts of the Tennessee Valley Authority. A first major focus of the study is on characteristics of the job situation and of the individual which may be relevant to achievement on the job. This aspect of the study represents, in part, an attempt to extend some of the stimulating work on achievement motivation from the laboratory to the industrial setting.

The theoretical approach underlying the analysis is based on the work of John W. Atkinson, David C. McClelland, and their associates. However, whereas these investigators have conceived of the motive for achievement as being a relatively fixed personality characteristic, the motive for achievement is conceived here as something which may vary as the rewards for achievement in the work situation vary. Thus, this volume proposes a somewhat modified theoretical approach to achievement motivation and presents some data relevent to this conception.

In considering any job situation, there are a large number of job, organizational, and personal characteristics which may affect motivation. The general concepts of motive, incentive, and expectation, taken from the Atkinson model of achievement motivation, are used to bring order to these many aspects of the situation. Those job features most relevant to achievement incentive (i.e., the amount of achievement posssible), as well as to the expectancy that achievement will result from effort, are considered under the heading of *opportunities for achievement*. Those job and personal characteristics most relevant to the motive for achievement (i.e., how much achievement is valued) are considered under the heading of *rewards for achievement*.

In examining the relation of job and personal characteristics to motivation, to pride, and to symptoms of stress, I have tried to go beyond studies that have considered the effects of only one or a few such characteristics. Instead, the effects of each "causal" factor are examined in combination with other relevant factors and when other factors are held constant. Although such analyses necessarily lead to some complexity in the results and in their presentation, they provide a more sophisticated view than would be possible with simpler techniques.

The second major aspect of the study concerns employees' feelings of identification with the work organization—their sense of belonging, of common purpose, of loyalty. Relatively little work has been done to try to understand the conditions which produce identification with organizations. This may be due in part to the difficulty of measuring a relatively intangible characteristic like identification. The present study has the advantage of being able to draw upon prior measurement work from the same project which has provided a scale of organizational identification. This measure, though still a rough one, has some evidence of adequate reliability and validity. This study also is more extensive than most previous work on organizational identification in considering simultaneously the relation between organizational identification and a variety of job and personal factors.

Previous theoretical discussions of identification with groups or organizations have been few and generally unsatisfactory. The present work does not present a comprehensive theoretical treatment of this topic. However, it does offer some general ideas which, it is hoped, will be helpful in clarifying the conception of organizational identification and in furthering our understanding of its determinants. Although focusing on identification with organizations, the general approach to identification has implications for the study of individual identification with other social units—e.g., regligious groupings, political parties, ethnic groups, etc.

The data presented show the relation of organizational identification to a wide range of organizational and personal characteristics. However, they give particular attention to the relation between identification and employee participation in decision making. The rather dramatic effects of a participation program on employee attitudes toward the organization will be of interest, I believe, both to social scientists and to those with managerial responsibility in organizations.

The choice of the Tennessee Valley Authority as a site for this study was due primarily to a coincidence of our interests and those of TVA management in the topic of employee involvement. However, TVA turned out to have several characteristics that made it an especially good place to study job involvement. First, the existence of its ambitious program of labor-management consultation—the "cooperative" program—provided an opportunity to study some of the effects on employee job involvement of this type of participation program. Secondly, the wide range of jobs and types of units, and the geographical dispersion of units, provided considerable variation in many organizational and personal characteristics which may affect job involvement.

The primary focus of this work is on furthering our basic understanding of job involvement, rather than in offering specific suggestions to people in organizations. However, the findings presented here may be useful in indicating general guidelines for those who are interested in increasing employee involvement. Some fairly specific suggestions in this direction are given in the final chapter.

MARTIN PATCHEN

ACKNOWLEDGMENTS

Most of the work for this project was supported by grants M4514 and MH08624-01 from the National Institutes of Health to the University of of Michigan, with Donald C. Pelz and myself as principal investigators. Dr. Pelz participated actively in the early phases of the project and contributed to an earlier book on measures of employee motivation and morale (Patchen, Pelz, and Allen, 1965). However, a two-year assignment in India prevented him from taking part in the preparation of this volume.

Craig W. Allen also participated in the early phases of the project, particularly in exploratory work and writing of questionnaire items. Susanna Y. Hubley provided skilled assistance in a variety of tasks, expecially in processing the research data, during the first two years of the project, and Alison Clark took over these tasks in the latter part of the project. Nancy Robinson and Phyllis Kreger did an excellent job of typing successive drafts of the manuscript.

This study would have been impossible without the generous cooperation we received from the management, union officials and employees of the Tennessee Valley Authority. We are grateful to all the TVA people, from members of the Board of Directors to the least skilled workers who gave us their time, their encouragement, their suggestions and their help. While the list of persons who helped us is a long one, I must make special mention of the continual and vital assistance we received from Lloyd L. Huntington, staff officer (now retired) of the Personnel Division of TVA.

For their helpful comments on portions of the manuscript, I would like to thank Arnold Tannenbaum, Jerald Bachman, Ezra Stotland, and Harry Crockett, Jr. To my wife Suzie, I am grateful for her encouragement and for her help in reading proofs.

MARTIN PATCHEN

CONTENTS

IDENTIFICATION
WITH THE WORK III
ORGANIZATION

8 Organizational Identification: Its Meaning and Determinants   155

9 Organizational Identification at TVA   169

10 Participation in Decision Making and Identification   181

11 Other Correlates of Identification   200

CONCLUSION **IV**

BACKGROUND
AND SETTING

PART I

THE PROBLEM
OF JOB
INVOLVEMENT

It is a truism, but an important one, that most adult men, and many women, spend the largest single segment of their lives at a job. The quality of their experience at work thus becomes a large part of the quality of their experience of life. While work hours have become shorter and will likely become shorter still, the central importance of work continues. This is true not only because of the sheer amount of time spent at work but because, as Blauner (1964) points out, the nature of a man's work affects his social character and his sense of worth and dignity.[1]

Much of the commentary and systematic inquiry into the effect of the job on the individual may, for convenience, be loosely grouped into three general categories: (1) the personal goals which are present on the job; (2) the social identification which the job provides; and (3) affective feelings on the job. In the following sections, we will briefly outline some of the problems which have been discussed in the literature and will indicate in this context the concerns and scope of the present study.

---

[1]For data and discussions on the meaning of work, see Palmer (1957); Morse and Weiss (1955); Tilgher (1930); Havighurst (1954); Weiss and Kahn (1960); Hearnshaw (1954).

PERSONAL GOALS IN WORK

In discussing aspects of the "alienation" which may be characteristic of people in modern society, sociologists have pointed to several phenomena which closely relate to the presence or absence of personal goals.[2] Seeman (1959) clarified the somewhat vague concept of "self-estrangement" as referring "essentially to the inability of the individual to find self-reward-ing—or in Dewey's phrase, self-consummatory—activities that engage him." In discussing alienation in industry, Blauner (1964) writes of "self-estrangement" as a state where "work becomes primarily instrumental, a means toward future considerations rather than an end in itself" (p. 26). Self-estrangement, Blauner writes, is experienced as monotony, a height-ened awareness of time ("clock-watching"), and detachment. Its opposite is interest and involvement in the work.

A related aspect of alienation, discussed by Dean (1961), is "purposeless-ness." He defines this feeling, following McIver (1950), as in part the "absence of values that might give purpose or direction to life." He illus-trates the opposite of purposelessness with the case of Polish Jewish physi-cians in the Warsaw ghetto who continued medical research in the face of their impending slaughter by the Nazis.

Another relevant aspect of alienation discussed by sociologists—Seeman, 1959; Dean, 1961, and by Blauner (1964) specifically in a work context—is "meaninglessness." Because of the division of labor which occurs in large work organizations, the individual may not see, or may disparage, the contribution which his particular work makes to some larger product or effort. The result, says Blauner, is that the employee may lack "a sense of purpose in his work" (p. 22). A number of other observers, often using different terminology, have also pointed to the individual's lack of felt social purpose in doing a specialized job which is only a small part of a complex whole (Argyris, 1957; Walker and Guest, 1952; Baldamus, 1951; Walker and Marriott, 1951).

Whereas sociologists have discussed lack of felt purpose and personal goals in the job as aspects of alienation, many psychologists have been interested in some of the same problems under the heading of "job motivation" (Hertzberg, Mausner, and Snyderman, 1959; Vroom, 1964; Gellerman, 1963; Zaleznik, *et al.*, 1958; Likert, 1959). While most of the

---

[2]The concepts relating to alienation which are discussed here are only those which are relevant to the presence or absence of personal goals. Other phenomena which have been discussed under the heading of alienation include feelings of powerlessness, feelings of normlessness (where persons believe that socially unapproved behaviors are necessary), and feelings of isolation (where persons assign low value to goals which are typically valued in the society). See Seeman (1959).

interest in alienation stems from a concern with the well-being of individuals (and is often critical of modern society), much of the interest in job motivation stems from a management-oriented desire to get greater efficiency on the job. Yet the study of job motivation, like the study of aspects of alienation, is concerned with the kinds of goals and purposes which employees find in their work. The search for ways to motivate employees to perform more efficiently, in an era when management lacks its former coercive power, has led in part to a concern with the same personal goals, like achievement in work, which are valued by social critics concerned with alienation.

In the present study, we do not attempt to study all possible goals of employees on the job. We focus particularly on the wish to accomplish worthwhile things on the job. Other personal goals on the job, such as promotion and praise by superiors and co-workers, will be considered to the extent that they are linked to work accomplishment.

We will use the conceptual approach and language of motivational theory (Atkinson, 1964) instead of using alienation or other relevant concepts because motivational theory is better developed than other relevant theoretical frameworks and usually links up more closely with actual behavior than, say, theory about alienation.

SOCIAL IDENTIFICATIONS WHICH THE JOB PROVIDES

A man finds his personal identity and sense of belonging in the social roles which he plays—father, church board member, Army Reserve officer, engineer, assistant supervisor of the X section of the Y company (D. Miller, 1963; Sherwood, 1962; Hughes, 1951). While family, community, and church associations have also been traditionally important, a man's work role has long been one of the main ways in which to establish his place in society. The very names many men bear—Smith, Miller, Baker, Cook, Carpenter, etc.—testify to the traditional importance of work in setting a man's place in society.

In present American society, some of the traditionally important social groupings have weakened. With great intercity mobility (U.S. Census of Population, 1963; Lansing, et al., 1963), ties with larger family groups and with community are generally less strong than they were fifty or a hundred years ago. It is, thus, probably more important than ever before that people be able to derive a sense of social belonging from the occupational roles which they play.[3]

---

[3] For investigations of group and organizational identification, see Willerman (1959); Zander, et al. (1960); Riegel (1956); Elmer (1951); Sherif and Cantril (1947); Dearborn and Simon (1958).

Yet the individual often does not value his membership in a work organization. Blauner (1964) calls this "social alienation," wherein "the worker feels no sense of belonging in the work situation and is unable to identify or is uninterested in identifying with the organization and its goals." On the other hand, he says, "membership in an industrial community involves commitment to the work role and loyalty to one or more centers of the work community" (p. 24). Such a feeling of true membership may help provide the sense of social identity and belongingness which the individual needs. The question of loyalty to the work organization is, of course, also of some interest to management, especially when it is confronted with problems like high turnover rates (Mayo and Lombard, 1944; Ross and Zander, 1957).

The sense of "membership in an industrial community" need not come from organizational membership, however. It can come instead, or in addition, from membership in occupational communities (Becker and Casper, 1956a; Becker and Casper, 1956b). These occupational communities may center about unions or professional associations and may in some cases extend into social life outside the work situation (e.g., see Lipset, *et al.,* 1956; Shepard, 1949; Tannenbaum and Kahn, 1958). There has been some research interest in the determinants of occupational loyalties and also in the compatibility of union and company loyalty (Purcell, 1960; Stagner, 1954; Dean, 1954).

In the present study, we are interested in employees' perceptions and feelings concerning their place in the organization that employs them. In particular we focus on (1) the extent to which employees feel a sense of solidarity (i.e., of common interest and purpose) with other members of the organization, especially with the top leaders; (2) their willingness to label themselves as organization members; and (3) their apparent willingness to defend and support the organization. Data on the relation of a composite measure of organizational identification to various aspects of the work situation—and especially to opportunities for participation in decision making on the job—will be presented. We will also consider the relation of identification with one's occupation to organizational identification.

FEELING STATES ON THE JOB

Related to, but separate from, personal goals and social identity derived from the job are the feeling states which people experience at work. Much of the research interest in this subject has taken the form of the study of employee satisfaction on the job (e.g., Morse, 1953;

Hoppock, 1935; Schaffer, 1953; Seidman, 1943; D. Katz, 1954; Hertzberg, 1957).

Employee satisfaction has been of interest not only because of its intrinsic importance, but because satisfaction or dissatisfaction has consequences for such practical management problems as high absence rates (see, for example, Noland, 1945; Katz and Hyman, 1947; Metzner and Mann, 1953, Patchen, 1960).

Closely related to the question of satisfaction on the job are problems of employee mental health. Some aspects of what is usually considered poor mental health, such as depression and anxiety, are in themselves feeling states. Other symptoms of poor mental health, such as psychosomatic illnesses, derive in part from affective states like anger, depression, and anxiety. Problems of mental health have a dual significance to society, in terms of their human consequences and in terms of their pragmatic costs in illness and inefficiency.[4]

As other writers have pointed out (Katz and Kahn, 1951), the attention of many concerned with employees' feelings about their jobs has tended to center on aspects of the job extrinsic to the work itself—i.e., on satisfactions with pay, with benefits like pension and vacation plans, with the physical environment, with promotion chances, and with personal treatment by supervisors. While these aspects of the job are all important, the satisfactions and dissatisfactions derived from the work itself—pride in work accomplishment versus feelings of failure or of frustration—deserve more attention than they have received. Feeling states and physical symptoms which are related to the performance of the work itself are of special concern in the present study.

The study to be reported is thus concerned with personal goals (motivation), with identifications, and with feelings on the job. Where people are highly motivated, where they feel a sense of solidarity with the enterprise, and where they get a sense of pride from their work, we may speak of them as highly "involved" in their jobs. Our primary concern will be to discover those aspects of the job situation, and those individual characteristics, which affect the level of job involvement.

Of course, motivation, identification, and feelings of pride do not necessarily vary together. Given individuals, or groups of individuals, may be relatively high on one and relatively low on another of these characteristics. Thus we view the concept of job involvement as merely a convenient label to summarize several characteristics which make the job more important, more salient, and potentially more satisfying to the individual.

---

[4]For discussion and research data concerning the relation between work and mental health, see French, *et al.* (1959); Kahn, *et al.* (1964); Kahn and French (1962).

As we shall see, however, these aspects of involvement are, empirically, not entirely independent of each other.

Before turning to a consideration of each aspect of job involvement and its determinants, we present, in the next chapter, a description of the sites in which the study was carried out and a brief description of the study procedures.

2

THE PEOPLE
AND JOBS
STUDIED

CONCERN WITH JOB INVOLVEMENT AT TVA

This study was conducted by the Survey Research Center, University of Michigan, in selected units of the Tennessee Valley Authority (TVA). TVA is a semiautonomous agency of the United States government devoted to the overall development of the Tennessee Valley area through flood control, electric power production, agricultural improvement, forest development, and other services.

From the beginning of TVA in the 1930s, its management has been dedicated to the concept that all TVA employees are working together for common goals and that employees can and should get a sense of purpose and meaning in their work. In part to help create among employees such a sense of involvement and personal meaningfulness in their jobs, top TVA management has encouraged employees to participate in decisions affecting their work. The major mechanism for such participation is TVA's program of cooperative conferences and committees. This program, described in more detail in Chapter 10, consists essentially of a series of meetings within a branch or division between representatives of management and of employees to discuss a wide range of work problems. Each cooperative program, among other accomplishments, has been responsible for implementing a large number of work improvements suggested by employees.

The effects which it was hoped the cooperative program would have upon employees were defined in 1952 by Gordon R. Clapp, the Chairman of the TVA Board at that time. He said :

> *The big result, it seems to me, that comes from these arrangements, these chances for cooperation, is the new meaning for the individual. He gains an idea of the importance of what he can do to influence the results of an agency that means something to the lives of many people outside the employment rolls.*[1]

Similar ideas were expressed in 1954 by the then President of the Tennessee Valley Trades and Labor Council, Samuel E. Roper. He said :

> *When an employee sees his ideas welcomed and put to use, he looks more carefully at his job to see how he can improve it. When he knows what the whole job is about, he works more intelligently to make his part count for the most. He becomes part of a team—a task force, if you please. As one of our employees put it, the cooperative program "gives us a strong feeling of partnership."*
>
> *There is no way to measure the energies that are released or the values that are achieved when a man gains this feeling of partnership. But you can sense it when you sit in a cooperative committee meeting; you can see it when you watch men develop into better workmen, better leaders, better group members.*[2]

Similar sentiments about the value of employee participation, and especially the cooperative program, in stimulating the enthusiasm and creativity of employees continue to be echoed up to the present time.

Yet despite the real success of many of the cooperative programs, it is clear to both TVA people and the outsider that there is considerable variation among TVA units in the extent to which the ideal of high job involvement among employees is realized. For one thing, there is considerable variation among TVA units in the vigor and effectiveness of the cooperative program as a mechanism of employee participation in decision making. Moreover, there are other important differences among various units and individual employees which may affect their job involvement. For example, the nature of the work itself varies widely, including as it does traditional craft jobs, engineering work, jobs monitoring automated equipment, and other kinds of work. Promotional opportunities vary considerably among different job categories. The practices of the immediate superior—e.g., the extent to which he gives recognition for

---

[1] Transcript of remarks of Gordon R. Clapp at meeting of Federal Personnel Council, Washington, D.C., April 24, 1952.

[2] Remarks before a Hoover Commission task force on water resources and power, quoted in *Teamwork: The Cooperative Program of the Tennessee Valley Authority*, Central Joint Cooperative Committee, Knoxville, Tennessee, December, 1955, pp. 11-12.

good work—vary. So also do the personal characteristics which various individuals bring to the job—e.g., their sense of commitment to their occupations.

The object of our study was to assess some of the differences in job involvement which exist among certain TVA units (and among individual employees) and to try to see how these may be related to differences in the job situations and personal characteristics of employees in these units.

CHOICE OF UNITS TO BE STUDIED

Although TVA is not a very large organization in terms of total number of employees (it has approximately 18,000 employees), its operations cover a wide variety of functions and are spread widely over the several states of the Tennessee Valley. TVA has literally dozens of divisions and branches devoted to such diverse tasks as forestry development, steam plant power production, hydro power production, fertilizer production, chemical research, recreational facilities, maps and surveys, navigation, construction, power distribution, power marketing, and engineering design.

With the limited resources of time and money available for this study, it was clearly impossible to cover the entire TVA organization. Moreover, since the study was to be concerned with relationships among variables rather than with a description of TVA, we were not concerned with having a representative sample of any specified universe of employees or work units. Therefore, the people studied are not a systematic sample of TVA units or of TVA employees. Our choices were governed by these aims : first, we wanted to include a variety of types of occupations so that our measurement of job involvement and study of its determinants would not be restricted to a limited class of occupations—to, say, blue-collar craftsmen or professionals. Secondly, we wanted to cover a number of major units doing the same kinds of work so that differences among these major units could be studied. Thirdly, we wanted to include an adequate number of immediate work groups, composed of men reporting to the same immediate supervisor, so that differences among such work groups could be studied.

After visits to a number of TVA installations and extensive discussions with TVA personnel, we chose two engineering design divisions and three steam (power) plants.[3] Even this restricted set of units, however, presents

---

[3]The two engineering divisions are the only units of their type at TVA. The three steam plants were chosen from approximately seven major steam plants; it was expected, on the basis of reports by informants, that they would provide some variation in employee morale.

considerable variety in geographical location and types of work. The units are located in five different parts of the state of Tennessee. They include a wide range of different job settings and different occupations—engineers, draftsmen, power plant operating personnel, machinists, boilermakers, laboratory analysts, clerks, and a variety of other occupations. The following sections present a brief description of the types of employees and job settings covered by our study.[4]

ENGINEERING DIVISIONS

The two engineering divisions covered by the study perform basically similar types of work and employ similar types of employees, though there are certain differences between them.

Division of Design

The Division of Design, located in Knoxville, Tennessee, produces the blueprints for the major new construction jobs of TVA—steam plants, dams, etc. The division employs about six hundred persons. It is divided into three major branches—civil design, electrical design, and mechanical design—complemented by several auxiliary branches and services including administration, drafting, and architectural design.

The majority of employees are graduate engineers with specialties (civil, electrical, mechanical) corresponding to the major branches. Most are fairly young men (median age about thirty-five). There are also a number of "engineering associates" who do not have an engineering degree but whose experience has qualified them to do work similar to that of junior engineers. A number of "engineering aides" assist the engineers by performing such jobs as maintaining files of previous designs.

Many engineers are recruited directly from colleges all over the country. Beginning engineers generally spend their first year rotating among sections concerned with different design problems and then tend to specialize in structural steel design, heavy equipment design, etc. Below the formal supervisor of a section, there are several grades of engineers of varying experience. Those of greater experience and higher grade often check the work of less experienced men.

The work of this engineering division is fairly highly specialized, according to the type of installation and the aspect of construction being planned. For example, among the units within the electrical design branch

---

[4]See Appendix A for a further description of the sample.

are those which plan steam plant switchboard design and one which plans hydro plant conduit and grounding design. The division usually works under demanding time deadlines.

The physical setting for most of the engineers consists of very large rooms containing dozens of men, each at work at his place among many rows of drawing boards. However, basic work units are fairly small—groups of two to twenty men, with the average about nine. There is considerable communication among men in different units working on complementary parts of a structure and some shifting of men across units from time to time.

The largest group of nonengineers in this division are the draftsmen. Groups of draftsmen work side-by-side in drafting service units. These men also tend to be fairly young and most have a high school education. Other types of employees found in the division include architects and clerical workers.

Power Planning Division

The second engineering division covered in the study is the Division of Power Planning and Engineering, located in Chattanooga, Tennessee. Whereas the Division of Design plans major installations like steam plants, this division designs facilities which carry the power, including transmission lines and substations.

Of five branches in this division, three (the larger branches) are engaged in the design of various facilities. Two smaller branches are concerned primarily with future planning, rather than with designs for immediate construction. Within each branch there is specialization by sections which is generally similar to that described for the larger engineering division. This division employs only about half as many people as does the Division of Design—about three hundred. The occupations and backgrounds of employees in this division are, however, generally similar to those in the larger engineering division.

Most engineering personnel in both divisions are represented by the same employees' organization—the TVA Engineers Association. While not formally a union, the Engineers Association negotiates with management on such matters as wages, benefits, and grievances. Most nonengineering employees in these divisions are represented by the Office Employees International Union.

As in most other parts of TVA, there is a "cooperative program" in each of the two engineering divisions. In this program, employee and top management representatives meet to discuss work problems (e.g., improving work methods) which lie beyond the scope of ordinary union-management relations. The formal business of the program is carried on

at meetings held once a month, with subcommittee meetings held in
the interim to discuss specific problems.

POWER PLANTS

The three steam (power) plants studied are part of a network of
seven major TVA steam plants which were operating at the time of the
study. A steam plant produces electricity by converting coal to steam,
which powers giant electric generators. The plants studied were all
modern and fairly highly automated. Each plant has an almost identical
technology and administrative structure. Two, the Gallatin and Johnsonville steam plants, are located in western Tennessee and one, the
John Sevier Steam Plant, is in eastern Tennessee. Together with other
power facilities, their operations are coordinated by a central head-
quarters in Chattanooga.

The total number of employees is about the same (about 265) in two
of the plants. The third plant is somewhat larger, employing a total of
440 persons. There are five sections within each steam plant: operating,
mechanical maintenance, electrical maintenance, laboratory, and administration. The first four of these were covered by our study, either in whole
or in part. The administration section, which has only a small number of
employees in each steam plant, was not covered.

Operating Section

The operating section of each plant is responsible for checking and
guiding the operation of a largely automated complex of equipment. The
work of operators and assistant operators centers around control rooms
where a set of gauges, lights, and other indicators shows the state of various
plant equipment and functions. Operators and assistant operators (who
will eventually become operators) are a bright, able group who have been
highly selected by tests from among a large pool of job applicants. They are
generally fairly young men (median age about thirty-eight) with a high
school education. Assistant operators go through intensive training during
their early period at TVA and have to master material which includes
mathematics and chemistry as well as practical operations. While operators thus develop considerable skill and knowledge, there are only infrequent opportunities to actively apply this ability on the job. These
occasions arise when units are being put "on the line" or "off the line,"
or when some malfunction of operation occurs. Most of the time operators,
though alert and watchful, are not actively doing anything. Operators and
assistant operators are assisted by "auxiliary operators" whose work is less

skilled (checking valves, cleaning certain areas, etc.) and who tend to be less highly selected than the operators. Also included in the main operating section are switchboard operators who are responsible for connecting units into or removing them from the electrical system as required and varying electrical loading in emergencies. Among their duties, they operate and observe control boards and voltage regulating equipment.

On any one shift there are several groups of operating employees working, each responsible for one or more generating units. Each work group consists of operators, assistant operators, and auxiliary operators under the supervision of a "shift engineer." Since the production of electricity is a continuous process, there are three shifts. Employees rotate among the three shifts, which brings them under the supervision of different shift engineers. These operating employees are represented by the International Brotherhood of Electrical Workers.

Also included administratively in the operating section are "yard" employees, who operate heavy coal-moving equipment and do various kinds of common labor, and janitorial employees. (The "yard" employees were not included in our sample; see Appendix A.)

Mechanical and Electrical Maintenance Sections

The job of the mechanical and electrical maintenance sections in each steam plant is to maintain and repair the plant's equipment. The trades most heavily represented are machinists, steam fitters, boilermakers, and electricians. Other tradesmen found in each steam plant include painters, carpenters, asbestos workers, and structural iron workers. Generally each group of craftsmen work under their own foreman. These men are, in general, similar to those in similar occupations working elsewhere. They are less well educated than the operating employees (over half did not finish high school) and are, on the average, a little older (median age about forty-three).

Maintenance men as a rule work only on the regular day shift. They are represented by the unions which usually represent men in each of their crafts—the machinists' union, the electrical workers' union, etc. Relations between TVA and the trade unions have generally been good.

Laboratory Section

The primary task of the laboratory section of each steam plant is to handle the incoming coal shipments and to analyze the coal and water input of the plant. When the coal is brought in by rail or truck, it is recorded by men called "materials testers." The materials testers also take samples from the coal, grind it up, and prepare it for analysis in the laboratory. Individuals often rotate among these specific tasks and among shifts. A high school education is required for this job, and some materials testers have some college education. Many of these employees are Negro.[5]

The work of analyzing coal and water samples is done by analytical chemists and chemical lab analysts. Also included in the laboratory is a unit concerned with test studies and reports. This unit includes several mechanical engineers, engineering aides, and instrument mechanics. Most employees in the laboratory section of each steam plant are represented by the TVA Engineers Association, the employee organization which represents most employees in the engineering divisions.

Cooperative Programs

There are two cooperative programs within each of the three steam plants included in the study. The larger program covers employees in the operating section, the mechanical and electrical maintenance sections, and the instrument mechanics from the laboratory. The other and smaller cooperative program includes most laboratory employees, administrative employees, and a few engineers scattered throughout the plant. As mentioned above, the major activity of each cooperative program is a monthly meeting attended by plant management and employee representatives. Between these monthly meetings, subcommittees (such as suggestion committees) carry on the work of the program. The cooperative program in the power plant has placed great emphasis on encouraging and implementing suggestions for improvements in work efficiency, convenience, and safety.

TYPES OF DATA OBTAINED[6]

Measures of Job Involvement

In informal interviews with employees in the engineering design divisions and in the steam plants, we attempted to learn something about their experiences of interest or boredom in the work and about their sense of belonging to or of estrangement from the work organization. These interviews served to provide us with some insights into the

---

[5]Only 17 out of 834 persons included in our sample are nonwhite; most of these were among the materials testers.

[6]Further information about the way in which the study was conducted, including data about the development of the questionnaire, the sample of employees covered, and non-questionnaire data obtained are given in Appendix B.

way in which various TVA employees react to their jobs and to the work organization.

For the purposes of a systematic study of job involvement, however, we needed to obtain more quantitative data concerning involvement of employees in their jobs. Such data could come either from the reports of the employee himself or from objective information about his behavior.

With regard to objective information about employees' behavior, one set of available data is the number of absences for each employee. Data on number of absences for each employee was available in the records of most of the work units covered. Although absence data are not completely comparable between steam plants and engineering divisions, they can be used as one measure of job motivation—especially within each of these major organizational groupings.

However, other objective data about employees' behavior was less suited to a comparison of job involvement across our entire sample of TVA employees. The number of ideas which employees submitted to the cooperative program might be considered an indication of interest in work innovation. However, the fact that units differed in the extent to which the suggestion system was promoted as the major channel for new ideas makes it difficult to compare individuals across units. Moreover, the proportion of employees who submitted any suggestion in, say, the year preceding the study, was small, so that no differentiation was possible among most employees with regard to the number of suggestions each submitted.

Behavioral data were also available concerning individuals who had left TVA in the period preceding (and following) our formal study. Turnover rates might conceivably have been used to compare units. However, turnover was almost nonexistent in the steam plants around the time of the study so that a turnover rate measure would not give clues to differences in job involvement among units within the steam plants. Moreover, since the vast majority of employees whose job situations were studied did not leave TVA in the year following our study, turnover could not be used to distinguish among individuals with respect to job involvement.

Data on the work efficiency of individual employees were not available, nor were data available on which the productive efficiency of units could be meaningfully compared. Ratings by supervisors of the behavior of employees in their units were obtained in some units, but these ratings are not comparable across units.

It may be noted that this situation, where few behavioral indicators of motivation, acceptance of change, organizational identification, etc., are comparable for employees across a large number of units and occupational groupings, is not unique to the TVA setting. It is, in fact, almost universal.

Faced with the problem of getting measures of job involvement which would be roughly comparable across our diverse sample of employees, we have relied primarily on information obtained from employees themselves on questionnaires.[7] While the use of questionnaires permits us to tap directly the perceptions, feelings, and self-reported behavior of employees, we face the problem that some questions may not be valid indicators of employees' true feelings, nor related to their actual behavior on the job. We have, however, attempted to make sure that the questionnaire measures we used are related to actual behavior. While data on suggestions submitted, turnover, attendance, and supervisors' ratings could not be used as comparable criteria across the entire sample, these data were used within narrower groups to help assess the validity of the questionnaire measures.

Some of the evidence concerning the validity of questionnaire measures of job interest, interest in work innovation, and identification with the work organization (TVA) is cited later, in those sections where a particular measure is discussed. A more complete report on the reliability and validity of these (and several other) measures is contained in an earlier monograph (Patchen, Pelz, and Allen, 1965).

Also included in the questionnaire are some measures of employee reactions—e.g., feelings of nervousness, reports of physical distress—which were not subjected to a process of validation. These measures, which are described in the body of this report, must rest upon their face validity.

The Work Situation

In addition to data about employee reactions to their jobs, it was an important aim of the study to describe aspects of the job situation which might be related to job involvement. Aspects of the job situation in which we were interested include such things as the difficulty of the job, the amount of control over means of doing the work, the amount of feedback on work performance, the frequency of time deadlines, promotion opportunities, and the amount of encouragement of work achievement by peers.

The problem of obtaining adequate information about the job situations of various individuals and groups is a formidable one. Conceivably, researchers might personally observe and code the activities and interactions of each employee or of representatives of each type of work. But in a study like the present one, where many employees in a wide variety of different occupations and work units are being studied, such

---

[7] A total of 834 persons took questionnaires.

an observational procedure would be impractical. A second alternative would be to have a knowledgeable person—say, the immediate supervisor —rate the job situation of each employee on a variety of dimensions (just as we had supervisors rate employees on aspects of job involvement). Such a procedure would have certain advantages, the principal one being that description of the job situation would come from a source other than the same employee who is answering questions about his job involvement. However, such a procedure also has certain limitations. One limitation is that the supervisor himself has certain biases, especially where he is describing aspects of the job situation—e.g., autonomy enjoyed, feedback from supervisors—where he himself is involved. A second limitation of such ratings is that the supervisor does not have complete information about all aspects of the job situation experienced by employees—e.g., the extent to which employees may encourage each other to work hard or discourage each other from doing so.[8]

The method adopted for obtaining data about each employee's job situation was to ask the employee himself. This procedure has the advantage of asking the person who is most knowledgeable. The procedure, does, however, run the risk that information about the objective job situation will be influenced by the subjective feelings of job involvement which are reported on the same questionnaire. In other words, there is the possibility that perceptions of the job situation may be distorted by the extent of satisfaction, motivation, or organizational identification which individuals experience. While not dismissing this problem entirely as a possible source of some distortion in the data, the following considerations tend to reassure us that this distortion is minimal.

1. Objective nature of the questions. An effort was made to make the questions concerning the job situation objective and descriptive rather than evaluative. For example, in trying to learn about the extent of feedback on the job, we did not ask the employee whether he feels he gets enough feedback. We asked, instead, questions about how much of his work is checked or revised (categories from 100 per cent to 25 per cent), and how often he is told about the results of the checking (categories from "almost always" to "about one-tenth of the time or less"). The objective nature of most job description questions should cut down greatly on the amount of bias due to differences in feelings about the work situation.

2. Low intercorrelation among responses. The data show low correlations between descriptions of various job characteristics. For example,

---

[8]We did obtain ratings from knowledgeable TVA persons about the chances for jobs outside TVA which were available to various occupational groups at the time of our study. See Chapter 11.

for all TVA employees taking the questionnaire, scores on the index of control over work methods correlated .22 with reported chance to finish things, .37 with frequency of supervisor compliments, .09 with belief in TVA purposes, .18 with feedback on performance, .12 with job difficulty, and .19 with achievement as a means to peer approval. In light of the fact that some positive correlations may be rooted in objective reality, the magnitude of such correlations does not suggest a large halo effect whereby perception of one aspect of the job in a favorable light, or general high morale, will lead to uniformly favorable perceptions.

3. Checking of questionnaire data against knowledge of situation. A further safeguard against gross distortion in questionnaire descriptions of jobs lies in the fact that, with respect to many features of the job, we can check the questionnaire against general knowledge of job situations. For example, in examining data about control over means in the job situation, we know in advance that steam plant operating personnel, who work under detailed regulations, should score relatively low, and that steam plant craftsmen, who often work physically apart from supervisors, should score higher. By checking the questionnaire data against such expectations, based on general knowledge of the various work situations, we can, at least with respect to some variables, get added confidence in the questionnaire information.

Personal Characteristics of Employees

In addition to data concerning job involvement and the job situation, data were also obtained from the questionnaire concerning personal characteristics of the employee. One class of such data is background characteristics; e.g., age, education, length of TVA service, state in which employee grew up. Several measures of personality characteristics—the need for achievement and the need for affiliation—were included. These personality measures were borrowed or adapted from the investigators who developed them (see Chapters 6 and 11). Finally, some information was obtained concerning the union or professional activities of each employee, and a number of questions bearing on occupational identification were asked.[9]

From all the data collected, we hoped to shed light on two main questions. First, under what conditions are people highly motivated for achievement on the job? Secondly when do people come to have a sense of solidarity or identification with the work organization?

In the next few chapters we will consider the first of these general

---

[9]Specific questions asked are given in the sections where the relevant data are discussed.

topics—achievement motivation and pride on the job. Before looking at the data from TVA, it will be rewarding to pause first to think in general terms about the kinds of situation which may be expected to result in high achievement motivation on the job. We turn to this topic in the next chapter.

SUMMARY

This study was conducted in two engineering design divisions and three steam (power) plants of the Tennessee Valley Authority. TVA management has attempted, especially by a program of employee participation in work decisions, to promote among rank-and-file employees a sense of involvement in the work of the organization. However, it is apparent that there are differences among TVA units in the extent to which the ideal of high employee involvement is reached. The object of this study was to assess some of these differences in job involvement and to see how these may be related to differences in job situations and in personal characteristics of employees.

The engineering divisions and power plants studied include a wide variety of types of occupations and job settings. Questionnaires were administered to 834 nonsupervisory employees in these units in order to assess their motivation on the job, their sense of identification with TVA, and other reactions to the job situation. These questionnaire measures of job involvement had been shown previously to be related to such behavior as absence, submitting suggestions, and leaving TVA, and to supervisors' ratings of employees' behavior. Information was also obtained from the questionnaire concerning various aspects of the job situation and personal characteristics of employees.

MOTIVATION AND ACHIEVEMENT ON THE JOB

PART

3

MOTIVATION
AND ACHIEVEMENT
ON THE JOB
Theoretical Perspective

WORK MOTIVATION AND ACHIEVEMENT

A man may want to do his best on the job for a variety of reasons. He may see work as a direct means of earning more money—if, for example, he works under a money incentive system. He may be motivated in part by fear of losing his job—if, for example, he is a new salesman who has to justify his salary by making sales. He may even, as Adams and Rosenbaum (1962) suggest, wish to maintain a feeling of equity by truly earning the salary he is being paid.

We are not, however, directly concerned here with these motives for doing one's best on the job, nor with several other possible motives which might be mentioned. We are concerned rather with work motivation, i.e., the internal "push" to perform well on the job, as it is related to the desire for achievement or successful accomplishment. We focus on this source of work motivation for several reasons. First, there is good reason to think that the desire to achieve is a powerful potential motivator in work (Hertzberg, *et al.*, 1959). Secondly, the experimental work on achievement motivation (Atkinson, 1964; Atkinson and Feather, 1966) provides a useful theoretical background which it is challenging to try to extend to (and modify for) the industrial situation. Thirdly, and perhaps of most interest to us, are the personal consequences for employees of seeking achievement on the job. For employees who care about doing well on the job, the many hours they spend at work have meaning, instead of being merely a drudgery necessary to enjoyment off the job. The job becomes a place where one is interested and involved. For these reasons, it seems useful to examine closely the relation of work motivation to factors which make achievement on the job possible and which make it valued.

In analyzing the relation of job motivation to the motivation for achievement, we will begin with the theoretical approach which has been proposed by Atkinson (1958a),[1] an approach consistent with that of many other motivational theorists as well.[2] Atkinson's formula for predicting the level of aroused motivation for action, as it is related to the desire for achievement, is (rephrased slightly) as follows :[3]

(1) Aroused Motivation
to Complete Task X
(Job Motivation)

$$= f \begin{bmatrix} \text{Motive for} \\ \text{Achievement} \end{bmatrix} \times \begin{bmatrix} \text{Achievement} \\ \text{Incentive} \end{bmatrix} \times \begin{bmatrix} \text{Expectancy That Perform-} \\ \text{ing Task X Will Result in} \\ \text{Successful Achievement} \end{bmatrix}$$

A brief explanation of these terms may be helpful :

Aroused Motivation to Perform Task X is a tendency to approach task completion and would be reflected usually in behavior; that is to say, high aroused motivation to complete Task X would be reflected in hard work on Task X. (Where tasks on the job are concerned, we will refer to such aroused motivation as "job motivation.")

Motive for Achievement is the tendency to approach achievement (success measured against some standard of excellence). It is equivalent

---

[1]The general formulation proposed by Atkinson sees the aroused motivation for action as a function of the tendency to approach success minus the tendency to avoid failure. The tendency to avoid failure is not considered systematically in this volume, although it does enter into some of the theoretical discussion and empirical measures at various points.

[2]Atkinson's general model of motivation is similar to those of Lewin (1938), Rotter (1955), Davidson, Suppes, and Siegel (1957), Tolman (1959), and Vroom (1964). The principal distinction is that Atkinson breaks down the "valence" or "utility" of an outcome into two components, Motive and Incentive. This is useful in many cases in distinguishing between that portion of the utility which is due to the characteristics of the individual (motive) and that portion which is due to the nature of the potential reward (incentive).

[3]In a later discussion of motivation (1964, pp. 279–281), Atkinson suggests that the general formula for predicting level of aroused motivation needs to be supplemented by a Habit construct. While fully accepting this general position, we do not view Habit as an important determinant of achievement motivation on the job, and will not discuss Habit in this chapter.

to the extent to which achievement is valued, or the amount of satisfaction which is anticipated from achievement.

Achievement Incentive is the amount of achievement which is possible in the situation. Just as the size and quality of a steak might represent the amount of possible food reward in a given situation, so the magnitude of possible achievement represents the amount of this type of reward which may be obtained in a given situation.[4]

Expectancy That Performing Task X Will Result in Successful Achievement refers to the subjective probability in the mind of the individual that his working hard on Task X will result in his reaching the incentive (rewarding goal) of successful achievement.

Another way of thinking about equation (1) is that it states that aroused motivation for performance is, in part, determined by the extent to which the individual feels that performance of the task may be expected to bring satisfaction in achievement. That is to say, the term on the right side of equation (1)—Motive for Achievement × Achievement Incentive × Expectancy That Performing the Task Will Result in Successful Achievement—may be looked on as the satisfaction in achievement which performance of the task may be expected to bring.[5]

The major task of this chapter is to try to specify in some detail factors which will affect the Motive for Achievement, the Incentive for Achievement, and the Expectancy (perceived probability) That Effort Will Lead to Achievement. In so doing, we will conceptualize the Motive for Achievement somewhat differently than it has usually been conceived in the past. We will also postulate a relation between Achievement Incentive and Expectancy of Success which is different from what has been previously suggested. These changes in the conception of achievement motivation appear necessary in order to take into account all the important determinants—especially social determinants—of achievement motivation in the job situation. It is hoped that the theoretical approach may be useful in other empirical contexts as well.

THE MOTIVE FOR ACHIEVEMENT

Atkinson (1958a) defines a motive as "the disposition within the person to strive to approach a certain class of positive incentives (goals) or to

---

[4]One important reason why achievement may be rewarding is that it brings a feeling of pride. However, we will not assume that this is the only reason.

[5]This concept of expected satisfaction is equivalent to the concept of expected utility used in decision theory (Edwards, 1961).

avoid a certain class of negative incentives (threats)." In slightly different terms, the strength of a motive to reach some kind of goal (like food, or relief from anxiety, or achievement) may be seen as the extent to which goals of that class are valued.

Atkinson (1966, p. 13) defines the achievement motive in particular as "a disposition to approach success."[6] The reason why success is a goal (i.e., is rewarding), he indicates in several discussions (1958a, 1964), is because of the "sense of pride" and the "thrill of accomplishment" which may result from successful achievement.[7] In other words, success is valued because of the internal rewards which it brings. The achievement motive is conceived of by Atkinson, McClelland, and their associates as essentially a personality characteristic which is formed by early experiences. This perspective is backed by research which shows that people who show a high motive for achievement as adults are likely to have been rewarded often for achievement as children (McClelland, et al., 1953).[8]

We would note, however, that the value of achievement on the job may be determined by factors other than general personality characteristics derived from early experiences. Features of the present job environment may also contribute to the value of achievement. These include (1) factors affecting the intrinsic value of achievement; (2) factors affecting the value of achievement as a means to social approval and respect in the job situation; and (3) factors affecting the value of achievement as a means of gaining other rewards—e.g., money.

The Intrinsic Value of Achievement

It seems extremely unlikely that most individuals will value success or achievement equally regardless of the nature of the achievement involved. In early life, when achievement motivation is being learned, specific persons will find that one type of achievement (e.g., creative work) will be rewarded by parents, and later by others, more than other kinds of

---

[6]See McClelland, et al. (1953) for an account of the early research on and conceptualization of the achievement motive.

[7]It may be noted that the desire to experience pride in one's accomplishments is one of a number of motives for self-approval which have been discussed by various writers—including the desire for self-esteem (Argyis, 1964), the desire to perform consistently with one's self-concept (Lecky, 1945; Vroom, 1962), the desire for self-actualization (Maslow, 1943), and the motivation for competence (White, 1959).

[8]That achievement continues to be valued even when it is no longer rewarded by others is probably the result of two overlapping processes. (1) Parental and other figures from the past may continue to serve as rewarding figures in the actor's imagination. Thus, after doing a good job on something, the adult may in effect say to himself, "Wouldn't Dad be proud of me now" or picture Dad praising him. (2) The adult may have adopted as his own standards those of his parents and other early adult figures so that he is able to approve himself in the same fashion that his parents previously did.

achievements (e.g., rote memorization). Thus the value of, and the motive to strive toward, certain kinds of achievements will be higher than that of other kinds.

A number of characteristics of the job situation may be expected to affect the extent to which possible achievements on the job are ones which will be valued. These job characteristics include (1) the involvement of valued abilities; (2) the social importance of the task; and (3) the individual's part in setting goals.

1. Involvement of valued abilties.   The amount of pride which comes from success on a job may be expected to depend in part on the extent to which the person values the abilities which are necessary for success on that job. For example, success in a task which he sees as requiring high intelligence may be viewed with greater pride than one which requires only steady attention. Research data, consistent with this point, show that when valued abilities are required in a task, performance is better (Alper, 1946; Kaustler, 1951) and personal concern about work problems is greater (Slater, 1959).

Closely related to the question of whether a person values the abilities required in his job is the question of his sense of identification with his occupation. A man whose occupation (and the ability required by that trade) is an important part of his self-image is likely to feel greater pride in accomplishment than does a co-worker who would rather be in another occupation or whose success in other roles (church leader, athletic team member, etc.) is more important to him than achievement in his occupational role.

2. Social importance of the task. In early life experiences the individual is likely to be rewarded more for achievements that help a wider social group (e.g., helping the team to win a game) than for achievements that help only himself or a narrower group. Thus, most people come to feel considerable pride in socially valuable achievements. In the same way, pride in success on the job may also be affected by the social importance of the work. An engineer working on space capsules may take greater pride in success than one working on sewage lines. The workers producing bombers during World War II probably took greater pride in successfully handling a difficult problem than they did when producing planes before or after the war.

3. Part in setting goals.   A number of studies suggest that permitting people to participate in the setting of their own work goals will often result in greater effort toward the goals (see, for example, Coch and French, 1948; Whyte, 1955; Likert, 1961). It seems likely that this result is due in part to the individual accepting fully, and thus valuing highly, goals which he has set, or helped to set, for himself. We would expect that the greater the individual's part in setting his work goals, the more he will value such goals and the greater his pride in successfully reaching the goals.

Achievement as a Means to Social Approval and Respect

In addition to the direct and immediate satisfaction which achievement on the job may bring, it may also be valued because it brings approval and respect from co-workers and superiors.[9]

The following aspects of the work situation may be expected to help determine the extent to which the value of achievement on the job is affected by the hope of social respect and approval:

1. Degree to which approval of peers and superiors is valued. Clearly, achievement will be little valued as a means to social approval and respect if the latter are little valued. Thus anything which affects the value of co-workers' approval and respect may affect the value of achievement on the job. We may, for example, expect that a man who is in a cohesive, mutually supportive work group will value the approval of his co-workers much more than a man who is isolated or works in a group split by antagonisms.

2. Probability that achievement will bring approval or respect. It is also clear that the more likely achievement is to bring approval and respect from others on the job, the greater its value. Thus a superior who often praises successful work tends to raise the value put on achievement by the man praised. A work group which often ostracizes a "rate-buster" is likely to lower severely the value of achievement among its members.

It may be noted that the process described, by which reward from important persons affects the value of achievement on the job, is similar to the process by which reward from parents (important persons at that time) develops achievement motivation in the child (McClelland, *et al.,* 1953).

Achievement as a Means to Other Rewards

In addition to the rewards of personal pride and social approval, there are, of course, other rewards which may stem from achievement and thus increase its value. Successful performance on the job may lead to higher pay, more job security, a more comfortable office, etc. It is not hard to imagine various aspects of the job situation which may create a weaker

---

[9]Social approval and social respect are, of course, somewhat different and may for some purposes be examined separately. For convenience of presentation, they are lumped together here.

or stronger tie between achievement and these rewards. For example, in some organizations, promotion (and the additional money and status which it may bring) depend primarily on length of service or on family ties or on getting along well with people. In other organizations (or other parts of the same organization) promotion may depend mainly on work achievements.

The above discussion may be summarized by stating the following (hypothesized) relation between the strength of the achievement motive on the job and the rewards, or satisfactions, which achievement may bring :

$$
\begin{array}{l}
\text{Motive for} \\
(2)\ \text{Achievement} \\
\ \ \ \text{on the Job}
\end{array}
= f
\begin{bmatrix}
\text{Intrinsic Satis-} \\
\text{faction of Achieve-} \\
\text{ment on the Job}
\end{bmatrix}
+
\begin{bmatrix}
\text{Expected Satisfaction} \\
\text{in Social Approval and} \\
\text{Respect Which Job} \\
\text{Achievement Will} \\
\text{Bring}
\end{bmatrix}
+
\begin{bmatrix}
\text{Other Expected} \\
\text{Satisfactions} \\
\text{Which Job} \\
\text{Achievement} \\
\text{Will Bring}
\end{bmatrix}
$$

The expected satisfaction in social approval which achievement will bring would be as follows :

$$
\begin{array}{l}
\text{Expected Satisfaction} \\
(3)\ \text{in Social Approval} \\
\ \ \ \text{Which Job Achievement} \\
\ \ \ \text{Will Bring}
\end{array}
= f
\begin{bmatrix}
\text{Motive for} \\
\text{Social Approval}
\end{bmatrix}
\times
\begin{bmatrix}
\text{Approval Incentive} \\
\text{(Amount of Social} \\
\text{Approval Which Is} \\
\text{Possible in Job} \\
\text{Situation)}
\end{bmatrix}
\times
\begin{bmatrix}
\text{Expectancy That} \\
\text{Achievement Will} \\
\text{Result in Social} \\
\text{Approval}
\end{bmatrix}
$$

Parallel formulas would predict other expected satisfactions (e.g., higher status, money) which achievement may bring.[10]

---

[10]Note that by substituting the terms of equation (3) into equation (2), we get the following overall relationship:

$$
\begin{array}{l}
\text{Motive for} \\
\text{Achievement} = f \\
\text{on the Job}
\end{array}
\begin{bmatrix}
\text{Intrinsic} \\
\text{Satisfaction} \\
\text{of Achievement} \\
\text{on the Job}
\end{bmatrix}
$$

$$
+ \left[\left(M_{\text{approval}} \right) \times \left(I_{\text{approval}} \right) \times \left(E_{\text{approval}} \right) \right] +
$$

$$
\left[\left(M_{\text{money}} \right) \times \left(I_{\text{money}} \right) \times \left(E_{\text{money}} \right) \right] \text{ etc.}
$$

Thus, the motive for achievement is predicted by the same general Motive $\times$ Incentive $\times$ Expectancy formula which was used to predict aroused motivation to

What such a set of formulas asserts is that the motive for achievement
—i.e., the extent to which achievement is attractive and valued—is determined in part by the likelihood that achievement will lead to other positive
outcomes and the extent to which those other outcomes are desired.
This conception of the determinants of a motive is consistent with that of
Vroom (1964), who discusses the valence (attraction) of an outcome to a
person as a function of the valences of all other outcomes and his concep-
tions of the first outcome's instrumentality for the attainment of these
other outcomes.[11]

It should be clear by now that the concept of achievement motivation
is being used here somewhat differently than it has usually been used in
the past. In contrast to the cencept of the achievement motive as a fairly
enduring personality characteristic, our conception is in one way narrower
and in one way broader. It is narrower in that it is concerned with the
motivation to achieve specifically *on the job* rather than in a wide
range of life situations. It is broader in that it focuses not only on the
intrinsic satisfactions (i.e., pride) of achievement on the job but also
on the value of such achievement as a means for other possible satisfactions.

INCENTIVE FOR ACHIEVEMENT

The achievement incentive on the job represents the degree of achievement or success which is possible for the individual in the job situation.
What determines the amount of achievement incentive which is present
on the job?

Difficulty of Successful Performance

One important determinant of achievement incentive is the level of
task difficulty. Atkinson (1958a) has postulated that the incentive for

---

complete task X. This suggests that both the motive to complete task X and the motive for
achievement may be treated conceptually in the same way. This may become clearer if we
phrase the former as the motive to approach the goal of completion of task X, and the latter
as the motive to approach achievement. The motive to approach the goal of completion of
task X is, in part, a function of the expectancy that completing task X will bring achievement and the strength of the motive to approach achievement. Likewise, the strength of the
motive to approach achievement is, in part, a function of the expectancy that achievement
will bring other rewards and the strength of the motives to approach these other rewards.

[11]Vroom (1964, p. 15) uses the term "motive" to refer to the valence of a class of
outcomes. His term "valence" includes both motive and incentive in the terminology
used in this book. Note also the work of Thomas and Zander (1959) which considers the
instrumentality of one goal for another.

achievement equals one minus the probability of success. The rationale for this statement is that the less the probability of success, the more likely is success to be seen as a true accomplishment and therefore the greater the pride which can be derived from success. Laboratory experiments based in part on this theoretical assumption that Incentive$=1-\text{p}$ success have been consistent with this assumption (Atkinson, 1958a; Feather, 1967).

We may note too that, in addition to the spontaneous perception of the person himself, successes in difficult tasks are likely to be defined by others as being substantial accomplishments. For example, in a TVA power plant where the quality of incoming coal was a problem, it was publicly stated that the devising of a practical coal-sampler would be a great accomplishment.

There are, of course, dangers in making jobs too difficult. Motivation for doing a good job is affected not only by incentive (which increases with difficulty) but also by the expected probability of success (which decreases with difficulty). Atkinson (1958b) has shown that whereas motivation to approach a task increases as we go from low to medium difficulty, it goes down where difficulty is very high.[12] The problem for most jobs in our society, however, is not that of excessive difficulty, where motivation is paralyzed by a low probability of success. It is more often— in most production and white-collar jobs—the lack of enough difficulty to provide a challenge and to make successful performance an achievement. There are, on the other hand, some persons—e.g., some top executives, some scientists—whose jobs may present difficulties so serious that the effect on motivation of the increase in achievement incentive is overidden by the effect of the low probability of success.

Other Determinants of Achievement Incentive

Although the experimental literature on achievement motivation has focused on achievement incentive as a function of task difficulty (expectancy of success), there are a number of other conditions which appear important in creating a strong achievement incentive. These include:

1. The existence (and clarity) of standards of excellence against which success in performance of the task can be judged.

---

[12]Moderately difficult tasks are also most likely to lead to tendencies to avoid doing the task because of fear of failure (see Atkinson, 1958b). Performance in moderately difficult jobs would be expected to be good among those whose motivation for success is greater than their fear of failure. For those who have a strong fear of failure, moderately difficult jobs may, in addition to causing a tendency to avoid work, also lead to considerable anxiety.

2.   Personal responsibility for success—i.e., success in the task depends upon the individual's own ideas and efforts.

3.   Feedback on the individual's success in performing the task.

These additional conditions[13] for creating achievement incentive have been noted or implied before (Atkinson, 1964). However, perhaps because such conditions are easy to arrange in the laboratory, they have usually been taken for granted in research. They have received little attention as conditions which may vary and may, therefore, affect the amount of achievement possible in the task situation.

In the following paragraphs we will discuss further each of these factors affecting achievement incentive, with particular attention to the way in which these factors may vary in different job situations.

Clear Standards of Excellent Performance

If a man is to see an opportunity to successfully accomplish something difficult on the job, he must see some standard against which his effort can be judged. In some job situations, objective standards of performance may be available—e.g., a certain number of sales or a certain number of widgets produced or a certain number of dollars earned. In some cases, the excellence of performance is judged against an absolute number previously determined; in other cases, the excellence of performance is judged against the performance of other people doing the same job—e.g., when an auto salesman wins a prize for selling more cars than other salesmen that month.

Even where objective standards of excellence are available, they may not be completely clear to the individual. For example, the auto salesman may not be completely sure about the extent to which he is being judged on the sheer number of sales and the extent to which he is being judged on the profit margins of the sales he accepts. He may also not know whether he is being judged against men of his own experience or against the whole agency sales force.

Where objective standards of excellence are not available, or as a supplement to them, performance may be judged subjectively by superiors. If the person whose work is to be judged knows specifically who will judge his work and, perhaps more important, what standards will be used in this judgment, his achievement incentive may remain high. In many cases, however, these things are not clear to him. Thus, an engineer may not be sure whether his drawings will be judged primarily by how much he

---

[13]McClelland (1961) discusses similar conditions, including individual responsibility and knowledge of results, as among the characteristics of the high-achievement role of entrepreneur.

follows previous procedures in similar jobs or by the extent to which he shows imagination in devising new techniques to handle new problems. Where standards of excellent performance are not clear, the achievement incentive may be expected to drop.

Feedback on Performance

For a man to see an achievement incentive (i.e., to see the possibility of a certain kind of success), he must not only be aware of standards of excellence; he must also expect to learn how well he has done against those standards of excellence. In other words, there is little prospect of experiencing success if one suspects he will never know how well he has done. That feedback results in a higher motivation for performance, especially among those with high achievement motivation, has been verified in a number of studies (e.g., Arps, 1920; Manzer, 1935; French, 1958).

In some cases the individual can get feedback from his own direct observation, as in the case of boiler room workers who can see temperature and pressure gauges which show the success of their efforts. In other cases, feedback must come via communication from others, as in the "Well done!" which an engineer may receive from a checker who goes over his drawings.

On the basis of experimental studies of learning in the laboratory (see, for example, Deese, 1958) and common observation, one would expect that the more rapid the feedback, the more it will reinforce the achievement incentive. For example, a scientist about to begin a theoretical paper is likely to have more achievement incentive if he expects to receive comments from respected colleagues immediately upon completion of the paper than if he believes he will have to wait several months for reactions.

Responsibility for Success

A person cannot see success in some task as a personal accomplishment unless he feels he is personally responsible for this success.[14] On a job, this has a number of implications. It means first that the more chance the employee himself has to choose the methods for doing his tasks, the more success in those tasks will be seen as potential achievements to him. Thus, a boilermaker who has to decide himself how best to repair a defective boiler is likely to see success in this job as something of a personal achievement. The man who has to follow a specified procedure for such a repair

---

[14]This idea is fully accepted by those who have investigated the need for achievement. Need for achievement is thought to be relevant in instances where success in a task depends on ability rather than luck (see, for example, O'Connor and Atkinson, 1960).

or his supervisor's instructions is much less likely to see success as a personal achievement.

There is some research concerning the relation between employee influence on work methods and productivity which is relevant to this matter. Although not all the evidence is consistent (see Vroom, 1964, pp. 223–229), most of it indicates that high employee influence over work methods is likely to be associated with high performance. This, of course, would be expected if, as indicated here, personal responsibility for success brings high achievement incentive.

We have noted four major factors which may affect the achievement incentive on any particular task, but this list is not necessarily exhaustive. For example, the chance to *finish* a task may at times vary and have an impact on achievement incentive. However, regardless of other factors which may enter into the picture, each of the major factors discussed above is essential in order for achievement incentive to be present in strength. We expect, therefore, that these factors will have a multiplicative effect on incentive, in the folowing fashion :

$$
(4) \begin{array}{l} \text{Achievement} \\ \text{Incentive} \\ \text{of a Task} \end{array} = f \begin{bmatrix} \text{Extent to Which} \\ \text{Standards of Ex-} \\ \text{cellence Are} \\ \text{Clear} \end{bmatrix}
$$

$$
\times \begin{bmatrix} \text{Extent to Which} \\ \text{Feedback on Per-} \\ \text{formance Is Ex-} \\ \text{pected} \end{bmatrix} \times \begin{bmatrix} \text{Extent to Which} \\ \text{Person Is Per-} \\ \text{sonally Respon-} \\ \text{sible for Success} \end{bmatrix} \times \begin{bmatrix} \text{Difficulty} \\ \text{of the} \\ \text{Task} \end{bmatrix}
$$

PROBABILITY THAT EFFORT WILL LEAD TO SUCCESSFUL ACHIEVEMENT

The general formula (1) for predicting motivation to complete a job, as it is related to the motive to achieve on the job, shows that we have to consider not only the strength of the motivation to achieve on the job and the achievement incentive which is present in the job situation, but also the expectancy (perceived probability) that effort will actually lead to success on the job. Although there is, to our knowledge, little research on this matter, we will consider here some of the factors which may affect the expectancy that effort will lead to successful achievement. These are (1) previous experience of success in the same or similar tasks; (2) features of the present task which are different from those in previous similar situations; (3) generalized self-confidence.

Previous Experiences of Success in Similar Tasks[15]

Where a person has had considerable previous experience in a task of a certain kind, his expectation that he can be successful may be heavily influenced by his success in the past. The craftsman whose work has usually been praised, rather than criticized, by his boss; the executive whose past decisions have usually turned out right; the scientist whose previous work has won honors; the salesman whose persuasion has usually been effective; these men are likely to perceive a high probability of success in their present efforts.

Difficulties Specific to the Present Task Situation

Expectations of success carried over from previous experiences may be modified by the nature of the present task situation. The task itself may be somewhat different from previous tasks of a similar kind. The defective boiler may be damaged more seriously than it was previously; the present customer may be a "tougher nut to crack" than most others; the location of the new dam may create special problems for the engineer; the scientific problem at hand may be in an unexplored area; and so on.

Aside from the nature of the task itself, the perceived probability of success may be affected by external factors which either facilitate or interfere with successful effort. Anything which affects the availability of needed resources—money, information, tools, materials, and time to finish the job—will affect the perceived probability of success.

Generalized Self-Confidence

We would expect the perceived probability of success in specific tasks to be influenced also by the general self-confidence of the individual. The degree of self-confidence probably derives in large measure from past experience of success in the individual's total, and especially early, life experience.

Each of the three factors discussed—past experiences of success in similar tasks, difficulties specific to the present task, and generalized level of confidence—may be expected to exert an independent effect on the net perceived probability of success. Probably the net perceived probability of success will be some kind of weighted average of the probabilities suggested by each of the three factors. The weight of each factor will probably be determined by the degree of past experience with similar

---

[15]Atkinson (1964, p. 258) also briefly discusses the effects of previous success and failure. He also discusses the possibility that perceptions of the probability of success may increase as the motive for success (achievement) rises.

tasks and the extent to which the present task differs from previous ones. If the person has had considerable experience under closely similar job conditions, his past experiences are likely to carry the most weight in his perceptions of the likelihood of present success. If the present task is unique but well defined, the information he has about its difficulty will probably be decisive. If he has little past experience with such tasks and little solid information on which to judge present difficulties, his generalized self-confidence may have the most effect on his perceived probability of success.

THE RELATION BETWEEN ACHIEVEMENT INCENTIVE AND PERCEIVED PROBABILITY OF SUCCESS

Psychologists who have studied achievement motivation have postulated, as noted above, that the achievement incentive equals one minus the probability of success. We would expect this formula to be generally and very roughly true. The more difficult a task is, the more likely is success to be seen by the individual as a substantial achievement and the more likely it is to be socially defined as a notable achievement.

However, our analysis suggests that such a simple relationship between incentive and probability of success will rarely be exactly correct and sometimes may be far off the mark. First, even where a low or moderate probability of success may tend to create a strong achievement incentive, the incentive may be affected by the clarity of standards of excellence, the expectation of feedback on performance, and the degree of felt responsibility for the outcome.

Secondly, the incentive for achievement is, in part, socially defined independently of the individual's perceived probability of success. To illustrate, imagine the case of a rookie baseball player who is trying to hit .300 in his first major league season. Suppose further that on the basis of his past experience in the minor leagues, his look at major league pitching in Spring training, and his general self-confidence, this young man perceives that he has a 90 per cent chance of hitting .300. Does this mean that his achievement incentive in this situation will be low—i.e., 1 — probability of success?

We would expect that his perceived incentive—i.e., his perception of the amount of achievement possible—would not necessarily be low in this situation. Hitting .300 in the majors, especially for a rookie, is defined by millions as a substantial achievement. Because he is influenced by such socially defined standards of success, the rookie player also is likely to see this level of batting success as an achievement of considerable magnitude. He is also likely to value such an achievement, though perhaps more for the prestige, money, etc., that it will bring than because of personal pride. Examples may also be found in other job settings; e.g., the chemist who sees a chance to synthesize a sorely needed product, who feels confident that he can do it, and for whom this possible success is a considerable incentive. It is possible, therefore, according to our conception of achievement incentive and perceived probability, for both of these factors to be high at the same time.

THE RELATION OF THE STUDY TO THESE IDEAS

In our study of work motivation at TVA, we will not try to test all of the relationships that are hypothesized in this chapter, as summarized in Figure 3-1. In particular, we will not try to predict the level of motive for achievement on the job, of achievement incentive, or of expectancy of successful achievement. This is not our major interest and, in any case, we do not have measures of these variables. Our main effort, rather, will be in predicting motivation to do the job. The theoretical ideas presented above will be valuable for their implications about what aspects of the job situation and what personal characteristics are likely to be related to work motivation.

On the basis of the theoretical formulation outlined, it is clear that those job and personal factors which are expected to affect the motive to achieve on the job, or achievement incentive, or expectancy of success, may also be expected to affect work motivation. Thus, we will look at the associations between work motivation and many characteristics of the job situation and of the individual which have been discussed above. Because of the nature of the work situations studied and of the available data, we will pay relatively little attention to factors bearing on the expectancy of success. We will pay greatest attention to factors bearing on the achievement motive and on achievement incentive. Those factors bearing especially on the achievement motive will be considered under the heading of *rewards for achievement*. Those factors bearing especially on achievement incentive (and also on the expectancy of achievement) will be considered under the heading of *opportunities for achievement*.

It should be emphasized that a theoretical model of the type outlined in this chapter does much more than simply draw our attention to variables which may be related to work motivation. The key concepts—especially, achievement motive on the job, achievement incentive, and expectancy of success—provide focal points around which a great mass of otherwise unorganized data about the nature of the job situation and

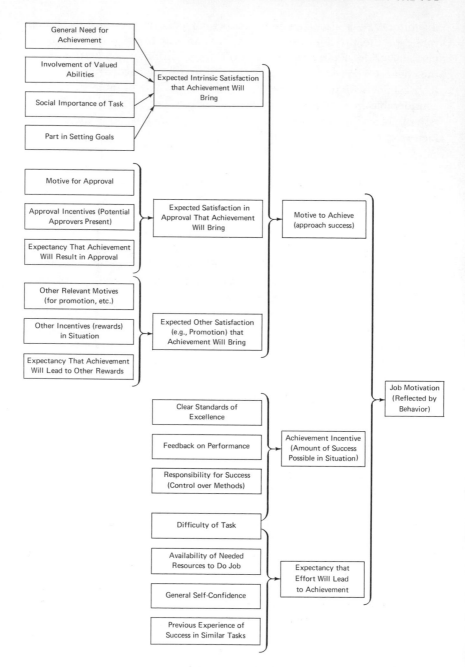

FIGURE 3-1 Hypothesized relation between job motivation and job and personal characteristics relevant to achievement

individual characteristics can be organized in a coherent fashion. The theoretical model will, in other words, provide a guide for the organization and analysis of our data about work motivation at TVA.

SUMMARY

In this study we are concerned with work motivation which stems from the anticipated satisfactions of personal achievement on the job. Following Atkinson, we see work motivation (insofar as it is based on the desire for achievement) as being determined by (1) the motivation for achievement; (2) the achievement incentive, or reward; and (3) the expectancy that work performance will lead to successful achievement.

The achievement motive has usually been treated as a fairly enduring characteristic which is part of the personality. However, because of factors in the job situation which may affect the value of achievement, we have conceived the achievement motive in a way which separates this motive from an exclusive linkage with personality. The level of achievement motivation on the job is seen as affected by factors which affect the intrinsic satisfaction which achievement on the job may bring. Achievement motivation on the job is seen as affected also by the extent to which achievement will bring social respect, social approval, and pragmatic rewards. The theoretical and practical implications of this view are that it directs us to the study of those present job factors (e.g., involvement of valued abilities, probability that achievement will bring approval from associates) which may affect the achievement motive on the job and ultimately may affect performance.

Achievement incentive, or the amount of achievement possible, has often been discussed solely as a function of the expectancy of success (difficulty of task). However, we have pointed to three other variables whose effects on achievement incentive need to be explicitly studied. These are (1) the extent to which there are clear standards of excellence; (2) the extent to which feedback on performance is expected; and (3) the extent to which the person is responsible for success. It was hypothesized that all of these job characteristics, along with at least moderate task difficulty, must be present in order for achievement incentive to be high and that their effect on achievement incentive is multiplicative. The impact of these incentive-relevant job features on job motivation will be the focus of much of the data to be presented in this portion of the book.

Some determinants of the expectancy that effort will lead to successful achievement were also discussed. These are (1) previous experience of success in similar tasks; (2) difficulties specific to the present task situation; and (3) general self-confidence.

Finally, the relation between achievement incentive and expectancy of successful achievement was discussed. An important implication of our discussion is that achievement incentive is seen as not simply a function of the probability of success. This is true in part because factors other than difficulty of the task (i.e., clarity of standards of performance, anticipation of feedback, and responsibility for outcome) can affect achievement incentive. It is seen as true also because the magnitude of achievement has a social as well as a personal definition.

In the study of work motivation at TVA, we will not test *directly* most of the theoretical ideas presented. However, in trying to explain variations in job motivation, we will be guided by the implications of the theoretical formulation as to what job and personal characteristics may be expected to affect motivation on the job. The theoretical model will also serve as an important framework for organizing a mass of data about specific job situations.

Before trying to explain some of the differences in job motivation at TVA, we will look, in the next chapter, at the nature of some of these differences and at the kinds of data available for assessing motivation and other individual reactions on the job.

4

JOB
MOTIVATION
AT TVA

The measurement of a person's motivation to perform his job (job motivation) is a difficult task. In this study we have focused on several kinds of data which we have reason to believe are indicators of job motivation. These are (1) general interest in the job; (2) interest in innovation on the job; and (3) number of absences from the job. A closely related phenomenon which we are interested in studying is pride in one's accomplishments in the job.

This chapter will illustrate some of the differences in job interest, interest in innovation on the job, and pride in work which we have found among employees in various jobs. Secondly, it will describe the questionnaire measures which we used to gather systematic data concerning motivation and pride on the job, as well as supplementary data concerning symptoms of stress. Thirdly, the relative standing of various occupational groups on measures of motivation and pride will be described.

GENERAL INTEREST IN THE JOB

For some people, the meaning of their work is primarily in the "living" it brings them—i.e., something to be endured in order that one

may live outside of work hours. An electrician at a TVA steam plant
seemed to reflect this general feeling when he answered an interviewer's
question concerning what he liked about his job :

> *Money—it's what we're here for. Fringe benefits, annual leave, sick leave. We get more
> than we would in a private concern.*

Another person for whom the job appeared to hold little intrinsic
interest, a woman clerk-typist, said when asked what she liked about her
job :

> *We get more money than most and it's not a hard job. Working conditions are perfectly
> all right. I'd prefer working as a legal secretary, but there's more money in this job. But
> a legal secretary has more prestige.*

A beginning civil engineer said :

> *It's steady; not hard work. You more or less set your own pace. There's no one really
> pushing you. Very few times that you really have to push yourself. The money is compa-
> rable to any place that I've worked.*

In another part of the interview, this engineer mentioned that he was
doing "not as good a job for TVA as I have done for other people."

Compare those answers with the answers of the following people to
the same question : "In general, what things do you like most about
your job?"

A payroll clerk :

> *Figures always have been fascinating to me. When a job becomes routine to you, you
> don't like it. I like to take a conglomeration of odd numbers and bring them down to where
> they mean something. I like to bring proofs about.*

An engineering aide in the laboratory of a steam plant :

> *Any test work here where we use various test instruments. My first love was instruments.*

A beginning electrical engineer :

> *Some engineers think they should start at the top with high class mathematics. But I'd
> rather learn a little at a time. To learn the details of a job, you have to start at the bottom.
> I learn a little every day. That's another thing I like about TVA.*

Clearly, these two sets of answers reflect differences in the amount of
interest which employees have in their work. To more systematically assess

job interest of various employees, we have used an index score based on employees' answers to the following questions :

1. On most days on your job, how often does time seem to drag for you?
   - (1) ——————— About half the day or more
   - (2) ——————— About one-third of the day
   - (3) ——————— About one-quarter of the day
   - (4) ——————— About one-eighth of the day
   - (5) ——————— Time never seems to drag

2. Some people are completely involved in their job—they are absorbed in it night and day. For other people, their job is simply one of several interests. How involved do you feel in your job?
   - (1) ——————— Very little involved; my other interests are more absorbing
   - (2) ——————— Slightly involved
   - (3) ——————— Moderately involved; my job and my other interests are equally absorbing to me
   - (4) ——————— Strongly involved
   - (5) ——————— Very strongly involved; my work is the most absorbing interest in my life

These questions were selected from a much larger number of questions relevant to job interest and job motivation which were asked at TVA. They were selected because they were most strongly associated with supervisors' rankings of employees on "concern for doing a good job" and with attendance.[1]

Differences Among Units

Average scores on the index of general job interest were computed for each of ninety work groups in various parts of TVA. Each group reports to a different immediate supervisor. Although average job interest is generally high at TVA, there is considerable variation among units, with average scores varying from 4.6 to 8.0.

It is interesting to examine the types of work units which score especially low and especially high on job interest. Among the work groups scoring *lowest* in job interest are two civil engineering sections; three drafting service sections; a group of steam fitters; a group of instrument mechanics; a switchboard (power plant, not telephone) operators' group; and a group of engineering aides in a steam plant laboratory.

Work groups scoring *highest* in job interest include civil engineering

---

[1]Data on the reliability and validity of this measure are presented elsewhere (Patchen Pelz, and Allen, 1965, pp. 26-39). The Index score was computed by adding the scores on each of the two questions.

units; a mechanical engineering unit; several engineering planning units; a machinist group; a carpenters' group; a material testers' (steam plant lab) group; an architectural design unit; and a lab engineering aides unit. Note that several occupational titles—civil engineering and engineering aides—appear both in the list of the units with highest job interest and among the units with lowest job interest. Other occupational titles in the lowest interest group—e.g., steam fitters and instrument mechanics—are similar to occupations represented among the highest interest units—e.g., machinists and carpenters—in that all are skilled crafts.

Moreover, there are other wide variations in job interest scores among identical occupational groups in different job locations. For example, in contrast to the instrument mechanics unit found among those groups lowest in job interest, another instrument mechanics unit doing similar work in another plant ranks near those units highest in job interest.

These discrepancies in job interest scores among those doing similar types of work appear to indicate that factors other than the intrinsic nature of the work itself have an important bearing upon job interest.

INTEREST IN INNOVATION

Another possible indicator of motivation on the job is the extent to which the individual is alert to new and better ways of doing things, instead of being content to do his job in a routine and mechanical fashion. Top management at TVA tries to encourage employees to contribute their work improvement ideas, in part through a system of cooperative conferences in which management and employee representatives discuss problems of mutual interest.

In interviewing employees at TVA, we asked : "Do you get much chance on your job to try out your own ideas?" Here are some examples of innovative behavior which people mentioned :

An electrician at a steam plant said :

We do that very frequently; for example, this past week I suggested that the electrical power should be taken from one elevation to another and the supervisor went over the situation and agreed.

A supervisor of the maintenance section in a steam plant said :

We completely redesigned the clinker here. It was a combination of the ideas of supervisors and craftsmen. Then we built a number of valves.

A boilermaker said :

On burner tilts which wore out, we used to have to screw them out. (Name) and another, and myself, made this jig to work on hydraulic jacks. This was on exhibit at one of the employees' exhibits. TVA sponsors these exhibits, for hydro plants, steam plants, and all. It was not done through the co-op committee. It was done through the foreman and the men.

On the other hand, some employees—sometimes for reasons beyond their control—take little initiative in trying to improve ways of doing the job. Asked about chances to try out ideas on his job, a steam fitter in a power plant said :

There was more interest at (another TVA installation)—more interest in making suggestions and more interest in receiving them. Since it was a small installation, you got more recognition for your suggestions to the cooperative committee . . . they have the same system here, but there aren't as many suggestions and not so much notice since it's so big.

To try to systematically assess the degree of interest in innovation found in various units at TVA, we included these questions in the questionnaire :

1. In your kind of work, if a person tries to change his usual way of doing things, how does it generally turn out?

    (*1*) _____ Usually turns out worse; the tried and true methods work best in my work

    (*3*) _____ Usually doesn't make much difference

    (*5*) _____ Usually turns out better; our methods need improvement

2. Some people prefer doing a job in pretty much the same way because this way they can count on always doing a good job. Others like to go out of their way in order to think up new ways of doing things. How is it with you on your job?

    (*1*) _____ I always prefer doing things pretty much in the same way

    (*2*) _____ I mostly prefer doing things pretty much in the same way

    (*4*) _____ I mostly prefer doing things in new and different ways

    (*5*) _____ I always prefer doing things in new and different ways

3. How often do you try out, on your own, a better or faster way of doing something on the job?

    (5) —————— Once a week or more often
    (4) —————— Two or three times a month
    (3) —————— About once a month
    (2) —————— Every few months
    (1) —————— Rarely or never

4. How often do you get chances to try out your own ideas on the job, either before or after checking with your supervisor?

    (5) —————— Several times a week or more
    (4) —————— About once a week
    (3) —————— Several times a month
    (2) —————— About once a month
    (1) —————— Less than once a month

5. In my kind of job, it's usually better to let my supervisor worry about new or better ways of doing things.

    (1) —————— Strongly agree
    (2) —————— Mostly agree
    (4) —————— Mostly disagree
    (5) —————— Strongly disagree

6. How many times in the past year have you suggested to your supervisor a different or better way of doing something on the job?

    (1) —————— Never had occasion to do this during the past year
    (2) —————— Once or twice
    (3) —————— About three times
    (4) —————— About five times
    (5) —————— Six to ten times
    (6) —————— More than ten times had occasion to do this during the past year

Employees' scores on an index of interest in work innovation based on these questions showed positive correlations with supervisors' rankings of the extent to which employees are "looking out for new ideas." Further evidence of the validity of the measure is provided by the fact that those employees who submitted suggestions to the cooperative program (according to records) score significantly higher than other employees on the index of interest in innovation.[2] Scores on the interest in innovation index, for ninety work groups, have a moderate association (r = .46) with group scores on the general job interest index.

As with the job interest index, the types of work groups which rank lowest in interest in innovation do not differ appreciably in occupational

---

[2] See Patchen, Pelz, and Allen (1965) for data on the reliability and validity of the Index of Interest in Work Innovation.

type from those groups which rank highest. Among the ten units which rank lowest on the interest in innovation measure are four engineering units (two electrical, one civil, one mechanical); a unit of analytical chemists; a drafting unit; two clerical units; and two steam plant operating units. At the other extreme, among the ten groups scoring highest on interest in innovation, we find the following : eight engineering units (four civil, two mechanical, two planning); an architectural procurement unit; and a unit of instrument mechanics in a steam plant. One of the civil engineering units, which is among the lowest in interest in innovation scores, designs exactly the same type of equipment as a unit which ranks among those highest in innovative interest.

Several craftsmen's units (machinists, carpenters) and several laboratory units (analytical chemists, material testers) have close to the lowest interest in innovation scores while other craftsmen's units (painters, boilermakers) rank close to the highest. In contrast to the clerical groups which are among the lowest in innovation, a clerical group in another location ranks close to the top. This pattern of the relative standing of various work groups suggests again that factors other than the intrinsic nature of the work can have an important effect on job motivation.

PRIDE IN JOB ACCOMPLISHMENT

In interviews with TVA employees, we asked : "Can you think of the last time that you accomplished something on the job that you were especially proud of?" Many people talked with some enthusiasm about things they had recently done on the job about which they felt proud. Here are a few such answers :

A chemist in a power plant :

There are about nine units, about four different levels checking on the water treatment, and changes are advised and made by us. If I come in the morning and check things and leave it better in the evening, I feel good. Now I'm a stickler for cleanliness in analysis, maybe too much so. Nevertheless, the area that I work in is known to be spic and span. The supervisor brings men to inspect my area. Also, if you are suspicious of something in analysis and if you have something and it saves thousands of dollars—a feeling of elation comes from this.

A draftsman in an engineering division :

Well, I did some work on our extra high voltage line and I figured I did pretty well, and I got quite a lot of compliments for it. Also, some drawings on it got into some big magazines. Of course, that was earlier when I didn't have as much experience, so maybe that's why I got such a kick out of it.

An engineering aide in the laboratory of a steam plant :

They ran an acid cleaning condenser and checked the iron and copper in the inlets and outlets. They wanted somebody to draw a graph, which would be part of the chemist's job usually—but the chemist wouldn't do it and they asked me to do it. It was a complex graph. I was proud of it because I was allowed to use my own initiative.

A few people, however, had difficulty thinking of instances where they had done something on the job of which they felt proud. Here are several such answers :

A woman clerk-typist :

On the job, no. I do lots of things outside of the job—in my church work, for instance, that I'm very proud of, but not anything on the job . . . I feel like a piece of machinery here. I've worked for lawyers and district attorneys, so I got a sense of achievement which I don't get here at all.

A civil engineer :

No, I haven't done anything major—mostly miscellaneous . . . I'm not doing as good a job as I have done for other people. Your work is such a small part of the overall thing. You never really see what you've done. I've been working on drawings now for two or three days. When it's all over, I'll never see it . . . In the other organization, we were into the job further. We were trying to get a job done, rather than drawings done. I had more ideas about how everything fit together than you do with this organization. The projects that I worked on were much smaller. You might want to weld something in a slightly different way, but it's so minor it wouldn't really matter.

To try to get systematic information about the amount of pride which various employees feel in their work, the following questionnaire items were used :

1. How often do you feel really proud of something you've done on the job?
    - (5) ——————— Almost every day
    - (4) ——————— Once every few days
    - (3) ——————— About once a week
    - (2) ——————— Once every few weeks
    - (1) ——————— About once a month or less
2. How often do you tell your wife or other family members about something you've accomplished on the job?
    - (5) ——————— Almost every day
    - (4) ——————— Several times a week
    - (3) ——————— About once a week
    - (2) ——————— About once a month
    - (1) ——————— Rarely or never
    - ——————— No family members to talk to

In general those work units which score high on the job interest index and on the interest in innovation index tend to score high on the pride in work index (see Appendix 0). Groups which score high on job pride also have fewer absences, especially in the power plants where the correlation between job pride and total number of absences is $-.61$ (p<.001).

Craftsmen's units tend to appear prominently among those work groups scoring highest on the pride in job index. There are four such craftsmen's groups (two machinists' units, a boilermakers' unit, and an asbestos workers' unit) among the ten groups scoring highest on the job pride index. However, there is one craftsmen's unit (a steam fitters' group) among the ten groups scoring lowest in job pride.

Three of the top ten units scoring highest on the job pride index are engineering groups, but six of the ten units scoring lowest on the index are also engineering groups.

Also among the units scoring lowest in job pride are two groups of analytical chemists and a steam plant operations unit. The procurement staff of an architectural unit is among those groups scoring highest in job pride.

ATTENDANCE

Previous studies indicate that poor attendance is often associated with low job satisfaction,[3] including a low level of liking for the job itself. It seems reasonable to assume, therefore, that variations in job motivation will tend to be reflected in variations in attendance.

At one of the two TVA engineering divisions and at all three of the steam plants covered by our study, we were able to obtain data concerning the attendance records of employees who took the questionnaire during the twelve months prior to its administration. In accord with procedures found desirable by Metzner and Mann (1953), we scored *instances* of absence rather than number of days. An instance was defined as any continuous period of absence. Thus, a lengthy absence due to serious illness or injury was counted as only one instance and did not unduly affect attendance scores. Instances of part-day absences (working only part of a day) as well as instances of absences of one or more days were tabulated. A total number of absence instances (full day plus part day) was also

[3]See a summary of some of the evidence in Vroom (1964). See also Katz and Hyman (1947); Mayo and Lombard (1944); and Noland (1945).

tabulated for each individual. Finally, average numbers of absence instances for the ninety work groups were computed.

There was considerable variation in absence among work groups at TVA, ranging from an average of 2.0 absences during the year in one architectural design unit (both full day and part day) to an average of 11.0 absences in one mechanical engineering unit. The mean total number of absences for all work groups was 5.6 and the standard deviation was 2.3, indicating that about two-thirds of the groups had an average of between 3.3 and 7.9 total absences during the year covered.

Full-day absences were much more frequent in power plants than in the engineering division, while part-day absences were much more frequent in the engineering division.[4] Within the power plants, absences were somewhat less frequent among operating personnel than among other units, probably reflecting the fact that replacements for absent operating employees must be found among off-duty employees.[5]

Because of these differences in patterns of absence, which appear unrelated to job motivation, attendance data will sometimes be presented separately for two types of employees : (1) engineering division personnel; and (2) power plant nonoperating personnel (i.e., maintenance men and lab people). It appears legitimate to combine employees from the three power plants when studying absence, since the power plants do not appear to differ consistently in relative number of absences. Also we will at times compare all ninety groups with respect to total number of absences since the total of full- and part-day absences are roughly comparable between engineering and power divisions.

SYMPTOMS OF STRESS

Although our major focus is job motivation and job pride, we are interested also in symptoms of stress which individuals experience. On the questionnaire which employees filled out were the following items :

---

[4]Full-day absences are generally most strongly related to differences in work conditions in the engineering division while total number of absences (both full day and part day) are most strongly related to work conditions in the power plants. Thus, later tables will present data on full-day absences for engineering and on total number of absences for power plants. In both cases, only the absence data for men are used since women have been shown to be absent more often than men.

[5]Because of this difference in attendance between operating and nonoperating personnel, data on attendance in the power plants alone will generally be presented for nonoperating employees only.

1. Listed below are some common physical problems which often bother people. How often does each of them happen to you?

    A. Trouble getting to sleep

        (6) —————— Several times a week
        (5) —————— About once a week
        (4) —————— Several times a month
        (3) —————— About once a month
        (2) —————— Once every few months
        (1) —————— Almost never

    B. Headaches
    C. Upset stomach
    D. Gas or bloated feeling

2. Most people have days when they feel pretty "blue" or depressed during most of the day. How often does this happen to you?

        (5) —————— Two or three times a week
        (4) —————— About once a week
        (3) —————— Once or twice a month
        (2) —————— About once a month
        (1) —————— Less than once a month

3. Most people have days when they feel tired or worn out during a good part of the day. How often does this happen to you?

        (5) —————— Two or three times a week
        (4) —————— About once a week
        (3) —————— Once or twice a month
        (2) —————— About once a month
        (1) —————— Less than once a month

4. How often do you feel nervous, tense, or edgy while on the job?

        (6) —————— More than 50 per cent of the time
        (5) —————— About 50 per cent of the time
        (4) —————— About 25 per cent of the time
        (3) —————— About 10 per cent of the time
        (2) —————— About 5 per cent of the time
        (1) —————— Very rarely or never

For each individual, an index of physical symptoms of stress, based on questions 1A, 1B, 1C, and 1D, and an index of psychological symptoms of stress, based on questions 2, 3, and 4, were computed.[6] Index scores for individuals working under the same immediate supervisor were then averaged to provide scores for each of the ninety work groups.

Although the items of these indices are similar to items found on some

———————————

[6]In computing these indices a score was assigned to each response which corresponds to the number to the left of each response. It may be noted that question 3 is more physical and less psychological than the other items in the index of psychological symptoms of stress.

inventories of psychiatric symptoms,[7] most of them were prepared for this study and, unlike our measures of job interest for which there is evidence of validity, there is no independent evidence which shows that responses to these questions really reflect meaningful differences in physical and psychological health. However, the items obviously refer to symptoms which are both fairly common and universally agreed to be associated with stress. They appear therefore to possess a reasonable amount of "face validity."[8] The indices of symptoms of stress will be particularly useful in assessing whether job conditions which increase motivation do so at the cost of undesirable symptoms of stress.

SUMMARY

General job interest, interest in work innovation, and absence are probable indicators of job motivation. Comments by employees illustrate variations in general job interest and interest in innovation, as well as variations in pride in work. To provide more systematic data on these topics, questionnaire measures of general job interest, interest in work innovation, job pride, and symptoms of stress, along with absence data, were obtained. Brief comparisons of the types of work units which scored especially low or especially high on our measures of job motivation and job pride indicate that there is considerable variation in these characteristics among units doing similar work.

In the following chapters we will try to isolate some of the personal and situational factors which may help to account for variations in job motivation. The next chapter will focus on opportunities to achieve on the job. Later chapters will consider rewards for achievement in the work situation and combinations of opportunity and reward for achievement as they are related to job motivation and other reactions to the job.

---

[7]See, for example, the scale of nervous symptoms which forms part of the California Test of Personality or the Cornell Index of Psychosomatic and Neuropsychiatric Symptoms (Buros, 1959).

[8]A standard psychiatric inventory was not used because there was not sufficient room in the questionnaire and because many of the items in such inventories were judged inappropriate for our sample of generally normal men.

5

OPPORTUNITY
TO ACHIEVE
ON THE JOB

We discussed in Chapter 3 various aspects of the job situation which may affect (1) the achievement incentive, i.e., the amount of achievement possible on the job; and (2) the expectancy that task effort will result in achievement on the job. Where achievement incentive and the expectancy of success are high (or, more exactly, when the product of these variables is high), we may speak of a good *opportunity for achievement* on the job. What effects do differences in opportunity for achievement have on job motivation? And what effects do such job differences have on pride in work and on symptoms of stress?

In this chapter, we consider primarily job differences which seem likely to affect achievement incentive. We have already discussed, in Chapter 3, four relevant job characteristics : (1) the extent to which the individual is personally responsible for success (has control over the methods of doing his work); (2) the difficulty of the work; (3) the extent to which feedback on one's performance can be expected; and (4) the extent to which standards of excellence are clear. In this chapter, we will examine these four determinants of achievement incentive, as well as several other job characteristics—chance to learn and chance to finish things—which appear relevant to achievement incentive. Also, we will consider an aspect of the job—the availability of resources to do the job—

which seems relevant to the probability of successful achievement. After looking at concrete examples of differences in these job characteristics, we will examine their relation, singly and in certain combinations, to job interest, to absence, to job pride, and to symptons of stress.

PERSONAL RESPONSIBILITY FOR SUCCESS

There are fairly wide differences among different occupations and different work units in the amount of personal control which employees have over the means of doing their work and thus over their success or failure. Comments from interviews with TVA employees give the flavor of some of these differences in personal responsibility. Some employees who appear to enjoy little control over means of doing the job commented as follows :

An engineering associate :

Most everything is standard. If new equipment is to be used, somebody else decided on it. If you get off the beaten path, someone else will call you down. Part of it is because some old tried methods are good, but it seems to be more than that. It is also, "if it's not my idea, we won't use it." Now I've got jobs to check. I have to check them according to the old method. If I don't change them to correspond to the old ways, someone else will change it for me.

An auxiliary operator in a power plant :

My work involves checking equipment and operating equipment under direct supervision. You are not supposed to deviate from the established operating procedures.

An engineering aide in one of the engineering divisions who keeps records of leaves and of materials sent by manufacturers, routes various materials, and checks in materials when they are returned :

It's sort of like the Army . . . If I felt I had a good idea, I would promote it; but I think things work out pretty well the way they are. There's less chance to make errors if you have a pattern to go by. TVA and Army Finance work about the same way. In both cases, there is an account system, numbers to learn. I might be in a rut, but if a thing is proven, if a system is proven to work satisfactorily, that's the answer.

On the other hand, some employees have the kind of jobs and the kind of supervision which give them considerable leeway in deciding how to do their work.

An electrician in a steam plant :

My foreman knows nothing about construction and I do, so he asks my advice all the time. He'll say, "Should we do it this way or that way," or "Go ahead and do it your way."

An architect in an engineering division :

This is a one-man proposition. I set my own rules. I can change anything I want to.

A store clerk in a steam plant :

There is quite a lot of opportunity to try out ideas. With such things as the shortening of a report or where to distribute a report. We make suggestions to send in more information than we do now. Everyone can do their individual work as they see fit.

Questionnaire Index

To assess more systematically the extent of control over job methods exercised by various employees, the following questions were asked :

1. In some jobs, there are detailed rules about what is the right way to do the job. In other jobs, a person can choose between several possible ways of doing the job.
   How is it with your job?
   - (*1*) _____ Almost everything is covered by rules
   - (*2*) _____ Most things are covered by rules
   - (*3*) _____ About half and half
   - (*4*) _____ On most things I have a choice of ways of doing the work
   - (*5*) _____ On almost everything I have a choice of ways of doing the work

2. If you suggest to your immediate supervisor a way of doing some job, how often does he go along with your suggestion?
   He goes along with my suggestions:
   - (*1*) _____ About one-tenth of the time or less
   - (*2*) _____ About one-quarter of the time
   - (*3*) _____ About half of the time
   - (*4*) _____ About three-quarters of the time
   - (*5*) _____ Almost always
   - _____ I never suggest a way of doing some job

3. When you get a job to do, how often is it completely up to you to decide how to go about doing it?
   - (*1*) _____ About one-tenth of the time or less
   - (*2*) _____ About one-quarter of the time
   - (*3*) _____ About half of the time
   - (*4*) _____ About three-quarters of the time
   - (*5*) _____ Almost always

4. How often do you get chances to try out your ideas on your job, either
    before or after checking with your supervisor?

    (5) ——————— Several times a week or more
    (4) ——————— About once a week
    (3) ——————— Several times a month
    (2) ——————— About once a month
    (1) ——————— Less than once a month

Scores on these questions[1] were averaged for each individual to form
an index of control over means.[2] For each group of employees working
under the same immediate supervisor, an average score on control over
means was also computed. Scores on the index tend to cluster within
work groups,[3] indicating that people in similar jobs under the same supervisor tend to report a similar situation.

Average scores on the control over means index vary widely among
the ninety immediate work groups.[4] As might be expected, operating
units at steam plants, which must work under standard operating procedures, all score below the median in control over means—though there
is some variation among these groups. Engineering, crafts, and other
groups, however, are found at all positions on the control over means
index. In some cases, groups doing very similar work in different branches
are at opposite extremes of the control over means continuum. Thus, a
steam fitter's unit in one steam plant scores lowest among all groups in
control over means, while steam fitters in another steam plant score very
close to the top on the same index. The same wide discrepancy in control
over means scores is found between two groups of painters in different
steam plants and between two sections in the same branch of one of the
engineering divisions. Evidently, for most types of jobs at TVA, supervisors have a fair amount of discretion about how much to permit
employees to choose among methods of doing the job.[5]

——————————

[1]Numbers preceding each response category represent the scores assigned to those
responses.

[2]Scores on the index of control over means have a moderate association ($r = .47$ for
834 employees) with answers to a question which may be viewed as a rough indicator of
achievement opportunity: "How much chance do you get to feel at the end of the day
that you have accomplished something?"

[3]A statistical test shows that variance between work groups is significantly greater than
variance within work groups ($F = 2.25$; $p < .01$).

[4]The range of group scores on the control over means index is 1.5 to 4.7. The mean
score is 2.25 and the standard deviation is 1.18.

[5]Another possible explanation of the wide discrepancy in control over means scores
among similar job units is that the measure is not valid at all. In view of the fact that
scores tend to be similar within the same group, it seems unlikely that the measure is
seriously misleading.

Relation to Job Involvement

What effects does the amount of control over job methods have on people's reactions to their jobs? To shed light on this question, correlation coefficients (rs)[6] were computed to show the associations between scores on the index of control over means and scores on job interest, absence, pride in work, and symptoms of stress. These correlations were computed both for individuals and for work groups. Partial correlations were also computed;[7] these show the associations when other variables which might affect job motivation are held constant statistically.[8]

The results for individuals and for work groups are generally parallel, but the relationships are slightly stronger for groups. Table 5-1 shows these data for the ninety work groups. The data indicate that the more control employees in a group exert over means of doing the job, the greater their general job interest ($r = .42$) and the greater their interest in work innovation ($r = .31$). When other variables affecting job interest are controlled for, these positive associations become smaller, but are still statistically significant (i.e., not likely to have occurred by chance). There are, moreover, small negative associations between level of employee control over means and the average number of absences (more control, fewer absences).

Along with the greater job interest which accompanies control over job means, such control is also associated, as shown in Table 5-1, with greater pride in job accomplishments ($r = .36$). But while generally appearing to be more highly involved in their job performance, those in groups which have greater control over means report fewer psychological symptoms of stress (nervousness, depression, being tired all day) ($r = -.37$).

---

[6] A correlation coefficient (r) is a measure of the amount of variance on one characteristic which is associated with, or "explained" by, variance on another characteristic. The value of r may range from $+1$, which indicates perfect positive association, through -1, which indicates that scores on the two characteristics have a perfect negative association (when one goes up, the other goes down proportionally). A value of zero indicates no correlation. The value r^2 equals the proportion of variance on one characteristic which may be "explained" by variance on the other characteristic.

[7] Partial coefficients were not computed for group absences separately in engineering divisions and power plants because the number of engineering groups and steam plant groups was too small to make such analysis statistically meaningful.

[8] For the partial correlation analysis for groups, the independent variables included in the analysis were the following: (1) need for achievement; (2) extent to which achievement brings peer approval; (3) extent to which achievement leads to promotion; (4) clarity of goals; (5) difficulty of work; (6) feedback on performance; (7) effect of own work on others' work; (8) identification with occupation; (9) opportunity for comparison of own work with others' work; (10) praise of good work by supervisors; (11) control over goals; (12) control over means; (13) frequency of time limits; (14) chance to do what employees are best at; (15) chance to learn new things; (16) chance to finish things.

For groups, there is no association between control over means and physical symptoms of stress, but there is a small, statistically significant negative association (more control, fewer physical symptoms) for individuals ($r = -.14$, $p < .01$).

TABLE 5-1   Control of Means of Doing Job as Related to Various Reactions to the Job, for Ninety Work Groups[a]

(Product-Moment Correlations)

	r	Partial r[‡]
General job interest	.42**	.21*
Interest in work innovation[b]	.31**	.22*
Full-day absences, engineering division (N = 34)	−.16	—
Total absences, power plants, nonoperating (N = 29)	−.12	—
Total absences,[b] all sites (N = 63)[c]	−.17	−.21
Pride in work	.36**	—
Psychological symptoms of stress	−.37**	—
Physical symptoms of stress	−.01	—

  * p<.05, two-tailed test
 ** p<.01, two-tailed test
  ‡   Correlations in this column are those which appear when other factors which may affect motivation on the job (see footnote 8) are held constant.
  a   Partial r's for control over means index A with pride in work, psychological symptoms of stress and physical symptoms of stress are not available.
  b   In computing correlations for this row of table, control over means index B was used. Control over means index A is used for other rows of table. Index B is based on first three of four questions listed in text while index A uses all four items.
  c   Includes six power plant operating groups.

Overall, the data of Table 5-1 indicate that those in work groups which have substantial control over the methods of doing their jobs have higher job motivation, feel greater pride, and are more relaxed on their jobs than those whose freedom to decide how to do their work is more limited.

DIFFICULTY OF THE WORK

A second job characteristic which affects achievement incentive is the difficulty of the work. As difficulty increases, success constitutes a greater achievement. As we have noted above (Chapter 3), both theoretical analysis and laboratory studies suggest that motivation to perform a task will be highest when the probability of success in a task is moderate rather than very high or very low.[9] In the jobs covered by this study—design

---

[9]This is because the arithmetic product of probability of success and incentive for success (approximately $1 - p$ success) is higher when the probability of success is moderate.

engineers, machinists, power plant operators, etc.—there are almost no instances where the probability of success is very low. TVA could not operate efficiently if too many engineers' drawings had serious defects or if machinery was often repaired or operated incorrectly. The probability of complete success on job tasks appears to vary between moderate and very high—i.e., between those jobs where there is some challenge and chance for misjudgment and those jobs which are almost completely routine. Thus, we expect in this setting that greater difficulty of work (lower probability of success) will increase job motivation. In other words, we expect that, within the range of job difficulty considered, the dampening effect on motivation of lower probability of success will be more than counterbalanced by the increased achievement incentive.

Two major factors which may affect the probability of successful completion of job tasks are (1) the extent to which problems are routine and solutions are standard; and (2) the amount of time available to complete the work.

Routine Versus Novelty

In some jobs, novel or unique problems which do not have standard solutions are rare. For example, an engineering aide in a steam plant lab commented :

My job is to conduct routine tests of all different natures . . . my general duties are calculations of a simple nature.

A mechanical engineer, telling about blueprints he had just made up, said :

It was fairly routine. There is not a whole lot to it. It's nothing too complicated.

At close to the other extreme is the work of a woman mathematician in one of the engineering branches, who described her work in this way :

I take an engineering problem considered suitable for the computer. The engineer sets up the problem and then I translate it into machine language and do as much of the formula as I can . . . Problems on this might take several days and then you'd discover that one little number at the beginning was wrong which makes the whole thing wrong. This would be your fault and it would mean that the work of two or three others would be wrong too.

Jobs at TVA vary considerably in degree of routinization. Although the engineer's job is always skilled and almost always calls for some problem solving, many engineers work on specialized design problems (e.g., hydro plant conduit and grounding design) which have been thoroughly worked out previously for similar jobs and so demand little new problem solving. Other engineering jobs—e.g., in planning features of transmission systems for future area needs—provide much greater challenge.

The work of most tradesmen in the steam plants—e.g., steam fitters, boilermakers, machinists—appears to be intermediate in degree of routinization versus challenge. Work techniques are generally fairly standard and maintenance work is fairly routine, but many repair problems offer some challenge. The work of some other blue-collar workers—e.g., painters, truck drivers—is more routine. Jobs in the steam plant laboratories (materials testers, instrument mechanics, chemical analysts, engineering aides) are, in general, intermediate in degree of routinization.

Time Pressures

Jobs at TVA, as elsewhere, also vary in the amount of time pressure for completion of work. Employees in all kinds of jobs at TVA sometimes work under time deadlines. Time pressures at the time of our study appeared to be greatest in one of the engineering divisions.

An electrical engineer commented about his most recent work in these words :

We're in a rush program. The supervisors are in a rush to get all the work out. This drawing was supposed to be issued at the first of the month, but when it was explained that decisions were not yet made, they understood that it's not our fault.

Another engineer in the same division said :

It's pretty difficult. One thing—we were rushing on everything.

The remarks of a draftsman in another engineering division illustrates a different type of experience. He said :

We always seem to get our work done in plenty of time. We're so far out ahead now that we're kind of lacking work. Of course, there are times when they said, "We need something in a hurry," but even then no real pressure is brought on us.

Questionnaire Index

To assess systematically the difficulty of various job situations, the following questions were asked :

1. In your job, how often do *problems* come up which are hard to foresee?

   (5) —————— Very often
   (4) —————— Fairly often
   (3) —————— Sometimes
   (2) —————— Seldom
   (1) —————— Never

2. In your job, how often do you have to solve *tough problems* in order to do the job right.

      (5) —————— Once a day or more
      (4) —————— Several times a week
      (3) —————— About once a week
      (2) —————— Several times a month
      (1) —————— Once a month or less

3. How often during the whole workday is your work fairly routine and how often is doing the job well a real challenge to your ability or ingenuity? My work is:

      (5) —————— Almost always a challenge to my ability or ingenuity
      (4) —————— Usually challenging
      (3) —————— About half routine and half challenging
      (2) —————— Usually routine
      (1) —————— Almost always routine

4. About how many times out of 10 do you meet the time limits set for your work? (If formal deadlines are often ignored, answer for deadlines you actually shoot for.)

      (1) —————— 10 times out of 10
      (2) —————— 9 times out of 10
      (3) —————— 8 times out of 10
      (4) —————— 7 times out of 10
      (5) —————— 6 times out of 10 or less

5. When there is a time limit or deadline or target date for your work, how "tight" are these deadlines usually? (If formal deadlines are often ignored, answer for deadlines you actually shoot for.) Deadlines are usually set so that there is:

      (1) —————— Much more than enough time to do the job
      (2) —————— Ample time
      (4) —————— Just barely enough time
      (5) —————— Too little time to do the job

An index of job difficulty was computed for each individual by averaging his scores on each of these items.[10] An average score was also computed for each group working under the same immediate supervisor. For ninety work groups, scores on the index of job difficulty vary widely, ranging from 1.5 (very easy) to 4.0 (moderately difficult). However, most groups tend to cluster close to the middle of this range.[11]

---

[10]Scores for each response are indicated by the number in parentheses which precedes it. Scores on the index of work difficulty have a statistically significant though low correlation with answers to the question, "In connection with your job, how much chance do you get to feel at the end of the day that you have accomplished something?" ($r = .19$ for 834 employees; $p < .01$).

[11]The mean group score on the index of job difficulty is 2.65, with a standard deviation of .43.

In general, units composed of steam plant operating employees score lowest on the index of job difficulty (i.e., they report least difficulty). Engineering units score highest (most difficulty) and crafts and laboratory groups are intermediate. However, within each of these broad categories of job types, there is considerable variation among groups on the index of job difficulty.

Relation to Job Motivation and Feelings on Job

What relation is there between the difficulty of jobs and employee reactions to the job? Table 5-2 shows the correlations, for groups, between scores on the index of difficulty of work and scores on (1) general job interest, (2) interest in work innovation, (3) absence, (4) pride in work, (5) psychological symptoms of stress, and (6) physical symptoms of stress.

TABLE 5-2　Difficulty of Work, as Related to Various Employee Reactions to the Job, for Ninety Work Groups

(Product-Moment Correlations)

	r	Partial r‡
General job interest	.25*	.06
Interest in work innovation	.45**	.34**
Full-day absences, engineering division (N = 34)	−.28	—
Total absences, power plants, nonoperating (N = 29)	−.03	—
Total absences, all sites (N = 63)a	−.06	−.29*
Pride in work	.24*	.13
Psychological symptoms of stress	−.02	−.04
Physical symptoms of stress	.02	−.16

　* p <.05, two-tailed test
　** p <.01, two-tailed test
　‡　Correlations in this column are those which appear when other factors which may affect motivation on the job (see footnote 8) are held constant.
　a　Includes six power plant operating groups.

These results show, first, a substantial association between the average level of work difficulty in a group and the average amount of interest in work innovation (r = .45); this association remains fairly marked (partial r = .34) even when a variety of other factors affecting interest in innovation are held constant.[12] There is not, however, any association for groups between job difficulty and general job interest when other factors affecting general job interest are held constant. (For individuals, there is a

---

[12]See footnote 8 for a list of the variables included in the partial correlation analysis.

very small, though statistically significant, association (partial r=.10; p<.05) between work difficulty and general job interest.)

Average job difficulty in a group has a small negative association (r=−.28) with number of absences (greater difficulty, fewer absences) among groups in an engineering division, though not among groups in power plants. For groups in engineering units and power plants combined, the greater the work difficulty, the fewer the absences (partial r=−.29; p<.05).[13]

In general these data—especially the association between job difficulty and interest in innovation—indicate that increased job difficulty is associated with greater job motivation. This seems intuitively reasonable, since those faced with the challenge of novel problems and pressing time deadlines might be expected to be stimulated to search for new and better solutions to job tasks. One might wonder, however, whether greater job difficulty would at the same time bring more frustration and tension.

Table 5-2 also shows the correlations between job difficulty and several measures of employee feelings on the job. These data show that greater job difficulty tends to be associated with greater pride in job accomplishments, though this relationship is quite small. Of more interest, perhaps, are the findings that greater job difficulty is *not* associated with symptoms of psychological stress (nervousness, depression, all-day tiredness) or with physical symptoms of stress (headaches, upset stomachs, etc.). There is, in fact, a slight tendency for those in groups having the more difficult work to report fewer physical symptoms of stress.

In the range of jobs covered by our study, then, greater job difficulty does not bring greater motivation at the cost of stress on the individual. This may not be true in all job situations. Where job difficulties are more extreme than for most jobs in our study or where individuals feel that their abilities are not adequate to meet the difficulties posed by the work, increased job difficulty may cause the individual to become tense, angry, or depressed. However, granted the limits of generality, the present findings are of interest in indicating that, at least with a moderate range of job difficulty, more difficult jobs appear to bring higher motivation at no cost in greater tension on the job.[14]

---

[13]Partial correlations were not computed separately for engineering and for steam plant groups because of the relatively small number of groups in each of these sets.

[14]It is possible that those in more difficult jobs differ from those in less difficult jobs in modal personality and/or in extra-job sources of stress in ways which would affect these results. However, we do not have adequate data on these points.

STANDARDS OF EXCELLENCE

For there to be a maximum achievement incentive on the job, there must be clear standards of excellence (see Chapter 3 for a general discussion of this point). Standards of excellence may concern the quality of work and/or they may concern the speed with which it is done.

Sometimes a man is not too clear about what type of final product is expected of him. For example, we asked a mechanical engineer how clear he was when he started a certain piece of work about how the supervisor wanted the work done. He replied :

This job, pretty good, but some jobs it's not too clear. I hardly know what he wants. I guess I know all I'm supposed to know.

On the other hand, asked the same question about a job he had just done, a draftsman replied :

I know exactly. I've worked with him for ten years. I know what he likes.

With respect to time goals, there is also variation in the degree of clarity of the goals. For some people, there are seldom or never explicit time limits or deadlines. For example, asked whether he knew exactly when his group had to be finished with a certain job, a draftsman replied :

No. We just had to finish it whenever we could.

On the other hand, a steam fitter in one of the steam plants said on this subject :

There's a certain time limit. Last week we started on leave drains. That was on Monday. Tuesday evening the foreman told us they wanted to fire the boiler Thursday, so we worked to that limit.

Time deadlines are especially prominent in some of the engineering branches. An electrical engineer pointed to the pressing nature of some of these deadlines when he said :

We get the pour schedules and masonry schedules from the field . . . We look at what they are going to pour next.

Questionnaire Measures

We do not have a very good measure of the clarity of standards of excellence on the job. However, there are some data which are relevant.

First, the following question was asked concerning the *frequency of time limits for work:*

> About what per cent of your time on the job are you working with a time limit or deadline or target date for the work you are doing?
> There is a time limit or deadline or target date for my work:
>
> (6) ——————— 90 per cent or more of the time
> (5) ——————— About 75 per cent of the time
> (4) ——————— About 50 per cent of the time
> (3) ——————— About 25 per cent of the time
> (2) ——————— About 10 per cent of the time
> (1) ——————— Never

This question probably provides the most meaningful data relevant to standards of excellence, since we know that time limits are set for many TVA jobs and that the frequency with which this occurs varies considerably among jobs and work units.

Secondly, two questions concern the *clarity of instructions* on the job.

1. How often do you get conflicting instructions or advice from different people as to what you should be doing on the job or how you should do it?

   (1) ——————— Several times a week
   (2) ——————— About once a week
   (3) ——————— Several times a month
   (4) ——————— About once a month
   (5) ——————— Less than once a month

2. Has there ever been a time when you have had a misunderstanding with anyone about when some work you were doing should have been finished?

   (1) ——————— Yes, there have been *many* misunderstandings about ——————— this
   (2) ——————— Yes, there have been *some* misunderstandings
   (3) ——————— Yes, there have been *occasional* misunderstandings
   (4) ——————— Yes, but it has only happened *rarely*
   (5) ——————— No, this has *never* happened

Thirdly, since the performance of others may help to set a standard of excellence, two questions aimed at assessing the extent to which each employee can *compare his own performance* with that of other employees are relevant :

1. How often do you observe personally the work of persons doing jobs similar to your own?

    (7) ——————— Every day
    (6) ——————— Several times a week
    (5) ——————— About once a week
    (4) ——————— Several times a month
    (3) ——————— About once a month
    (2) ——————— Once every few months
    (1) ——————— Very rarely or never

2. How often do you hear anything said (including jokes) about how good a job someone else, whose work is similar to your own, is doing?

    (6) ——————— Several times a week
    (5) ——————— About once a week
    (4) ——————— Several times a month
    (3) ——————— About once a month
    (2) ——————— Once every few months
    (1) ——————— Very rarely or never

In addition to the scores which each individual received on each of these three measures,[15] mean scores for each group of employees under the same immediate supervisor were also computed for each measure. These scores, both for individuals and for groups, were correlated with the various measures of employee reactions to the work situations.[16]

Results for the ninety work groups, shown in Table 5-3, indicate, on the whole, little relation between the three indicators of clarity of standards of excellence and the indicators of job motivation. Groups which have frequent time limits, clear instructions, or opportunities for comparison of members' performance to that of others, tend to have fewer absences, when other variables affecting absence are controlled; this negative association with absence is statistically significant for the measure of frequency of time limits (partial $r = -.26$; $p < .05$). However, none of these three "clarity of standards" factors appears to contribute positively to the level of general job interest or to interest in work innovation. In fact, there is a tendency for those in groups which have frequent time limits to have low interest in the job. Similarly, those groups which have good opportunity for comparison are more likely than others to have low job interest.

With respect to the relation between frequency of time limits and

---

[15]Scores were assigned to each individual according to the numerical values shown above next to each response. Where there are two questions bearing on the same variable, a simple mean score for each individual was computed.

[16]For individuals, scores on the question concerning chances to get a feeling of accomplishment on the job have small but statistically significant negative correlations with frequency of time limits ($r = -.09$; $p < .05$) and with opportunities for comparison of own work with others ($r = -.11$; $p < .01$).

job motivation, the possibility suggests itself that this relationship may depend on the extent to which employees have a voice in setting time limits. Perhaps, we thought, frequent time limits are associated with high job motivation when the employees have had a part in setting the time limits. Data on the employees' role in setting time limits come from the following question :

> How much say or influence do you have (either alone or together with other people at your level) when it comes to setting the time schedules for jobs that you work on?
>
> (Five response categories from "no influence at all" to "a great deal of influence")

Work groups at TVA differ considerably in the average degree of such influence which employees report. For each of three sets of groups— those low, medium, and high with respect to employee influence on time limits—correlations were examined between scores showing frequency of time limits and scores on general job interest and interest in innovation.

TABLE 5-3   Job Features Relevant to Clarity of Standards of Excellence, as Related to Various Employee Reactions to the Job, for Ninety Work Groups

(Product-Moment Correlations)

	Frequency of Time Limits		Clarity of Instructions		Opportunity to Compare	
	r	Partial r‡	r	Partial r	r	Partial r
General job interest	.03	−.18	.19	−.04	−.22*	−.23*
Interest in work innovation	.21*	.03	.10	.03	−.09	−.02
Absences, full-day engineering division (N = 34)	−.15	—	.13	—	−.24	—
Absences, total power plants, nonoperating (N = 29)	.29	—	−.13	—	−.02	—
Absences, total, all groups (N = 63)a	.17	−.26*	−.06	−.15	−.19	−.23
Pride in work	−.33**	−.33**	−.08	−.11	.24*	.21*
Psychological symptoms of stress	.15	.06	−.27**	−.19	.13	.10
Physical symptoms of stress	−.04	−.02	−.26	−.31**	.29**	.28**

* p <.05, two-tailed test
** p <.01, two-tailed test
‡ Correlations in this column are those which appear when other factors which may affect motivation on the job (see footnote 8) are held constant.
a Includes six power plant operating groups.

However, contrary to expectation, the association between frequency of time limits and job interest does not systematically increase as employee influence over time limits increases.

These data indicate, then, that having clear time standards—even when employees have a voice in setting them—does not necessarily contribute to higher job motivation. Later in this chapter we shall examine further the relation of time standards to job motivation, when we consider the combination of time standards with other factors relevant to achievement incentive—i.e., with control over means, job difficulty, and feedback on performance.

With respect to feelings about the job, Table 5-3 shows also that members of groups which have frequent time limits express significantly *less* pride in their work. There is no relation between frequency of time limits and our measures of psychological or physical symptoms of stress.

Getting clear instructions is associated with fewer physical symptoms of stress in a group (partial $r = .31$; $p < .01$), while having the opportunity to compare one's work to that of others is associated both with greater pride in work (partial $r = .21$; $p < .05$) and with more physical symptoms of stress (partial $r = .29$; $p < .01$).

It is difficult to draw any general conclusions from these data bearing on the relation between standards of excellence and employee reactions to the job. We do not have a good overall measure of the clarity of standards and it is hard to judge how much the differences in clarity of instructions and in opportunity for comparisons reflect differences in the clarity of standards of excellence. However, the data on frequency of time limits at work are especially interesting, since we have confidence that the question on time limits does reflect an important difference in the work situation faced by different groups. The finding that those who more frequently work under time limits are *not* more interested in their work and take *less* pride in their job (though their attendance tends to be better) is arresting. It may be that time limits, even when employees help set them, are not viewed as a standard of excellence by most employees in these job settings. Another possible explanation is that, while time limits may provide one standard of excellence, the attention which they focus on the speed of the work diverts attention from the possibility of doing work which is creative or innovative, thereby reducing achievement incentive.

FEEDBACK ON PERFORMANCE

In order for achievement to appear possible for an individual, he must believe, we have suggested in Chapter 3, that he will be able to tell how well he has done—i.e., get feedback on his performance. In some jobs and at some times, a person can tell by himself pretty well how he has done. An electrical engineer put it this way :

It's like a good musician. You usually know. Quite often you can go over it again and see how many errors or changes you have to make. Lots of times you might misinterpret something and catch yourself later.

In other job situations, however, the individual cannot tell very well by himself how well he has done and requires feedback from others. Such a situation is common in some engineering units at TVA where the "drawings" of an engineer are checked over by others. A civil engineer commented on some of the possible failures in feedback :

You may not know you've made a mistake until it's all over and you may not know it even then. The designer designs it and then there is a man who checks it, but a mistake may never get back to you. It develops that the designer will put down anything at all and says to himself, "Let the checker take care of it" . . . You don't get the drawings back. Changes made by the checker are not made back with the man who originally did it.

Another example of lack of feedback is provided by a unit operator telling about his group's "moving number 5 (unit) off the line for periodic inspection." He said :

It wasn't completely finished when we left. I never did hear about it. Another shift finished up.

On the other hand, some men get much greater feedback on their performance. A boilermaker in a steam plant said :

When I do a good job, they come around and tell us. Pat you on the back. This would be the foreman or the general maintenance foreman who would do this. Our foreman checks most things we do.

Measure of Feedback

We do not have complete information about the amount of feedback that employees in our study get about their work. We do not know, for example, to what extent various employees can tell themselves, without conversation with others, how well they have done a given job. There are, however, some relevant data about how much employees are told by others about the quality of their work. The relevant questions are as follows:

1. How much of your work is checked, inspected, or reviewed by someone else?

   (5) _____ 100 per cent of my work is checked, inspected, or _____ reviewed.
   (4) _____ About 90 per cent
   (3) _____ About 75 per cent
   (2) _____ About 50 per cent
   (1) _____ About 25 per cent of my work is checked, inspected, or reviewed.

2. When your work is checked or inspected, how often are you told what the results of the checking were?

   (5) _____ Almost always
   (4) _____ About three-quarters of the time
   (3) _____ About half of the time
   (2) _____ About one-quarter of the time
   (1) _____ About one-tenth of the time or less

3. If you do an outstanding job on something, how likely are you to be *complimented* by one of your *supervisors*?

   (6) _____ Almost always
   (5) _____ About three-quarters of the time
   (4) _____ About half of the time
   (3) _____ About one-quarter of the time
   (2) _____ About one-tenth of the time
   (1) _____ Almost never

4. If you do an outstanding job on something, how likely are you to be *complimented* by one of your *co-workers* (other than one of your supervisors)?

   (6) _____ Almost always
   (5) _____ About three-quarters of the time
   (4) _____ About half of the time
   (3) _____ About one-quarter of the time
   (2) _____ About one-tenth of the time
   (1) _____ Almost never

5. If you make a mistake or oversight, how likely is it to be called to your attention by someone other than a person responsible for checking your work?
   This happens:

   (6) _____ Almost always
   (5) _____ About three-quarters of the time
   (4) _____ About half of the time
   (3) _____ About one-quarter of the time
   (2) _____ Almost one-tenth of the time
   (1) _____ Almost never

For each employee, two indices of feedback were computed.[17] The first, Feedback Index A, is based on the average of scores in response to all five of the above questions. The second, Feedback Index B, is based on responses to questions 1 and 2.[18] Index B was computed in order to have a feedback measure which focuses on feedback of information as separate from social reward for achievement. (Measures of social reward for achievement, which include the latter three items above, will be discussed in Chapter 6.) For each work group, average feedback scores were also computed. Most work groups get a moderate amount of feedback, but there are considerable differences among groups in this respect.[19]

TABLE 5-4 **Feedback on Performance (Index B), as Related to Various Employee Reactions to the Job, for Ninety Work Groups**

(Product-Moment Correlations)

	r	Partial r‡
General job interest	.11	.03
Interest in work innovation	.22*	.09
Absences, total; all groups (N = 63)	.25*	.02
Pride in work	—.10	.06
Psychological symptoms of stress	.06	.06
Physical symptoms of stress	—.19	—.04

*p <.05, two-tailed test
‡Correlations in this column are those which appear when other factors which may affect motivation on the job (see footnote 8) are held constant.

Contrary to our expectation, neither measure of feedback shows firm associations with the indices of general job interest or interest in work innovation. There are some significant correlations among these variables, but they shrink to close to zero when other factors affecting job interest are held constant. The data for groups, using Feedback Index B, are shown in Table 5-4. For individuals in the engineering division, there

---

[17]Numbers preceding each response category indicate the scores assigned to those responses. Scores on the questions composing an index were averaged for each individual.

[18]Feedback Index B represents the percentage of time that the person is told the results of checking, multiplied by the percentage of time that his work is checked; it has a small but statistically significant correlation (r = .12; p<.01) for individuals with scores on the question, "In connection with your job, how much chance do you get to feel at the end of the day that you have accomplished something?"

[19]The mean group score on Feedback Index B is 52.2, which indicates that in the average group employees get feedback on their work performance from someone checking the work about 50 per cent of the time. The standard deviation is 24.8, indicating that two-thirds of the groups have a score on Feedback Index B between 27.4 and 77.0. The mean group score on Feedback Index A is 3.5 with a standard deviation of .6.

are some small but statistically significant correlations between both feed-back indices and absences.[20] Correlations between feedback measures and individual absence in the power plants are not significant.

In addition to the generally weak relation of feedback to indicators of job motivation, Table 5-4 indicates also that feedback has only small and nonsignificant associations with pride in work, and psychological and physical symptoms of stress.

In general, then, these data show feedback, in itself, to have little effect on feelings about the work. Interpretation of this result should be tempered by the fact, already noted, that there is often nonsocial feedback on performance which is not reflected in our measure of feedback. More-over, in a later section of this chapter we will see that feedback as measured here does have a greater impact on job interest for persons whose control over work methods is high or who are doing jobs which are relatively difficult.

CHANCE TO LEARN

In discussing achievement incentive on the job, we have considered factors which may affect the amount of success the individual can have in mastering his work environment. But there is another type of accom-plishment possible on the job—the improvement of oneself through learn-ing. For many employees at TVA, the opportunity to learn is a very salient aspect of the job. For example, we asked a young electrical engineer in an engineering division if he could think of the "last time that you accomplished something on the job that you were especially proud of." He told us:

> *Not accomplishments in the sense of evidence of some structure, but I'm most pleased about learning something new every day. In college you learn a wide base of principles; you don't specialize enough to learn about, say, relays. I feel that I learn quite a bit and apply knowledge learned in college in such a way as to produce results. I learn many things better now than I did in college because I have to apply them.*

Other types of employees covered by our study have jobs in which there is considerable chance for learning—especially the assistant operators in the power plants who are acquiring the knowledge necessary to be operators. On the other hand, in some jobs—e.g., most craftsmen's jobs,

---

[20]For individuals in the engineering division, Feedback Index A correlates $-.15$ ($p < .01$) with number of absences (partial $r = -.14$; $p < .01$); Feedback Index B correlates $-.20$ ($p < .01$) with number of individual absences in the engineering division. A partial correlation between absence and Feedback Index B was not computed for individuals.

materials testers, draftsmen—there is relatively little chance to learn new things.

A pertinent question asked of employees is the following :

> In connection with your job, how much chance do you get to learn new things?
>
> (*1*) ——————— Very little or no chance
> (*2*) ——————— Little chance
> (*3*) ——————— Some chance
> (*4*) ——————— A good chance
> (*5*) ——————— An excellent chance

For our sample as a whole, 25 per cent of employees said they have little or no chance to learn, 29 per cent said they have some chance, and 45 per cent said they have a good or excellent chance.

Each employee was given a score on the basis of his answer to this question (corresponding to the numbers shown above), and average scores were also computed for each of the ninety work groups in our sample.[21] Individual and group scores on chance to learn were then correlated with the various measures of employee reactions to the job. Results for groups are shown in Table 5-5.

The results show substantial correlations both for indivduals ($r = .31$; $p < .01$) and for groups ($r = .50$; $p < .01$) between chance to learn new things and general job interest. These associations are considerably

TABLE 5-5 **Chance to Learn New Things, as Related to Various Employee Reactions to the Job, for Ninety Work Groups**

(Product-Moment Correlations)

	r	Partial r‡
General job interest	.50**	.18
Interest in work innovation	.28**	−.10
Absences, full-day; engineering division (N = 34)	.00	—
Absences, total; power plants nonoperating (N = 29)	−.09	—
Absences, total; all sites (N = 63)a	−.08	−.27*
Pride in work	.27**	.07
Psychological symptoms of stress	−.43**	−.37**
Physical symptoms of stress	−.15	.00

* p <.05, two-tailed test
** p <.01, two-tailed test
‡ Correlations in this column are those which appear when other factors which may affect motivation on the job (see footnote 8) are held constant.
a Includes six power plant operating groups.

[21]The mean score for ninety work groups on chance to learn was 3.23, with a standard deviation of .61.

reduced when all other factors affecting job interest are held constant but still remain statistically significant for individuals (partial $r = .15$; $p < .01$) and close to significance for groups (partial $r = .18$). Also, for work groups in engineering and power plants combined, the more group members report a chance to learn on the job, the fewer the absences in the group (partial $r = -.27$; $p < .05$).

There are no significant relationships between chance to learn and interest in work innovation when other factors affecting interest in innovation are held constant. The lack of relation to interest in innovation might be expected, of course, since even interested learners are usually not yet ready to be innovators.

In addition to showing tendencies toward greater job motivation, the more a group's members report chances to learn on the job, the fewer the psychological symptoms of stress reported (partial $r = -.37$; $p < .01$).[22]

Overall, these data indicate that when people have a good opportunity to learn new things on their jobs, they will be more highly motivated in their jobs and happier while doing them.

OTHER FACTORS RELEVANT TO OPPORTUNITIES FOR ACHIEVEMENT

Several other factors in the job situation also appear relevant to achievement incentive or to expectancy of achievement. Among these job factors are (1) opportunities to finish tasks; and (2) availability of the resources necessary to do the job.

Chance to Finish Tasks

It seems likely that the achievement incentive, or amount of accomplishment possible, on the job will be reduced if a man may not be able to finish the task he is working on. While this is not a problem in many jobs, there are some employees in our sample—especially craftsmen in the power plants—who sometimes face this situation. For example, a steam fitter told us:

I felt bad about a pipe that I installed recently. It had (something wrong with it). It wasn't necessarily my fault—just one of those things—but I felt bad because it was quitting time and I couldn't fix it myself and someone who was coming on the job at that time would have the trouble of fixing it.

---

[22]The negative association between chance to learn and psychological symptoms of stress does not appear to be due to those who are learning being younger and therefore being less likely to report feeling tired or worn out (one of the items of the index of psychological symptoms of stress). The more chance to learn, the less often people report feeling "nervous, tense, or edgy on the job" ($r = -.46$ for ninety groups).

On the questionnaire, we asked :

In connection with your job, how much chance do you get to finish things?
(1) ——————— Very little or no chance
(2) ——————— Little chance
(3) ——————— Some chance
(4) ——————— A good chance
(5) ——————— An excellent chance

For our sample as a whole, 64 per cent said they had a good or an excellent chance, 22 per cent said they had some chance, and 12 per cent said they had little or no chance to finish things.

Scores for individuals and for work groups[23] were correlated with scores indicating various employee reactions to the job. The data (not shown) both for individuals and for groups indicate little relation between chance to finish things and the indicators of job motivation—i.e., general job interest, interest in work innovation, and absence (even with other things held constant). Nor is there a consistent relation between chance to finish things and pride in work or symptoms of stress. Thus it appears that, for the jobs covered at TVA, variations in the chance to finish tasks do not have any marked impact on job motivation or on feelings about the job. It may be that where variations in the chance to finish work are more dramatic, the influence of this job characteristic would be greater.

Availability of Resources

Another aspect of the work situation which appears relevant to opportunities for achievement is the extent to which the person can get the things he needs—e.g., information, tools, or materials—to do the job right. Where he meets blockage and frustrations in getting such necessary resources, it seems likely that his expectancy of being able to do the job successfully will be diminished.

It is possible that problems in getting resources will also make success seem more of an accomplishment than it would be otherwise—i.e., raise achievement incentive. However, it seems intuitively likely that the value of succeeding in a task will not be raised much by obstacles which are not intrinsic to the task itself. Moreover, blockages and frustrations in getting necessary resources introduce a cost into performing the task which is likely to reduce net motivation.

---

[23]Scores assigned for individuals correspond to the numbers shown before the response categories. Scores for groups were computed by averaging the scores of all group members. The mean score for groups was 3.73, with a standard deviation of .51.

To obtain relevant data on this matter, the following question was asked of TVA employees :

> In your job, how often do you find yourself concerned about . . . not being able to get information, tools or materials needed to carry out your job properly?
>
> (6) ——————— Several times a week
> (5) ——————— About once a week
> (4) ——————— Several times a month
> (3) ——————— About once a month
> (2) ——————— Once every few months
> (1) ——————— Never

For the TVA sample as a whole, relatively few employees reported frequent problems of this sort. Only 14 per cent said they found themselves concerned about getting necessary resources several times a week, or even once a week. However, there is some variation among work units in this respect, with some units having no employees frequently concerned about such problems while other units have about one-fourth (and in one case one-half) of their employees frequently concerned about this.

Scores regarding frequency of concern about getting necessary resources for the job, both for individuals and for work groups,[24] were correlated with scores on the various measures of employee reactions to the job situation. These data, not shown, indicate little association between concern about getting needed resources and the measures of job motivation—i.e., general job interest, interest in work innovation, and attendance. There are, however, some small but statistically significant correlations between the availability of resources and employee feelings relevant to the job. For the ninety work groups, the more people in a work group experience difficulty in getting needed information, tools, or materials, the more often they experience psychological symptoms of stress, like nervousness, depression, or tiredness (partial $r = +.27$; $p<.01$). It appears, then, that the main effect of difficulties in getting necessary resources is not so much to reduce motivation as it is to increase unpleasant feeling states on the job.

INTERACTION OF OPPORTUNITY FACTORS

So far we have examined separately the relation between employee reactions to their jobs and each of several job characteristics which help

---

[24]Scores were assigned to various answers according to the numbers indicated to the left of the response categories above.

to provide opportunity for achievement. The strongest of these separate relationships are summarized in Figure 5-1). We now look at the impact of various *combinations* of these job characteristics. What, for example, is the impact on job motivation of having both high control over means and frequent feedback on job performance? How about the effect of both a difficult job and frequent time limits? What if all four of these factors are present simultaneously?

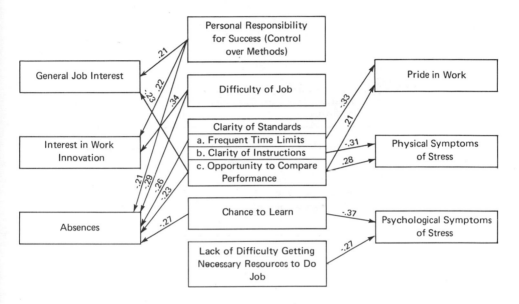

Note: Numbers are partial coefficients showing strength of each association independent of other relevant variables. See footnote 8 in this chapter for list of variables held constant in each partial correlation analysis.

FIGURE 5-1 Strongest relationships between job features relevant to opportunity to achievement and employee reactions to the job (for ninety work groups)

The most intensive analyses to study such questions were done with respect to two indicators of job motivation—the measures of general job interest and of interest in innovation.[25] These analyses consider the effects of four major factors (control over means, job difficulty, time goals, and feedback) which are relevant to the amount of achievement possible on the job; these analyses do not consider the chance to learn, which concerns a somewhat different kind of accomplishment. One analysis attempts to

[25] For another indicator of motivation—absence—which had to be studied separately in power plants and engineering divisions, the number of cases was too small for a four-way analysis of variance.

account for variations among individual scores on the index of general job interest and a second analysis treats individual variations on the index of interest in work innovation.

First, it is of some interest to look at the mean job interest scores of persons who experience different combinations of control over means, job difficulty, feedback, and time limits. Such data are shown in Table 5-6. They indicate large differences in general job interest and in interest in innovation between persons whose jobs provide many of the requisites for achievement incentive and those whose jobs provide few of these requisites. At the extremes, there are large differences in job interest be-

TABLE 5-6   Interest in the Job, for Persons Experiencing Different Combinations of Job Characteristics Relevant to Achievement Incentive

```
┌─────────────────────────────────────────────────────────────────┐
│                              CODE                                 │
│  A.  High control over means;   Ā.  Low control over means        │
│  B.  High job difficulty;       B̄.  Low job difficulty            │
│  C.  High feedback on performance;  C̄.  Low feedback              │
│  D.  Frequent time goals;       D̄.  Infrequent time goals         │
└─────────────────────────────────────────────────────────────────┘
```

Job Characteristic	N	General Job Interest (Index Score)		Interest in Work Innovation (Index Score)	
		Mean	Standard Error	Mean	Standard Error
ABCD	73	7.61	.14	3.75	.08
ABC$\overline{D}$	42	7.64	.20	3.57	.10
ABD$\overline{C}$	42	7.17	.24	3.49	.11
ACD$\overline{B}$	50	7.28	.19	3.36	.10
BCD$\overline{A}$	41	6.61	.22	2.90	.12
AB$\overline{C}\overline{D}$	30	7.03	.25	3.44	.13
AC$\overline{B}\overline{D}$	59	7.27	.16	3.00	.08
AD$\overline{B}\overline{C}$	35	7.11	.27	3.20	.14
BC$\overline{A}\overline{D}$	24	6.96	.31	2.75	.14
BD$\overline{A}\overline{C}$	50	6.37	.22	2.97	.11
CD$\overline{A}\overline{B}$	70	6.67	.23	2.90	.09
A$\overline{B}\overline{C}\overline{D}$	48	7.18	.22	3.07	.10
B$\overline{A}\overline{C}\overline{D}$	40	6.05	.28	2.72	.11
C$\overline{A}\overline{B}\overline{D}$	40	6.33	.31	2.67	.10
D$\overline{A}\overline{B}\overline{C}$	54	6.04	.23	2.65	.09
$\overline{A}\overline{B}\overline{C}\overline{D}$	85	6.05	.20	2.44	.07

tween those who have high control over means, high job difficulty, high feedback, and frequent time goals, and those who differ in all of these aspects of the job situation.

To test more systematically the importance of the joint effects of these four job characteristics, two analyses of variance were performed. These analyses show how much of the variance in job interest is due to each of these job features and, of greatest interest here, how much of the variance in job interest is accounted for by interactions among (i.e., joint effects of) these four job features. These analyses were done on data which are somewhat more refined than those shown in Table 5-6— i.e., each person could be scored high, medium, or low on each of the job characteristics rather than merely high or low. Table 5-7 shows the results of the analyses of variance.

The data of Table 5-7 indicate that, when the other three features relevant to achievement incentive are constant, control over means has a

TABLE 5-7   Analysis of Effects on Job Interest of Four Job Characteristics Relevant to Achievement Incentive[a]

(Analysis of Variance[b])

Job Characteristics	Predicting to General Job Interest F	Predicting to Interest in Innovation F
Control over means	35.9***	35.5***
Feedback on performance[c]	8.3***	7.8***
Time limits: frequency	0.0	6.5**
Difficulty of job	4.4*	29.8***
Control means × feedback	1.6	1.0
Control means × time limits	0.6	0.5
Control means × difficulty	0.3	1.5
Feedback × time limits	0.1	0.4
Feedback × difficulty	0.7	2.0
Time limits × difficulty	1.0	0.6
Control means × feedback × time limits	0.8	0.9
Control means × feedback × difficulty	1.0	2.1*
Control means × time limits × difficulty	0.8	1.2
Feedback × time limits × difficulty	3.0**	0.3
Control means × feedback × time limits × difficulty	1.2	1.8*

*p < .05
**p < .01
***p < .001
  a N = 736 individuals; each individual was scored as high, medium, or low on each of the four job characteristics.
  b Degrees of freedom among means are as follows: 16 for four-way interaction; 8 for three-way interaction; 4 for two-way interaction; and 2 for main effects.
  c Feedback Index B is used here.

marked relation both to general job interest and to interest in work innovation. The level of job difficulty also has a strong relation to interest in innovation (more difficulty, more interest) and a significant though smaller relation to general job interest. Feedback on job performance[26] is also related to both measures of job interest while having frequent time limits is associated only with interest in work innovation. These results generally parallel the results of the correlation analysis.[27] It is of interest to note that by far the greatest part of variation in job interest is "explained" by the single job characteristics—especially control over means and job difficulty—operating independently, rather than by interactions among (specific combinations of) these characteristics.

There is, however, some evidence of the kinds of interaction among these job features which we expected to find.

Control Over Means and Job Difficulty

There is, first, a tendency for interaction between control over means and job difficulty. This interaction tendency occurs with respect to the relation of these job features to interest in innovation, though not with respect to their relation to general job interest. Table 5-8 shows the mean

TABLE 5-8   **Mean Interest in Innovation Scores for Persons Differing in Control over Means and in Job Difficulty**[a]

Control over Means	Job Difficulty		
	Low	*Medium*	*High*
Low	2.71 (91)	2.77 (97)	2.94 (83)
Medium	2.91 (66)	3.08 (86)	3.33 (98)
High	3.06 (76)	3.25 (55)	3.75 (84)

Note: Figures in parentheses indicate number of persons.
a   See Table 5-7 for analysis of variance.

[26]The feedback measure used here is Feedback Index B.

[27]However, when all factors affecting individual job interest are held constant in the correlation analysis, the relation of both feedback and time goals to job interest falls below statistical significance.

interest in innovation scores for nine categories of persons who represent different combinations of control over means and job difficulty. Either greater control over means or greater job difficulty brings an increase in interest in innovation, regardless of the level of the other variable. But increases in control over means have greatest impact when job difficulty is high and vice versa. While this interaction does not reach statistical significance, it seems noteworthy that the cell in which the greatest interaction is apparent (high control over means, high difficulty) is the one which was predicted to show this effect.[28]

Control Over Means and Feedback

A second instance in which some interaction tends to take place is between control over means and feedback on work performance. This interaction is apparent in the joint effect of these job characteristics on general job interest. Table 5-9 shows the average job interest scores of persons having different degrees of control over means and different amounts of feedback on job performance. These data show that, in general, either greater control over means or greater feedback on performance brings an increase in general job interest. However, the impact of increases in either characteristic is greatest when the other is also high. Thus, greater control over means brings the greatest increase in job interest when feedback on job performance is high and vice versa. Although the interaction effect falls short of statistical significance, we may note again that the specific nature of the interaction is the one predicted.

Feedback and Difficulty

A third instance in which some evidence of interaction between two of these job characteristics appears is the combination of feedback on job performance and job difficulty. Table 5-10 shows the average interest in innovation scores for those who experience various levels of feedback and job difficulty. Where feedback is low, increases in job difficulty show only a small tendency to bring greater interest in innovation. But where feedback is medium or high, increases in job difficulty have more association with increased interest in innovation. Conversely, where job difficulty is low (or medium), increases in feedback on performance have little association with interest in innovation; but when job difficulty is high, greater feedback has a somewhat more marked effect on interest in innovation. This interaction effect is a little short of statistical significance, though the nature of the interaction is generally in the predicted direction.

---

[28]The statistical test for interaction does not take account of whether the interaction occurs in a cell where it was predicted to occur or not.

TABLE 5-9   General Job Interest Scores for Persons Differing in Control over Work Means and in Feedback on Job Performance[a]

Control over Means	Feedback on Performance		
	Low	*Medium*	*High*
Low	5.91 (104)	6.57 (74)	6.15 (93)
Medium	6.95 (82)	7.04 (81)	7.35 (87)
High	6.91 (57)	7.39 (99)	7.63 (59)

Note: Figures in parentheses indicate number of persons.
See Table 5-7 for analysis of variance.

TABLE 5-10   Mean Interest in Innovation Scores for Persons Differing in Feedback on Job Performance and in Job Difficulty[a]

Feedback on Performance	Job Difficulty		
	Low	*Medium*	*High*
Low	2.85 (84)	2.84 (80)	3.06 (79)
Medium	2.85 (82)	3.15 (74)	3.54 (98)
High	2.95 (67)	3.00 (84)	3.37 (88)

Note: Figures in parentheses indicate number of persons.
a   See Table 5-7 for analysis of variance.

Combinations of Three Opportunity Components

Among the possible combinations of three opportunity components, the analysis of variance (Table 5-7) shows two interactions which are not likely to have been due to chance. The strongest three-way interaction takes place among feedback on performance, frequency of time limits, and job difficulty, as they relate to general job interest. Looking at various combinations of these three job characteristics (see Appendix C), we see that by far the lowest scores on the general job interest scale are obtained by people who have frequent time limits for their work but whose work is of low difficulty and who get little feedback on their performance. The highest general job interest is shown by those who face time limits relatively infrequently, whose jobs are more difficult, and who get high feedback on their performance.

A second statistically significant three-way interaction takes place among control over means, feedback on performance, and job difficulty, with respect to their effect on interest in work innovation. Inspection of the scores of those with various combinations of control, feedback, and difficulty (see Appendix D), indicates that the interaction occurs primarily between control over means and job difficulty. A combination of high control and high difficulty brings a jump in innovative interest. The impact of feedback is minimal relative to the impact of the other two factors.[29]

Combination of Four Opportunity Components

The analysis of variance also shows a significant interaction effect among all four of these job characteristics relevant to achievement incentive—i.e., the effect of all four in combination is greater than the sum of their individual effects (or of the effects of pairs or triplets). The nature of this four-way interaction is a little hard to specify, both because of the large number of combinations (eighty-one)[30] and because of the small number of persons in some of these combinations. In general, however, the data show that the highest scores, especially on interest in innovation and also on general job interest, are found among persons who are relatively high on all four, or at least three, of the requisites of achievement incentive; the lowest scores are generally found among those who stand relatively low on all four, or at least three, of these characteristics.

---

[29]Differences in feedback may serve to reduce variation within categories of persons whose average scores are influenced most heavily by control over means and job difficulty.

[30]Since each individual can score high, medium, or low on each of the four incentive components, there are eighty-one possible combinations.

The Multiplicative Model

We had expected, on the basis of the theoretical ideas presented in Chapter 3, that the major job characteristics relevant to achievement incentive—control over methods, difficulty, feedback on performance, and clarity of standards of excellence—would have a multiplicative effect on achievement incentive. If this were true, one would expect that the interaction effects between two or more of these job features would be large relative to the main effects of a single job feature. Yet the data of Table 5-7 do not show this pattern. Instead, the effects of the single job characteristics—especially control over means and job difficulty—are much larger than the effect of various interactions among these characteristics. Interaction effects of the kind predicted are, indeed, found, but they are relatively small. The overall picture is that the job characteristics are largely additive in their effects on motivation. How can this pattern be explained? Can increases in one requisite for achievement incentive bring increases in motivation even when the other requisites are not present?

It should be noted first that none of the requisites for achievement incentive was ever at a zero level—or even very close to it—in the job situations studied. Employees in the engineering divisions and steam plants almost always had some ways of judging excellence, some control over the way they did their jobs, some degree of difficulty in the work, and some feedback on their performance. If we had somehow found (or artificially arranged for) situations in which one or more of these requisites were entirely absent, then larger interaction effects would probably have been found. For example, control over means may show an association with job interest only when there is some way of judging excellence, some feedback, and some job difficulty present. In other words, the present data do not indicate that any of the incentive requisites considered can be safely ignored if only one or two other requisites are increased enough.

These data may indicate, however, that once there is present some necessary minimum of all requisites for achievement incentive, increases in a single requisite—especially control over means of doing the job—may bring large increases in job interest. To the extent that several incentive requisites—e.g., control over means and job difficulty—are increased simultaneously, the data also indicate that some extra impact or motivation from the combination of these factors will occur.

Predicting to Pride and Symptoms of Stress

In addition to the complex analysis relating job interest to job characteristics which are relevant to achievement incentive, we did a less formal analysis relating various combinations of these same job characteristics to job pride and to symptoms of stress on the job.

For this analysis, we first categorized each individual according to whether he scored high or low on each of four job features—control over means, difficulty of work, feedback on performance, and frequency of time goals.[31] There are sixteen possible high-low combinations of scores on these factors. For each of the sixteen categories, mean scores were computed on measures of pride in job performance, of psychological symptoms of stress (nervousness, depression, or tiredness) and of physical symptoms of stress (headaches, upset stomachs, etc.). These data are presented in Appendix E.

With respect to pride in job performance, there is a suggestion in the data that the combination of high job difficulty and high feedback on performance is most effective in producing high job pride. Two out of the three categories of individuals who have high job difficulty and high feedback have the two highest mean scores on the index of pride in job performance. However, the sheer number of the four job features which favor high achievement incentive appears to have little effect on job pride.

In general, there is little association between the number of incentive-relevant factors present on the job and symptoms of psychological or physical stress. The greatest average number of both physical and psychological stress symptoms was shown by people who hold difficult jobs which have frequent time limits but who have low control over means of doing the job and low feedback on performance. Where there are time limits and work is difficult but there is more control over means and more feedback, reports of nervousness and other symptoms of anxiety are much less frequent. Even lower in reported symptoms of anxiety are those who have difficult jobs but have only infrequent time deadlines as well as high control over means and high feedback on performance.

SUMMARY

In this chapter we have examined the relation between opportunity for achievement on the job and employee reactions to the job. Among those job characteristics which appear relevant for achievement incentive (i.e., the amount of achievement possible), control over means of doing the job and difficulty of the job show the strongest associations with indicators of job motivation. The more employees have control over the means of doing their jobs, the more interest they take in their work and the fewer absences they have. Employees with high control over means also express greater

---

[31]For this analysis, individuals were divided into two approximately equal categories on each of the four job characteristics. Feedback Index B was used for this analysis.

pride in their work and fewer symptoms of stress on the job. The more difficult jobs are—e.g., in presenting nonroutine problems to solve—the more interest in innovation employees show and the fewer absences they have. Another job factor which shows some evidence of a positive association with job motivation, and a negative association with stress symptoms, is the chance to learn new things on the job.

Several other job factors which were expected to help provide opportunities for achievement showed little positive association, in themselves, with motivation on the job. Measures of feedback on job performance had little relation to job interest, absence, pride, or symptoms of stress. Evidently feedback on performance does not produce favorable reactions to the job unless other achievement-relevant job features are also present. Several indicators of the clarity of standards of excellence (frequency of time limits, clarity of instructions, and opportunity to compare) generally showed little association with measures of interest on the job, although they did have some negative associations with absence. However, the more often employees work under time limits, the less pride they express in their work. Any advantages which frequent time limits have in providing a standard of excellence is counterbalanced evidently by negative effects of time pressures.

The chance to finish things on the job was not related either to indicators of job motivation or to employee feelings on the job. Variations among jobs in our sample with respect to chances to finish things may not be large enough to make this factor important in this setting. Finally, a measure of the availability of necessary resources (information, tools, and materials) to enable employees to do their job right had little relation to job motivation. However, the more employees experience difficulty in getting such resources, the more frequent their symptoms of stress, like nervousness and depression.

In addition to examining the separate effects of each job feature which is relevant to achievement incentive, we also studied the joint effects on job interest of four of these job features—control over means, job difficulty, feedback on performance, and frequency of time limits. Job interest tends to be increased by combinations of (1) high job difficulty and high control over means; (2) high control over means and high feedback; (3) high job difficulty and high feedback. There are also some specific combinations of three job features which bring especially high or especially low job interest. Particularly high job interest is found among those who face time limits relatively infrequently, whose jobs are difficult, and who get high feedback on their performance. Particularly low job interest is found among people who have frequent time limits but whose work is of low difficulty and who get little feedback on their performance. The analysis of interaction among the job characteristics also shows, however, that the effects of specific combinations of job characteristics are quite small in comparison with the main effects of each characteristic alone. These data may indicate that once there is present some necessary minimum of all the requisites for achievement incentive, increases in a single relevant factor—especially control over means of doing the job or difficulty of the job—may itself bring large increases in job motivation.

6

REWARDS
FOR ACHIEVEMENT
ON THE JOB

In our general discussion of achievement motivation on the job (Chapter 3), we have argued that the motive for achievement—i.e., how much the individual values achievement on the job—may be much affected by the rewards for achievement which the job situation provides, as well as by personal characteristics of individuals. If this is true, we would expect to find differences in job motivation among those whose jobs provide differing amounts of reward for achievement or whose personal characteristics make achievement more or less valuable. In this chapter we will look at some data from TVA which bear on this topic.

First, we will look at the effect on job motivation of several factors which may affect the extent to which achievement on the job is intrinsically satisfying. Secondly, we will examine the effect on job motivation of factors which make achievement on the job a means to approval from peers and superiors. Finally, we will see how job motivation is affected by the extent to which achievement is seen as a means to promotion.

INTRINSIC VALUE OF ACHIEVEMENT: PRIDE

Achievement may be valued not because it is a means to other rewards, but because it brings directly the satisfaction of personal pride. To what extent will achievement on the job bring personal pride? We have discussed in Chapter 3 the following factors which may make job achievement a means to pride and thus increase job motivation : (1) personality needs; (2) the extent of identification with one's occupation; (3) the amount of opportunity to use one's skills; and (4) the extent of influence over work goals. We will next consider the relation of each of these factors to job motivation and to other reactions on the job.

PERSONAL NEEDS

Need for Achievement

The motive, or need, for achievement, as it has been conceptualized by McClelland, Atkinson, and their associates, is the disposition to derive satisfaction from success or, alternatively, to approach success (Atkinson and Feather, 1966). This motive has been conceptualized by these authors as being, in adults, a fairly fixed personality characteristic. There is evidence (McClelland, *et al.,* 1953) that persons develop high need for achievement when, as children, they are rewarded and praised by their parents and other adults for successfully and independently performing various tasks.

To measure the need for achievement, we have used a short version of the Achievement Risk Preference Scale (ARPS) developed by O'Connor and Atkinson (1960). This scale is designed to measure, more exactly, the relative strength of need for achievement as compared to fear of failure. Psychologically, a high ARPS score represents a greater concern with the satisfactions to be derived from success in a situation which tests one's aptitudes than with the possible pain from failure in such a situation. The scale used consists of eleven items derived from the theory of need for achievement. Examples are the following (with high need for achievement responses starred) :

I would enjoy a party at which was played:

＿＿＿＿＿ Roulette

＿＿＿＿＿ Shuffleboard or horseshoes*

If I were a relief pitcher, I would like to be called into the game when:

＿＿＿＿＿ My team was losing 6 to 12

＿＿＿＿＿ The score was tied*

Once I am sure I can do a task:

＿＿＿＿＿ I become bored with it*

＿＿＿＿＿ I enjoy it most

High need for achievement responses are those which show a disposition (1) to like activities in which performance based on ability (not luck) is evaluated against some standard of excellence; (2) to choose activities in which success is neither certain nor so unlikely that failure can cause little shame; and (3) to focus on the satisfactions of success rather than on the embarrassments of failure. This scale has been found to be correlated with other measures of need for achievement (Atkinson and O'Connor, 1966; Kasl, 1966), with liking for jobs of moderate difficulty (Kasl, 1966), with the grades of high school students (cited by Eckerman, 1963), and with the work performance of salesmen under specific circumstances (Eckerman, 1963).[1]

Most people in our own sample at TVA tended to be at an intermediate position on the measure of need for achievement (an average of 51 per cent high need for achievement responses). However, there was a fair amount of variation in scores both for individuals and for groups.[2] In general, the engineering groups score higher on need for achievement than do the steam plant (blue-collar) groups. This ordering is far from uniform, however; some engineering groups score toward the bottom on need for achievement while some steam plant units score toward the top.

What is the relation of need for achievement scores to scores on our indicators of motivation and of feelings on the job? Table 6-1 shows, first, that, both for individuals and for groups, need for achievement has little relation to the measure of interest in work innovation. Nor do need for achievement scores have a positive correlation with the index of general job interest. There is, in fact, a very small but statistically significant *negative* association for individuals, such that the greater the need for achievement, the less the overall job interest ($r = -.09$; $p < .05$). This association remains significantly negative even when other factors affecting job interest are held constant;[3] it tends to be found also for

---

[1]Atkinson and O'Connor (1966) report substantial correlations between the ARPS measure and a measure of need for achievement (TAT) minus test anxiety. Kasl (1966) reports a moderate correlation of the ARPS with the slope of the regression line of job attractiveness ratings on job difficulty, although Eckerman (1963) did not find such an association. Kasl (1962, 1966), studying industrial workers, also reports associations of the ARPS measure with educational attainment and with liking for jobs which require skill, along with several other associations consistent with theoretical expectations. However, Atkinson and O'Connor (1966) report a lack of association between ARPS scores and achievement-oriented performance in an experimental situation.

[2]For individuals, the standard deviation is 17 per cent high need for achievement responses. For work groups, the range is a mean of 41 per cent to a mean of 82 per cent high need for achievement responses with a standard deviation of 8 per cent.

[3]The overall negative association between need for achievement and general job interest was found in the engineering division A where the correlation was $-.25$ ($p < .01$) but was not found among steam plant and nonoperating employees. Correlations between these variables were not computed separately for engineering division B or for power plant operating employees.

TABLE 6-1 Need for Achievement, as Related to Various Employee Reactions to the Job

(Product-Moment Correlations)

	Individuals[a]		Groups[b]	
	r	Partial r‡	r	Partial r‡
General job interest	−.09*	−.09*	−.16	−.09
Interest in work innovation	.04	.06	.08	.10
Full-day absences, engineering	−.11	−.14	.10	—
Total absences, steam plant nonoperating	.02	.03	.09	—
Total absences, all sites	—	—	.18	.15
Pride in work	−.06	−.04	−.30*	−.13
Psychological symptoms of stress	.04	.03	.17	.09
Physical symptoms of stress	.05	.06	.08	.14

*p <.05, 2 tailed test

‡ Correlations in this column are those which are found when other factors which may affect job motivation (see footnote 8, Chapter 5) are held constant.

a N for individuals is approximately 800 for each row of table, except for rows concerning absence. N for engineering division absence data is 160, N for power plant absence data is 226.

b N for groups is approximately 90 for each row except for absence data. For absence data, N is 34 for engineering groups, 23 for power plant nonoperating groups, and 63 for groups in all sites, including 6 power plant operating groups.

groups. The only correlation in the expected direction is between need for achievement and absence in the engineering division (the higher the need for achievement, the fewer the absences), but this association is small (partial r = −.14) and of marginal statistical significance. Overall, these data indicate that those with higher personal need for achievement are not more highly motivated on the job than are those with lower need for achievement. These findings could indicate that need for achievement (at least as measured) does not have much of an impact on job motivation at TVA or that the level of achievement incentive for most TVA jobs is too low to permit its effect to be noticeable in the sample as a whole. Further results which show the relation of need for achievement to job motivation under varying levels of opportunity for achievement (Chapter 7), as well as other data to be presented in this chapter, will help to throw further light on this matter.

Importance of Challenge

An indication of desire for achievement more specifically on the job comes from responses to a question concerning "the things that are most important to you in a job." Each employee was asked to rank eight aspects of a job in the order in which these are important to him. One was "having work which is a challenge to my ability." Other job aspects listed concerned (1) pleasant working conditions; (2) chance to use one's abilities; (3) learning new things; (4) good wages; (5) friendly co-workers; (6) promotion opportunities; and (7) steady employment. For engineering employees and for power plant employees separately, the ranked importance of each aspect of the job was correlated with job interest scores and with absence.

Among the various aspects of the job which were ranked, the challenge of the job showed the strongest relation to job motivation—in particular, to interest in work innovation. The more employees valued work that was a challenge to their abilities, the more interest in work innovation they showed. The relationships are small (r = +.23 for engineering and +.19 for power plants), but are highly significant statistically with samples of this size.[4] However, the ranked importance of challenge on the job did not have any sizable association with either general job interest or with absence.

Overall, the data indicate that valuing challenge on the job specifically has a somewhat greater effect on job motivation than does general need for achievement.[5] While neither valuing challenge on the job nor need for achievement has a positive effect on general job interest (i.e., periods of time "dragging," feeling of involvement with the job), valuing challenge on the job seems to be more likely to lead to seeking opportunities for achievement (i.e., interest in innovation). Those with high need for achievement, though they may be willing to respond to challenges on the job, do not seem to go out of their way to find such challenges. These results suggest that the need for achievement, instead of being a unitary personality trait, is stronger for given individuals as it concerns success in specific areas of endeavor (e.g., the job, sports, home handyman skills, etc.).[6] Thus, knowing how much a man values achievement on the job specifically would be a better predictor of his job motivation than would a more general measure of his need for achievement.[7]

---

[4]We do not know if the association between the ranked importance of challenge and interest in innovation would remain statistically significant if other variables affecting interest in innovation were held constant. At the time that further analysis had to be halted, such partial correlations were not available.

[5]In order to make a more direct comparison with the associations reported between interest in innovation and the ranked importance of challenge to one's abilities, it may be noted that the correlation between need for achievement and interest in innovation is .00 for steam plant (nonoperating) employees and .01 for engineering division employees.

[6]Eight of the eleven items on the ARPS scale of need for achievement concern sports or games, one concerns "work," and two concern a "problem" or "task."

[7]Although self-report measures of the need for achievement have generally not proved useful, the present measure of the importance of "challenge to my ability" on the job has the advantage of calling for a ranking of the importance of challenge in comparison to seven other socially acceptable job criteria. Thus, it is more likely to be sensitive to real differences than is a question which simply asked people how important challenge on the job is to them.

IDENTIFICATION WITH ONE'S OCCUPATION

A man whose occupational role (engineer, carpenter, steam plant operator) is important to his self-image is, we have hypothesized (see Chapter 3), likely to get more pride from achievement on the job than someone whose occupation matters little to him. To assess "identification with one's occupation" we asked TVA employees these questions:

1. If you were to start life over again with the same opportunities you had, how likely would you be to go into the same type of work or occupation you are now in?

   (Five alternatives from "Probably I would go into something different" to "definitely would go into the same type of work")

2. Suppose there was a series of lectures on the topics listed below, and you could attend only some of these. Rank order the topics according to how *interested* you would be in hearing an informed person talk on each topic.

   (Six topics listed including "New work techniques in your occupation")

3. If someone asked you to describe yourself and you could tell only one thing about yourself, which of the following answers would you be most likely to give? (Which one . . . would you choose second? . . . Which one . . . would you choose third?)

   (Five alternatives listed, including "I am a (my occupation or type of work)")

4. How much time do you spend in your off-hours *reading about or studying things closely connected to your occupation*? (Do not include any work you take home with you.)

   (Six alternatives from "More than five hours a week" to "Very little or no off-hours time in extra reading")

5. Some people's family names were originally chosen according to their occupation; for example, Cook, Baker, Goldsmith, and Farmer. Suppose that, for some reason, everyone had to choose a different name than he now has. How would you feel about being called by your occupation?

   (Five alternatives from "Would like it" to "Would definitely not like it")

6. If you have or were to have a son, how would you feel if someone suggested that he enter the same occupation you are in? (If you are a woman, answer for a daughter.)

   (Five alternatives from "Would completely approve" to "Would strongly disapprove")

7. Please list the names of any *professional or occupational* organizations to which you belong. *Do not include* organizations not connected with your occupation such as church groups, civic groups, social groups, etc. *Do include* employee associations, unions, professional societies, etc. If you belong to more than three such organizations, list only the three in which you are most active.

Now answer the following questions for each of the organizations listed above:

A. Have you ever been an officer of this organization? (Yes—No)
B. Have you ever served on any committee of this organization? (Yes—No)
C. About how many meetings of this organization and its committees have you attended in the past year? ("Zero" through "six or more")

For each individual an index score on occupational identification was computed on the basis of answers to these questions. Also, for each of ninety work groups (persons under the same immediate supervisor), a mean score on the index of occupational identification was computed. Mean scores vary widely among groups, ranging from a low of 1.8 to a high of 4.5 on a scale which ranges from 1 to 5.[8]

Highest in occupational identification scores are a small number of architectural units. Next come engineering units; as might be expected these units are generally above the median in occupational identification and many engineering units are close to the top. However, there is considerable variation among engineering units and a number of these units are below the median in occupational identification scores.

Craftsmen's units generally fall below the engineering units in occupational identification scores. There are some exceptions, however; in particular, several electricians' groups, several machinists' groups, and several instrument mechanics' groups are on a par with or above most engineering units.

Laboratory groups, which include a variety of skill levels, have fairly widely dispersed scores. Most of these groups, including materials testers and analytical chemists, are below the median for all TVA groups. More uniformly below the median, though not at the bottom, are groups in the operating sections of steam plants. Among the very lowest on occupational identification are several clerical units and several drafting service units.

If there are wide variations in occupational identification, what difference do such variations make for motivation and feelings on the job? Table 6-2 shows data on the relation between occupational identification and measures of various employee reactions to the job. For both individuals and units, the higher the occupational identification scores, the higher the scores on measures of general job interest. Also, the higher the occupational identification, the greater the employee interest in work innovation. These associations, though reduced, remain significant when other variables affecting job interest are held constant.

---

[8]The overall mean score for groups on the index of occupational identification was 3.16 with a standard deviation of .51.

TABLE 6-2   Identification with Occupation, as Related to Various Employee Reactions to the Job

(Product-Moment Correlations)

	Individuals[a]		Groups[b]	
	r	*Partial r‡*	*r*	*Partial r‡*
General job interest	.30**	.20**	.32*	.30*
Interest in work innovation	.25**	.10*	.46**	.28*
Full-day absences, engineering	.14**	.25**	.36	—
Total absences, power plant nonoperating	—.06	—.03	.17	—
Total absences, all sites	—	—	.39*	.59**
Pride in work	.13*	.05	—.03	.08
Psychological symptoms of stress	—.14**	—.14**	—.13	—.11
Physical symptoms of stress	—.09*	—.07	—.08	—.05

* p <.05, two-tailed test
** p <.01, two-tailed test
‡   Correlations in this column are those which are found when other factors which may affect job motivation (see footnote 8, Chapter 5) are held constant.
a   N for individuals is approximately 800 for each row of table, except for rows concerning absence. N for engineering division absence data is 160; N for power plant absence data is 224.
b   N for groups is approximately 90 for each row except for absence data. For absence data, N is 34 for engineering groups, 23 for power plant nonoperating groups, and 63 for groups in all sites, including 6 power plant operating groups.

But while those with high occupational identification are likely to be more interested in their job than others, they are also more likely to be absent, particularly in the engineering division. The surprising positive association in the engineering division, and for all sites combined, between occupational identification and absence holds even when a large number of other variables including education, age, and length of service are held constant.

The relation of occupational identification to feelings on the job is also shown in Table 6-2. For individuals there is a small but statistically significant negative association between occupational identification and reported psychological symptoms of stress (more occupational identification, fewer symptoms of stress).

Overall, these data indicate that increased occupational identification is associated with greater job interest and with more positive feelings on the job but, rather inconsistently, with more absences—especially among engineering personnel. It seems likely that the greater number of absences among those with high occupational identification is related to the fact that men who are high in occupational identification are also high in chances for jobs outside TVA (r = .51).[9]

---

[9]Chances for jobs outside TVA was not among the factors held constant in the partial correlation analyses predicting to indicators of job motivation. See Chapter 11 for information about the measure of this factor.

Thus, those with the strongest occupational ties also have the least dependence on TVA as an organization. This independence may make those with higher occupational identification somewhat less concerned than others about the organizational standards and sanctions relating to absence.[10]

Yet the fact that those with strong commitment to their occupations permit themselves relatively frequent absences—despite their high interest on the job—suggests that strong commitment to one's occupation usually reflects only liking for a certain type of work and satisfaction in filling a certain occupational role. Apparently it does not necessarily reflect a strong desire for outstanding achievement in that role. (Further evidence which tends to support this conclusion will be presented in Chapter 7.)

CHANCE TO USE ABILITIES

Another factor which we expected to affect the amount of personal pride which achievement brings on the job is the extent to which the job requires valued abilities. Where the individual's most prized abilities are involved, we reasoned (Chapter 3), the value of achievement should be great and thus job motivation should be high.

Employees were asked this question on the questionnaire :

> In connection with your job, how much chance do you get to do the kind of things you're best at?
>
> (1) —————— Very little or no chance
> (2) —————— Little chance
> (3) —————— Some chance
> (4) —————— A good chance
> (5) —————— An excellent chance

A score was assigned to each individual on the basis of his response to this question. Mean scores were also computed for each group of persons working under the same immediate supervisor.

Among all 834 respondents at TVA, 23 per cent said they had little or no chance to the do the things they're best at, 33 per cent said they had some chance, and 41 per cent said they have a good or excellent chance (3 per cent gave no answer). Responses to this question vary according to type of job. Among the small group of architectural design people, 90 per cent say they have a good or excellent chance to do the things

---

[10]It may be also (though there is no evidence on this point) that those persons who have the strongest occupational identification are in jobs where supervisors give them most leeway to be absent.

they're best at. Engineers in one division and tradesmen in the steam plants are next highest—with about half in these job categories saying they have a good or excellent chance. Draftsmen and engineers in the second engineering division and steam plant laboratory employees are next, with about 40 per cent saying good or excellent. Operating employees in the steam plants—the men who check and monitor the automated equipment—are least likely to feel they have a good or excellent chance to do the things they're best at. Less than one-fourth of these employees give the most positive responses.

What is the relation, first, between perceived chances to do the things one is best at and indicators of motivation on the job? Table 6-3 shows that the more chance an individual gets to do what he is best at, the greater his general job interest (r = .33 for individuals, .43 for groups). The size of this association is reduced considerably when other factors which may affect motivation are held constant but remains statistically significant for individuals (partial r = .12; p < .01).

There is also a positive association between innovative interest and chance to do what one is best at. However, when other variables affecting motivation are held constant, this association essentially disappears. The

TABLE 6-3   Chance to Use Abilities, as Related to Various Employee Reactions to the Job

(Product Moment-Correlations)

	Individuals[a]		Groups[b]	
	r	Partial r‡	r	Partial r‡
General job interest	.33***	.12**	.43**	.14
Interest in work innovation	.21**	.02	.36**	.12
Full-day absences, engineering	—.18*	—.09	.09	—
Total absences, power plant nonoperating	—.16*	—.06	—.18	—
Total absences, all sites	—	—	.04	.31*
Pride in work	.24**	.04	.29**	.14
Psychological symptoms of stress	—.18**	—.05	—.26*	—.05
Physical symptoms of stress	—.17**	—.08	—.17	—.07

*p < .05, two-tailed test
**p < .01, two-tailed test
***p < .001, two-tailed test
‡   Correlations in this column are those which are found when other factors which may affect job motivation (see footnote 8, Chapter 5) are held constant.
a   N for individuals is approximately 800 for each row of table, except for rows concerning absence. N for engineering division absence data is 158; N for power plant nonoperating absence data is 219.
b   N for groups is approximately 90 for each row of table except for absence data. For absence data, N is 34 for engineering groups, 23 for power plant nonoperating groups, and 63 for groups in all sites, including 6 power plant operating groups.

association between chance to use one's best abilities and number of absences is inconsistent; for individuals a greater chance to use abilities tends to go with fewer absences, but for all groups, greater average chance to use abilities is associated with more frequent absence when other things are held constant.

The data of Table 6-3 indicate also that those who are able to use their best abilities are slightly more likely to feel pride in their work accomplishments and slightly less likely to report psychological symptoms of stress (nervousness, depression, tiredness) or physical symptoms of stress (headaches, upset stomach, gas, trouble sleeping).

Overall, the data of Table 6-3 indicate that having a chance to use one's best skills does contribute to greater interest and more positive feelings on the job. However, the small size of these relationships, when other factors are held constant, indicates that the chance to use one's skills, in itself, exerts only a relatively small effect on job motivation. (Further data on the effects of chances to use one's best abilities in different job situations are presented later in this chapter and in Chapter 7.)

INFLUENCE ON WORK GOALS

Another factor which may be expected to affect a person's pride in work achievement is the amount of say which he has in setting his own work goals. In the TVA units we studied, the major goals of work—e.g., designing a given part of a construction job, repairing a boiler, drafting blueprints for specific jobs, keeping steam plant units operating smoothly —are set, of necessity, by outside requirements and by management planning. There is, however, some variation in the extent to which employees can help set their own immediate goals on the job.

Of particular importance are time goals. In most parts of the engineering divisions studied, each branch and each section of a branch must meet time schedules for the various engineering design jobs they do. In the steam plants, time schedules are not quite so prominent but are frequent nevertheless. Laboratory reports must often be prepared by a certain time. Craftsmen must make repairs on equipment within a certain period. Even operating personnel face time limits at intervals, as when they must take a unit "on" or "off the line" within a certain interval.

There were indications from our early interviews that some employees have more influence in setting these time goals than do others. With the wide range of jobs covered by the study, we also expected differences in the extent to which people can decide the order in which they do things and the extent to which they are able to influence the quality goals in their work.

To assess the amount of control over goals which is exercised by various employees, the following questions were included in the questionnaire:

1. When you have several things to do on the job, how often is it up to you to decide which you will do first, and how often are you expected to do things in a set order?

   (Four response categories from "Almost always expected to do things in a set order" to "Almost always up to me to decide which I'll do first")

2. When you finish a given piece of work, how often do you have any say at all about what work you'll be doing next?

   (Five response categories from "About three-quarters of the time or more" to "Extremely rarely or never")

3. When schedules or time limits are being set for work you are doing, which of the following appears to be the *most important* influence on how these limits are set? (Put a number 1 next to the most important influence.)[11]

   _____ Requirements of *people outside* your own section

   _____ Your *own estimate* of how long the job will take (or the estimate of yourself and other people at your level)

   _____ Your *supervisor's estimate* of how long the job will take

   Now go back and put a *number 2* next to the *second* most important influence on what the time limits or schedules are. Put a *number 3* next to the *third* most important influence.

4. Before your supervisors set deadlines, time limits, or target dates which involve your work, how often do they ask your opinion—either alone or as a member of a group—concerning how long the job will take?

   (Five response categories from "9 times out of 10 or more" to "1 time out of 10 or less")

5. How much say or influence do you have (either alone or together with other people at about your level) when it comes to setting the time schedules for jobs that you work on?

   (Five response categories from "No influence at all" to "A great deal of influence")

6. In judging the quality of your work, how much is the person who checks your work influenced by what you tell him about the *special problems or conditions you met in doing the job?*

   (Five response categories from "A great deal" to "Not at all")

7. When your work has been looked over by a supervisor or checker, how much say or influence do you have in deciding whether it should be *changed or done over?*

   (Five response categories from "No say at all" to "A great deal of say on this")

---

[11]Those who never have time limits in their work were instructed to skip the questions concerning how time limits are set.

For each individual, an index score on influence over work goals, based on his responses to these items, was computed. Average scores on this index were also computed for each work group under the same immediate supervisor.

Mean scores for the ninety work groups vary widely, from a low of 1.9 to a high of 4.2 on a scale ranging from 1 to 5.[12] In general, groups in one engineering division score lower on the influence over goals index than do those in the second engineering division—though there is some overlap. This result is consistent with many respondents' comments and with other questionnaire data indicating that influence by employees in the one engineering division is generally lower than influence of employees in the other division. Steam plant operating groups, which work under well-defined rules of procedure, score moderately low on the influence over goals index. Steam plant laboratory groups score moderate to high; scores of craftsmen's groups in the steam plants vary widely.

What relation do the data show between influence over goals and indicators of job motivation? Table 6-4 shows that having greater influence over job goals does not lead to higher scores on our measure of

TABLE 6-4 Employee Influence on Work Goals as Related to Various Employee Reactions to the Job

(Product-Moment Correlations)

	Individuals[a]		Groups[b]	
	r	Partial r[‡]	r	Partial r[‡]
General job interest	.22**	.01	.24	.03
Interest in work innovation	.27**	.16**	.09	.01
Full-day absences, engineering	−.16*	−.13	−.17	—
Total absences, power plant nonoperating	−.14*	−.02	.13	—
Total absences, all sites	—	—	−.09	.17
Pride in work	.24**	.14**	.18	−.03
Psychological symptoms of stress	−.15**	−.01	−.05	.25*
Physical symptoms of stress	−.11*	−.01	.06	.07

  * p <.05, two-tailed test
 ** p <.01, two-tailed test
 ‡ Correlations in this column are those which are found when other factors which may affect job motivation (see footnote 8, Chapter 5) are held constant.
 a N for individuals is about 800 for each row of table except for absence data. For absence data, N for engineering division is 157 and N for power plant nonoperating is 218.
 b N for groups is about 90 for each row of table except for absence data. For absence data, N is 34 for engineering groups, 23 for power plant nonoperating groups, and 63 for groups in all sites including 6 power plant operating groups.

---

[12]The mean for groups on the control over goals index is 2.80; the standard deviation is .58.

general job interest.[13] However, there is a significant tendency for individuals who have more influence over goals to have greater interest in work innovation and a tendency for such persons, especially in the engineering division, to be absent less often. For work groups, however, the average amount of influence on goals which employees exert has little relation to their average degree of job interest, absence, pride in work, or physical symptoms of stress on the job. High average influence on goals exerted by employees is associated with a somewhat higher average occurrence of psychological symptoms of stress.[14]

In general, these data indicate that increased influence over goals does tend to increase job motivation, but not substantially. The smallness of this effect suggests that helping to set goals at work does not in itself raise the value of achievement greatly.[15] Later in this chapter and in Chapter 7, we will consider evidence which suggests that influence over goals has a greater effect on job motivation when other circumstances favoring achievement motivation are favorable.

COMBINATIONS OF FACTORS
AFFECTING PRIDE IN ACHIEVEMENT

We have looked at the way in which people's reactions to their work are related to each of four factors which may affect the extent to which achievement is a source of personal pride. But one may wonder whether certain combinations of these factors—i.e., need for achievement, identification with one's occupation, influence over job goals, and chance to do what one is best at—may produce effects together that could not be predicted from a knowledge of the separate effects of each.

To examine the combined effects on job interest of pride-related factors, we categorized employees as high or low on each of the four factors. With two possibilities (high or low) for each of four factors, there are sixteen possible categories into which employees fall. Table 6-5 shows the mean job interest and job pride scores for persons in each of these categories.

---

[13]However, data presented in Chapter 7 show significant positive correlations between influence over goals and measures of job interest when opportunity for achievement is high.

[14]These small associations for groups occur despite the fact that there are significant differences ($F = 2.43$; $p < .01$) among the ninety work groups on the index of control over goals.

[15]The small associations of influence over goals with indicators of job motivation may be due in part to possible weaknesses in the measure of influence over goals. While time goals are definitely relevant in most jobs at TVA, it is not clear to what extent the other questions in the index tapped matters which are important to employees.

TABLE 6-5   Job Interest and Job Pride, for Employees Experiencing Various Combinations of Factors Relevant to Making Achievement a Source of Pride

> **CODE**
> A. Need for Achievement
> B. Identification with Occupation
> C. Influence Over Work Goals
> D. Chance to Do What Best At

High on Following Factors Making Achievement Means to Pride	N	Interest in Work Innovation		General Interest in Work		Pride in Job Accomplishment	
		Mean	S.E.ᵃ	Mean	S.E.	Mean	S.E.
ABCD	79	3.61	.08	7.65	.13	3.19	.11
ABC	63	3.19	.10	7.19	.18	2.63	.12
ABD	45	2.98	.13	7.45	.16	2.89	.14
ACD	50	3.18	.10	6.78	.21	2.78	.12
BCD	52	3.41	.10	7.49	.18	3.24	.12
AB	80	2.92	.08	6.53	.17	2.37	.12
AC	64	2.95	.10	6.18	.19	2.65	.15
AD	30	2.77	.16	6.97	.35	2.38	.18
BC	24	3.34	.16	7.30	.26	2.67	.25
BD	25	2.95	.13	7.50	.32	2.86	.26
CD	26	3.20	.15	7.27	.23	2.90	.22
A	81	2.77	.08	5.57	.22	2.29	.12
B	37	2.90	.15	6.70	.23	2.32	.19
C	30	2.82	.14	6.77	.32	2.83	.19
D	20	2.83	.15	7.05	.38	2.73	.27
None	41	2.66	.10	6.15	.30	2.41	.16

a   Indicates standard error of mean

As might be expected, the highest average job interest and close to the greatest job pride are shown by persons who stand high on all four pride-related factors (row ABCD).[16] However, the combination of occupational identification, influence over work goals, and chance to use skills (row BCD) results in scores which are almost as high as for those high in all four factors.

Perhaps the most notable feature of Table 6-5 is that the lowest scores on general job interest are obtained by those who are *high* in need for achievement but *low* on the other three factors of identification with

---

[16]Other data, not shown, also indicate that fewest symptoms of stress are reported by those who score high on all four pride-related factors while most symptoms of stress are reported by those who score low on all these factors.

occupation, influence over work goals, and chance to use skills (Row A in table).[17] These persons are also lowest in job pride and second lowest in interest in work innovation.

Even when one or two other factors facilitating pride in job achievement are present, high need for achievement tends to be associated with lower general job interest (for example, compare row AC with row C). Only when circumstances are most optimal for pride in work (i.e., all three other factors are high), is high need for achievement not associated with lower job interest. On the other hand, even when other pride-relevant factors are optimal, there is no evidence that high need for achievement greatly increases job interest.

Additional data concerning the effects of need for achievement are shown in Appendix F. These data are for selected persons who were uniformly low or uniformly high on all three factors of occupational identification, influence on work goals, and chance to use skills. For each of these three categories, the effect of variations in need for achievement is shown. The data, consistent with those of Table 6-5, suggest that when other circumstances do not favor pride in work (i.e., the three other factors are low) increases in need for achievement are associated with lower interest in the job.[18] When other circumstances do favor pride in work (i.e., other factors are all high), need for achievement has no substantial effect on job interest.

That those with high need for achievement tend to have low interest in their jobs in circumstances which provide little chance for them to feel pride in their work seems fairly easy to understand. The achievement needs of such men are more likely to focus on activities (e.g., sports, home projects) in which they can feel a greater pride in accomplishment.

However, it is less easy to explain why, even when circumstances do favor pride in work, those with high need for achievement do not show greater job interest than do others. We will be in a better position to discuss the relation between need for achievement and job motivation after we have looked at this relation under varying levels of opportunity for achievement (see Chapter 7).

---

[17]The difference between the mean general job interest scores in rows "A" and "None" does not reach statistical significance. Note, however, that for the entire sample the negative correlation between need for achievement and general job interest is statistically significant.

[18]Although these results are not statistically significant, they indicate that the statistically significant negative correlation between need for achievement and job interest tends to occur among those for whom other circumstances do not favor pride in work.

INTERACTIONS AMONG PRIDE-RELEVANT FACTORS

To try to understand more systematically the way in which job interest is related to factors which make achievement a source of pride, two analyses of variance were performed. The first analyzes the effect of the pride-relevant variables on general job interest and the second analyzes their effect on interest in work innovation.[19]

The analyses of variance (results of which are shown in Appendix G) show a sizeable relation between both measures of job interest and (1) control over job goals, (2) identification with one's occupation, and (3) chance to do what one is best at. These results parallel the correlation data presented in Tables 6-2, 6-3, and 6-4, which show positive associations between these variables. The analyses of variance also show little overall association between need for achievement and job interest. This result generally parallels the correlation data shown in Table 6-1. (The more refined correlation analysis showed that there is, in fact, a small negative association between need for achievement and general job interest.)

The new information which the analyses of variance provide, which the correlation analysis did not provide, concerns interaction among (i.e., joint effects of) the factors relevant to pride in achievement. Overall, there is very little evidence of interaction among these factors. The single inter-action of any size is between control over job goals and chance to do what one is best at. More detailed analyses of the data (not shown here) indicate that the nature of this interaction is not consistent. With respect to general job interest, the impact of either chance to use one's best skills or influence over work goals is greater when the other factor is low than when it is high—as though each tends to compensate for a lack of the other. However, interest in innovation tends to require both influence over goals and chance to use one's best skills; each pride-relevant factor, especially chance to use one's skills, has a greater impact on innovative interest when the other factor is high than when it is low. It may be that the activity directed toward better ways of doing the job reflects a particularly high level of motivation for which a combination of factors making achievement a means to pride are required.

There are no other substantial interaction effects among other combinations of the four pride-relevant factors. It appears, therefore, that the impact on job interest of occupational identification, control over work goals,

---

[19]These analyses were done with data more refined than those shown in Table 6-5. Each person could be scored as high, medium, or low on each of the four pride-relevant factors with the exception of chance to use one's skills, on which persons were scored as high or low. There are fifty-four possible categories into which each person can fall, representing the possible combinations of positions on the four factors.

and chance to do what one is best at, is largely additive. In general (with the exception of the small interaction between control over goals and chance to use skills), an increase in any of these three factors is accompanied by an increase in job interest, irrespective of the level of the other two factors.[20]

REWARD FROM PEERS FOR ACHIEVEMENT

Another thing which can make job achievement more or less valued by a man on a job is the reaction of his co-workers to the kind of job he does. Achievement may be valued in part because it brings the approval and respect of co-workers. There is evidence (e.g., Seashore, 1954; Patchen, 1962) that group pressures will sometimes work to improve attendance and performance on the job. On the other hand, it is well known, and has been documented by several studies (e.g., Roy, 1952; Roethlisberger and Dickson, 1939), that doing "too good" a job (e.g., being a "rate-buster") may in some job situations be cause for disapproval by co-workers.

In informal exploratory interviews we asked employees in various kinds of jobs whether there were cases where someone was criticized by his co-workers and what would happen if someone were not "carrying his load." Many respondents maintained that all employees in their units always did their best so that censure of laggards was not an issue. A few employees mentioned instances of employees who sometimes "goofed off" but said that discipline was left to supervisors. For example, an engineering associate who told about several men who "goof off" was asked whether any of their co-workers would say anything to them. He replied :

I doubt seriously if anyone would say anything. They might kid them a little. A man would probably get fighting mad if someone on his own level said anything seriously.

An electrician, asked whether there were any instances where someone didn't cooperate with the others, said :

Yes; one person has a chip on his shoulder all the time. He just is that way. No one did or does anything about it. We just try to let the thing work itself out.

---

[20]For individuals, an index of achievement as a means to pride, which represents a sum of scores on need for achievement, identification with occupation, chance to use skills, and influence over work goals, correlates .33 ($p < .001$) with the index of general job interest, .30 ($p < .001$) with the index of interest in work innovation, $-.15$ ($p < .01$) with absences in the engineering division, and $-.16$ ($p < .01$) with absences among steam plant nonoperating employees. For groups, the index of achievement as a means to pride correlates .41 with general job interest and .47 with interest in innovation.

Just as our interviews did not elicit instances of men rebuking their co-workers for poor work (or for "too good" work), so too we did not encounter descriptions of situations where men in a unit were cheering each other on to better performance. While some compliments and some rebukes occur among co-workers, the impression gained from reading the limited number of interviews we conducted is that clear group sanctions based on performance are not found in most work situations within the engineering divisions and power plants at TVA.

This impression is supported by responses to the following question :

If a person on your job were known as a fast, energetic worker, how would this affect his chances of being close friends with people on his own level on the job?

(Five response categories from "Would make it much harder to become close friends" to "would make it much easier to become close friends with people on his own level")

In response to this question, 56 per cent of all TVA employees taking the questionnaire said that whether a man was "a fast, energetic worker wouldn't matter one way or the other" as far as being accepted was concerned. Sixteen per cent thought that such an energetic worker would find it harder to make friends, but 27 per cent thought that hard work would make it easier for a man to be accepted in their units. Approximately the same distribution of responses occurs within each of twenty-one major work units, like an engineering division branch or a steam plant mechanical maintenance section. In other words, throughout the parts of TVA studied, responses indicate neither substantially greater nor lesser acceptance by employees of an exceptionally energetic worker. Moreover, mean responses to this question do not differ significantly among work groups in engineering divisions nor among work groups in steam plants, indicating that immediate work groups do not differ greatly in their generally indifferent attitudes toward energetic workers. In view of the emphasis which has been given to work group pressures in some literature, these data are interesting in indicating that group sanctions, either pro-efficiency or anti-efficiency, may be rather weak in many work situations.

However, responses to questions concerning co-workers indicate that both compliments for good work and reminders of mistakes do occur with some frequency. Asked "If you do an outstanding job on something, how likely are you to be complimented by one of your co-workers (other than one of your supervisors)?" over one-third (37 per cent) of all TVA employees say this happens more than half the time. Asked "If you make a mistake or oversight, how likely is this to be called to your attention

by someone other than a person responsible for checking your work?"
over one-fourth say that mistakes are usually called to their attention by
co-workers. There is considerable variation among work units on these
questions, particularly among power plant units, concerning the frequency
of compliments for good work.

On the basis of his answers to these questions, and to the question
concerning attitudes toward "a fast, energetic worker," each person was
given a score on an index of group sanction for achievement. Average
scores on this index were also computed for each of the ninety work
groups.

Group Solidarity

In addition to the kinds of group sanctions which are exerted on
employees, it is important also to know the amount of solidarity within
work groups, which may make these pressures more or less effective.
Seashore (1954) has found that, whatever the direction of group pressures,
the uniformity of behavior in a group depends on the degree of group
cohesiveness. Where employees feel a sense of cohesiveness or solidarity
with their co-workers, they may be expected to value greatly the approval
and respect of these co-workers.

To assess the degree of solidarity which each employee feels with his
co-workers, the following questions were asked :

1. Compared to people you've worked with elsewhere (other firms, other parts
    of TVA, the Armed Forces, etc.), how close do you feel to the people you
    work with in your present job?

    (Five response categories from "much closer now than to other people I've
    worked with," to "much less close than to other people I've worked with")

2. Compared to people you've worked with elsewhere (other firms, other parts
    of TVA, the Armed Forces, etc.), how much do the people you work with
    in your present job help each other out?

    (Five response categories from "much less than other people I've worked
    with" to "much more than other people I've worked with")

3. Following are some kinds of people with whom you may now have or have
    previously had contact. Rank them according to *how close you feel to them
    personally.* Put a *number 1* next to the kind of group which, in general, you feel
    closest to; put a *number 2* next to the group you feel next closest to; put a
    number 3 next to the group you feel least close to.

    _____ Your neighbors
    _____ Your relatives, other than your immediate family
    _____ People you work with at TVA

For each individual, an overall index score on peer reward for achievement was computed by multiplying the average of scores on questions concerning group sanctions for achievement and the average of scores concerning solidarity with co-workers. For each work group too, a mean score on peer reward for achievement was computed.

To what extent is work motivation at TVA associated with the extent to which good work will bring reward from co-workers? Table 6-6 shows, both for individuals and for groups, the correlations between scores on the index of peer reward for achievement and scores showing various employee reactions to the job. These data show a positive association between peer reward for achievement and general job interest, but this relation is small and becomes smaller yet when other factors affecting job interest are held constant. So too, there are only very small associations between peer rewards and interest in work innovation, pride in work, and symptoms of stress when other things are held constant.

There is, however, evidence of a definite effect of peer rewards on the number of absences. The greater the peer rewards for achievement in a group, the fewer the average number of absences. Although this association is small (in the .20s), it is found both in the engineering division and in the power plants and also for all sites combined. When other factors affecting absence are held constant (for groups in all sites combined), the association with absence becomes a little stronger and statistically significant.

The question may be raised as to whether the lower absence rate in groups which give higher reward for achievement is due to more frequent

TABLE 6-6   Reward for Achievement by Co-Workers, as Related to Various Employee Reactions to the Job, for Ninety Work Groups

(Product-Moment Correlations)

	r	*Partial r*‡
General job interest	.26*	.18
Interest in work innovation	.06	.11
Full-day absences, engineering (N = 34)	−.24	—
Total absences, power plant nonoperating (N = 29)	−.27	—
Total absences, all sites combined (N = 63)ᵃ	−.21	−.26*
Pride in work	.34**	.07
Psychological symptoms	−.15	−.07
Physical symptoms	−.07	−.12

* p <.05, two-tailed test
** p <.01, two-tailed test
‡   Correlations in this column are those which are found when other factors which may affect job motivation (see footnote 8, Chapter 5) are held constant.
a   Includes six power plant operating groups.

sanctions or to greater solidarity in such groups. (Both of these factors are included in the index of peer reward for achievement.) The data show that both group sanctions and group solidarity are associated with fewer absences.[21] Thus, compliments and criticisms bearing on the work, rather than merely the general attraction of a friendly group, help to account for the relation between peer rewards and lower absence.

It may be noted that another aspect of employees' relations to their co-workers also has an association with attendance. Employees were asked, "If you didn't do a good job on something or didn't do it fast enough, how often would this create problems for someone you have contact with on the job?" They were also asked how many people would be affected in such circumstances. An index of effect on others' work was computed for individuals and for work groups. The more effect the members of a group have on the work of others, the fewer their absences (partial $r = -.33$; $p < .01$). This association is independent of the impact of peer rewards for achievement, just as the association between absence and peer rewards is independent of the extent to which employees' work affects the work of others. However, it seems likely that there are sanctions for absence, not covered in our measure of peer rewards, which would be applied when a man whose work greatly affects the work of others is absent. He is likely to be told by others of how his absence created problems for them and, implicitly at least, criticized for being away. Thus, the association between the measure of effect on others' work and absence may be another instance of the relation between peer sanctions and absence.

In general, the data cited in this section indicate that, when co-workers are alert to the kind of job a man is doing and are interested in his work, he is more likely to want to come to work. However, there is little evidence that peer rewards have any appreciable impact on job interest or job pride. The better attendance of men in groups which reward good work may be due to a heightened sensitivity of men in such groups to the opinions of their peers (which presumably include a negative attitude toward absence), rather than to any great increase in internalized motivation.

SUPERVISORY REWARD FOR ACHIEVEMENT

A person's motive to achieve may be strengthened also if he expects that doing a job well will bring approval from supervisors whose approval

---

[21]The respective association with absence of the group sanctions and group solidarity measures are as follows: for the engineering division, $-.18$ and $-.20$; for steam plants, $-.13$ and $-.29$; for all groups combined, $-.25$ and $-.09$.

he values. Some TVA employees feel that if they do outstanding work this will be recognized and acknowledged by their supervisors. A secretary in an engineering unit said :

> *If you do a pretty table, you're complimented and they always say so on the service review if you've done a good job. Supervisors are very good about this in this branch—they always make a point to say something.*

A boilermaker commented :

> *When I do a good job they come around and tell us. Pat you on the back. This would be the foreman or the general maintenance foreman who would do this. Our foreman checks most things we do.*

A chemist in the laboratory of a steam plant said :

> *We have a man here at the labs who is very good about that. If a man needs a reprimand, he needs to be pushed into giving it, but he gives a good word often—although it doesn't help in promotion.*

Other employees, however, feel that good work does not bring recognition from their supervisors. An assistant unit operator said :

> *You don't see too much of patting men on the back. If you do a good job, nothing happens. Something goes wrong, you hear about it real quick. They seem to take a good job for granted. Myself, I don't care.*

A draftsman said :

> *The main method of recognition is through the service reviews and these are based pretty much on personalities. If the boss likes you, you get a higher rating. I've never gotten "fully adequate." I don't like the way they store things up all year and then put them on your service review. They seem very reluctant to pat you on the back. They never tell you one way or the other until you get your service review at the end of the year. But it isn't too bad. If you try real hard and do good and no one notices you, you think "What the heck."*

An engineer commented :

> *It depends not on what you do but what you don't do. If everything is alright and you don't create problems, people are satisfied. If you put out three times as much work as someone else and one thing comes back, that's what they remember.*

In the questionnaire which employees filled out, the following relevant question was asked :

If you do an outstanding job on something, how likely are you to be *complimented* by one of your *supervisors?*

(6) ——————— Almost always
(5) ——————— About three-quarters of the time
(4) ——————— About half of the time
(3) ——————— About one-quarter of the time
(2) ——————— About one-tenth of the time
(1) ——————— Almost never

The wide differences among the few people quoted above are paralleled in the responses by the 834 employees in our sample. Of these, 23 per cent said a supervisor "almost never" compliments them for outstanding jobs while 33 per cent reported that a supervisor "almost always" compliments them. Other responses were scattered fairly evenly among the other categories.

Mean scores for responses to this question were also computed for each group of persons working under the same immediate supervisor.[22] Scores vary fairly widely among groups.[23] There are sizable differences among units doing comparable work (e.g., among steam plant laboratories) indicating that the frequency of compliments for good work is chiefly a function of the supervisors' personal styles.

What is the relation between the frequency of supervisors' compliments for good work and our measures of employee reactions to their jobs? Both for indivduals and for the ninety work groups, there are positive correlations in the expected direction between frequency of supervisory approval and general job interest, interest in innovation, and pride in work. (Table 6-7 shows the data for groups.) However, when other variables affecting motivation are held constant, frequency of supervisors' compliments no longer has a significant relation to any of the indicators of job motivation or of feelings on the job. In work units at TVA, approval from peers seems to have more of an effect on job motivation (especially as reflected in absence) than does approval from supervisors.

Since, as we have indicated, the presence or absence of supervisory acknowledgment of good work appears to be quite important to many men and often spoken of with obvious emotion, its small association with job motivation and pride is rather surprising. It may be that when a man expresses resentment about lack of appreciation by supervisors, this more often represents an expression of general hostility towards the supervisor,

---

[22]Scores were assigned to each response corresponding to the numbers shown above to the left of each response.

[23]The mean group score is 4.00 ("about half the time") and the standard deviation is 1.20.

TABLE 6-7 **Supervisory Compliments for Good Work, as Related to Various Employee Reactions to the Job, for Ninety Work Groups**

(Product-Moment Correlations)

	r	Partial r‡
General job interest	.34	.10
Interest in work innovation	.25	.05
Full-day absences, engineering (N = 34)	−.09	—
Total absences, power plants nonoperating (N = 29)	.03	—
Total absences, all sites (N = 63)a	.05	.14
Pride in work	.28**	.15
Psychological symptoms of stress	−.14	.13
Physical symptoms of stress	−.08	.10

 * p <.05, two-tailed test
 ** p <.01, two-tailed test
 ‡ Correlations in this column are those which are found when other factors which may affect job motivation (see footnote 8, Chapter 5) are held constant.
 a Includes six power plant operating groups.

toward the work organization, or toward the job as a whole, than it does a real desire to have the approval of the supervisors. The results suggest that, for most people, the approval of supervisors is not really greatly valued, especially when, as one person quoted above commented, his compliments don't help for promotion. Of course, power over promotion is not the only thing that may help to increase the value of the supervisor's approval or disapproval. Admiration and liking, based on positive personal contacts, are also likely to have this effect. In many work groups, both at TVA and elsewhere, employees may not like and admire their supervisors enough to make them strive for these supervisors' approval.

PROMOTION AS A REWARD FOR ACHIEVEMENT

Another reason why a person may strive to do outstanding work on the job is that such performance may lead to promotion. Promotion means more money, higher formal status; and not least important for many, it is a tangible sign of recognition of one's value by the organization. For good work to be a path to promotion, there must be opportunities for promotion and ability—rather than seniority—must be an important basis for promotion.

In general, the parts of TVA studied were fairly static in size, and promotion opportunities were fairly limited. There were generally better promotion chances in the engineering divisions than in the steam plants.

Most young beginning engineers could expect to be promoted to a higher "grade" about three times before reaching a position below the section supervisor, where promotion became more difficult. However, many engineering division employees had already been promoted as far as they could easily go.

In the steam plants, promotion opportunities were more limited. For most craftsmen, the only possible promotion was to section supervisor (foreman). But the number of such jobs was small. As one electrician put it : "We have twenty electricians and two foremen. If the foreman dies, then someone gets promoted." In the operating sections of the steam plants, there is a usual advancement for some employees from assistant unit operator to operator but at that point advancement stops for most men.

To obtain the perceptions of employees concerning their promotion chances, the following questions were asked :

1. In your opinion, about what percentage of people in TVA of your grade and seniority, doing your type of work, will be promoted to a higher grade in the next five years?

   (Seven categories, from "90% or more" to "less than 5%")

2. How many grades up can you expect to be promoted during the rest of the time you work for TVA?

   (Five categories from "None" to "Four or more grades up")

In the engineering divisions, there is considerable spread in answers to the first question, with the median response being that "about 25 per cent" of people like themselves will be promoted in the next five years. However, 46 per cent think that half or more of people like themselves will be promoted in the next five years. The median response to the second question is between one and two grades.

In the steam plants, 60 per cent of all employees said that 5 per cent or less of people like themselves would be promoted in the next five years. Only 10 per cent thought that 50 per cent or more in their category would be promoted in the next five years. Concerning the number of promotions to be expected at any time in the future, the median expectation in the steam plants was for one promotion.

But if, for some at least, there are opportunities for promotion, there is still the question of what the linkage is between promotion and good work.

Some employees see ability as having an important effect on the possibility of promotion. A draftsman said :

I think I've advanced real well. I suppose I've been lucky, but advancement is always there if you have the qualifications.

A heavy equipment said concerning promotion:

I think they're fair about that too. If a man can handle a higher job, he'll get it.

Other employees who were interviewed, however, felt that doing a good job often counted little for promotion in comparison to sheer seniority and being liked by supervisors. Commenting on the system of filling jobs by "posting" them throughout the TVA system, an engineering aide said:

People apply but they don't get them. The general feeling, too, is that a lot are awarded on the basis of personality and politics, not strictly through qualifications and seniority.

Asked what promotion depends on, a civil engineer answered:

Time is number one. From grade 4 up, it's politics mostly. (Q. Below grade 4 how much does merit count?) They try to say it does, but I think it is mostly a matter of time. The boys who do most work get it quicker, but everyone gets it sooner or later.

To systematically assess the perceptions of TVA employees concerning the bases of promotion, we asked the following question:

1. Promotions can be based on seniority, ability to do the job, and being liked by the supervisors. Which of these three things do you think will count *most* in determining how soon you get promoted? (Put a *number 1* next to this item.)

    _____ Seniority (beyond the minimum required for promotion)
    _____ Ability to do the job
    _____ Being liked by the supervisors
    _____ No chance at all for promotion

    Which do you think will count *second* most in determining when you get your next promotion? (Put a *number 2* next to this item, above.) Finally, put a *number 3* next to the thing which you think will be least important in determining how soon you get promoted.

For all employees, 57 per cent ranked "ability to do the job" as first in importance, while 25 per cent ranked it second and 12 per cent ranked it third. (Six per cent gave no answer.) Being liked by supervisors received the next largest percentage of first-place rankings (29 per cent) while seniority received fewest first-place and most last-place rankings.

For each employee, an index score of the extent to which good work is perceived to be a path to promotion was also computed. This index was derived by multiplying the person's score on Q1, that concerning the percentage of people like himself who will be promoted in the next five years, by the ranking given to ability as a requisite for promotion.[24] Mean scores on the index of achievement as a means to promotion were also computed for each group of employees under the same immediate supervisor.

What is the relation between the extent to which good work is a means to promotion and the indicators of work motivation? Results show that, both for individuals and for groups, there are no significant associations between achievement as a means to promotion, on the one hand, and general job interest, interest in work innovation, or number of absences, on the other hand. Nor are there significant associations, either for individuals or for groups, between the index of achievement as a means to promotion and pride in work, psychological symptoms of stress, or physical symptoms of stress. (The data for groups are shown in Table 6-8.)

These data indicate, then, that at least in the job situations covered by this study, hope of promotion is not an important contributor to job motivation. It is interesting to speculate about why this might be so. It may be that, despite the fact that many employees ranked ability as the prime criterion for promotion, it is a "reasonable" amount of ability and effort and not truly outstanding performance which is required for promotions into most of the jobs at TVA. In this respect, ability may be less crucial for promotion in most of the jobs covered than in, say, some salesmen's jobs or some academic jobs. Secondly, it may be that, while promotion is a real possibility for most employees, it is for most a rather

TABLE 6-8   **Extent to Which Good Work Is a Means to Promotion, as Related to Various Employee Reactions to the Job, for Ninety Work Groups**

(Product-Moment Correlations)

	r	*Partial r**
General job interest	.04	.16
Interest in work innovation	−.02	.03
Full-day absences, engineering (N = 34)	−.03	—
Total absences, power plant nonoperating (N = 29)	−.05	—
Total absences, all sites (N = 63)[a]	.16	.16
Pride in work	−.10	.16
Psychological symptoms of stress	.17	.13
Physical symptoms of stress	−.06	.10

* Correlations in this column are those which are found when other factors which may affect motivation (see footnote 8, Chapter 5) are held constant.
a   Includes six power plant operating groups.

[24]In computing this index, the ranking scores were re-coded so that three became one and vice versa.

far distant possibility—something that may happen in a year, two years, or five years. It would be difficult for such a distant reward to raise greatly the motivation experienced on the job today.

There are, of course, some jobs for which outstanding work may serve as an essential and fairly immediate path to advancement. One might think, for example, of a young growing company where outstanding salesmen or executives quickly shoot up to higher positions. Yet such situations are probably a small minority of all job situations. Probably the great majority of people work in jobs which are fairly similar to those at TVA —where reasonable competence is needed for promotion but where the proper formal qualifications of education and training, along with the required seniority, will bring a number of promotions at intervals of several years each during the work career. Reflection on this type of job situation, along with the present data, suggests that, while the eventual chance for promotion may encourage a person to do his work with reasonable diligence, the promotion reward cannot be expected to inspire a continuously high level of interest, energy, and enthusiasm on the job.

COMBINATIONS OF DIFFERENT REWARDS FOR ACHIEVEMENT

So far we have looked at the relation between job motivation and each of several rewards for job achievement (pride, peer approval, supervisory approval, and promotion) which may make achievement more valued and thus create a motive for achievement. (The strongest separate relations are summarized in Figure 6-1.) But is the effect of one reward

Note: Numbers are partial correlation coefficients. Those in parentheses are for all (834) individuals; others are for all ninety work groups. Each partial correlation shows the strength of the association independent of other relevant factors. See footnote 8, Chapter 5, for a list of variables held constant in each partial correlation analysis.

FIGURE 6-1 Strongest single relationships between factors relevant to reward for achievement and employee reactions to the job

for achievement dependent on the presence or absence of other rewards? For example, does the fact that job achievement brings supervisory approval have a different effect on motivation when achievement also brings peer approval than when peer approval is absent?

In this section we examine the effects on job interest of various combinations of rewards for achievement.[25] As a first step in studying the joint effect of various rewards for achievement, employees were coded as either high or low (in about equal numbers) in getting each of the four types of reward for achievement—i.e., pride,[26] peer approval, supervisory approval, and promotion. With two possible positions (high-low) on each of four rewards, this results in sixteen categories of persons. For each of these categories, representing one possible combination of rewards for achievement, an average score on general job interest and on interest in work innovation was computed. Table 6-9 shows these data.

A number of things stand out in these data. One is the importance of the reward of personal pride in achievement. Men for whom compliments from supervisors, approval from peers, and promotion advantages are all absent nevertheless score relatively high in general job interest if they get personal pride from achievement (row D). When all other rewards for achievement are high but personal pride rewards are low (row ABC), general job interest is only moderate. (A seeming contradiction to this pattern is the fact that those high only in supervisory approval and peer approval for good work, but not in pride (row AB), score quite high on general job interest. However, a more refined analysis of the data, which trichotomizes individuals on each reward, shows that when personal pride rewards are lowest, the combination of supervisory and peer approval does not bring high job interest.)

When the extremes are compared—i.e., those receiving personal pride rewards plus several other rewards versus those who receive no rewards for achievement—the differences in general job interest are considerable. These differences in general job interest are even greater for more refined data (not shown) which classify persons as high, medium, or low on each of the rewards for achievement. Differences in interest in work innovation

---

[25] Job interest is the focus of attention because our primary concern is with indicators of motivation; absences were not used as a criterion in this instance because this measure is less comparable across the whole sample of TVA employees.

[26] The measure of the extent to which achievement is likely to produce pride is an index based on the sum of scores on need for achievement, identification with occupation, chance to use skills, and influence over work goals.

TABLE 6-9   Job Interest for Persons Receiving Various Combinations of Rewards for Achievement

```
                        CODE
        A.  Supervisory Approval for Good Work
        B.  Peer Approval for Good Work
        C.  Good Work Improves Promotion Chances
        D.  Good Work Leads to Personal Pride
```

High on following Rewards for Achievement	N	General Job Interest		Interest in Work Innovation	
		Mean Score	Standard Error	Mean Score	Standard Error
ABCD	80	7.44	.17	3.38	.08
ABC	17	6.76	.39	2.85	.18
ABD	68	7.54	.16	3.30	.09
ACD	41	7.34	.20	3.25	.11
BCD	29	7.41	.21	3.19	.17
AB	30	7.63	.24	2.89	.13
AC	20	6.90	.37	3.06	.16
AD	27	7.19	.26	3.32	.14
BC	22	6.64	.30	2.89	.13
BD	45	6.98	.20	3.32	.10
CD	44	6.61	.25	3.21	.13
A	14	6.29	.51	3.06	.23
B	64	6.03	.24	2.74	.10
C	44	5.98	.26	2.65	.13
D	65	7.00	.18	2.99	.10
None	86	5.90	.19	2.87	.08

associated with different reward combinations are smaller than the differences in general job interest.[27]

To analyze more systematically the joint effect on job interest of the various rewards for achievement, analyses of variance were performed. These analyses are particularly valuable in permitting us to assess statistically whether the combination of any two, three, or four rewards has an effect on job interest which is greater than the simple addition of their separate effects. These analyses also show the effect on job interest of each reward factor, independent of other reward factors. The analyses of variance were performed with data somewhat more refined than those of Table 6-9 in that each person was scored as high, medium, or low on each reward for achievement rather than only high or low.[28]

---

[27]See Chapter 7 for an estimate of the overall amount of variance in job interest explained by factors most relevant to achievement reward, taking into account the effect of other factors affecting job interest.

[28]The only exception to this was that promotion rewards were still scored as either high or low, in order to provide cases for all possible cells of the analysis.

The results of these analyses, shown in Appendix H, indicate that the main effects of each of the achievement rewards, taken separately, are much greater than the effects of any interactions among these factors. By far the largest impact on job interest comes from the extent to which people can get personal pride from achievement. Peer approval and supervisory approval also show significant effects, especially on general job interest, but the extent to which good work is a means to promotion has no significant effect on job interest. These data, showing the effects of single rewards, are generally consistent with the results of the correlation analysis.

Looking at possible interactions among rewards, there is only one statistically significant interaction—that among promotion rewards, supervisory approval, and personal pride in achievement, as these affect job interest. Inspection of the data indicates that, where all three of these rewards are present together, the increase in job interest is somewhat greater than might be expected from the additive effects of the three separate rewards.

Peer approval and pride in achievement also tend to interact somewhat in their effects on interest in innovation. Data concerning the joint effects of peer approval and pride are shown in Table 6-10. These data

TABLE 6-10 **Interest in Innovation, for Employees Who Differ in Pride Rewards and Peer Rewards for Achievement (Mean Scores)**

Pride Rewards for Good Work	Peer Reward for Good Work		
	Low	*Medium*	*High*
Low	2.83 (80)	2.77 (64)	2.78 (41)
Medium	2.95 (86)	3.01 (101)	3.14 (79)
High	3.01 (55)	3.33 (88)	3.47 (99)

	F	df	p
Pride Rewards	24.2	2,640	.001
Peer Rewards	4.1	2,640	.05
Pride × Peer	1.9	4,640	N.S.

indicate that when achievement brings little personal pride, peer approval for good work has no effect on interest in work innovation; but when achievement brings considerable personal pride, increases in peer approval bring an increase in innovative interest. Conversely, increases in pride rewards for achievement have a greater association with innovative interest when peer approval for good work is high than when it is low. The combination of both pride and peer rewards for achievement brings a fairly marked increase in interest in work innovation.[29]

SUMMARY

In this chapter we have considered the relation of motivation on the job to characteristics of the job and of the person which may affect the amount of reward which achievement brings.

We considered, first, four factors which may affect the amount of personal pride which job achievement brings. The first factor relevant to pride in achievement is the individual's need for achievement. We found little relation between the level of general need for achievement and our indicators of job motivation. The valuing of achievement specifically on the job appeared to have a somewhat greater—though still modest —positive effect on job motivation. Although fuller discussion of the relation between need for achievement and job motivation is deferred until the next chapter, these results suggest that the need for achievement is probably variable across different situations (e.g., the job versus sports) instead of being a unitary personality characteristic which is equally relevant to all situations.

A second factor which is relevant to pride in achievement is the extent of identification with, or commitment to, one's occupation. Results show that those who feel strongly committed to their occupations are more interested in their work and also report fewer symptoms of stress. However, paradoxically, the more identified men are with their occupations, the *more* likely they are to be absent. The more frequent absence of those who are strongly committed to their occupations is probably due in part to the fact that those with stronger occupational ties are likely to have weaker ties to TVA as an organization and are therefore less subject to its control. However, these results appear also to shed light on the meaning of occupational commitment. They suggest that, while commitment to one's occupation usually reflects a genuine liking for that type of work and liking for that occupational role, it does not necessarily reflect the desire for outstanding achievement on the job.

---

[29]This apparent interaction tendency falls short of statistical significance, however.

Two other factors which were expected to affect pride in achievement are the chance to use one's best abilities on the job and influence over job goals. Both of these factors showed positive associations with at least one indicator of job motivation. However, the overall results indicate that each of these factors, in itself, has only a small effect on job motivation. The impact of each of these factors on motivation under varying levels of opportunity for achievement will be examined in Chapter 7.

Analyses of the effects of various combinations of the factors relevant to pride in achievement indicate that these factors are generally additive in their effects on job interest, with interaction effects relatively small. However, those who are high in need for achievement tend to have low interest in their jobs when other factors making achievement a means to pride are low. These results suggest that those who have a high need for achievement feel more frustrated than others in situations which are not conducive to pride in achievement. An overall measure of the extent to which achievement is a means to pride had a stronger association with job interest (though not with attendance) than do other rewards for achievement.

In addition to rewards of personal pride, this chapter has also considered the extent to which job achievement is likely to bring rewards from external sources—i.e., approval from peers, approval from supervisors, and promotion. While the level of reward for achievement from peers is not greatly associated with job interest, higher levels of peer reward for achievement are associated with fewer absences. These results appear to indicate that approval for good work from co-workers does not greatly increase the intrinsic interest of the job but does make individuals more concerned about meeting their job obligations. This conclusion is supported by data which indicate that absence is less frequent among men whose absence would have the greatest impact on the work of others.

Although approval for good work by supervisors (or the lack of such approval) is often commented upon by employees, there is little evidence that the likelihood of supervisory compliments for achievement has much impact on the level of job motivation. It may be that, for many persons, the supervisor is not liked and respected enough, nor has he sufficient power over promotion, for his approval to be valued greatly.

The extent to which achievement is a means to promotion also showed little relation to job motivation. Among the likely reasons for this result is that in most TVA jobs, as in most jobs elsewhere, the reward of promotion is usually rather distant in time; such a distant reward cannot be expected to evoke energy and enthusiasm in the present.

Finally, the effect on job interest of various combinations of rewards for achievement was examined. In general, the effects of the various rewards are additive. At the extremes, those who are likely to get personal pride plus several other rewards for achievement show much stronger job interest than those who are likely to get no rewards for achievement. There is also some evidence that a combination of different types of rewards—personal pride, plus supervisory approval, plus greater chance for promotion—brings an increase in job interest which is greater than might be expected from their separate effects added together. The data also suggest that peer approval for good work has a positive effect on innovative interest only when circumstances also favor personal pride in achievement. Conversely, the impact of personal pride rewards on innovative interest is greater when peer rewards for achievement are high.

7

OPPORTUNITY
AND REWARD
FOR ACHIEVEMENT
Joint Effects

In previous chapters we have examined separately the impact on job motivation of opportunity for achievement and of reward for achievement. One would expect, however, that good opportunities for achievement would be most likely to bring strong job motivation when the rewards for achievement are high, and vice versa. In fact, since many opportunity factors should raise achievement incentive and since rewards should strengthen the motive for achievement, the general formula presented in Chapter 3 would lead us to expect the effects of achievement opportunity and achievement reward to be multiplicative. In this chapter we will examine the joint effects of opportunity for achievement and reward for achievement on job motivation and on other reactions to the job.

INTERACTION BETWEEN OPPORTUNITY AND REWARD FOR ACHIEVEMENT

One way of examining the joint effects of achievement opportunity and achievement reward on job motivation is by categorizing people with regard to their position on both major variables (opportunity and reward). For example, TVA employees were divided into three approximately equal groups according to their scores on work difficulty (an aspect of achievement opportunity). Persons in each of these three categories were subdivided into three further groups according to their score on the index of overall reward for achievement.[1] Persons in each of the nine resulting categories were then compared with respect to their scores on the measures of job interest.[2] An analysis of variance among these scores permits us to answer these questions : (1) Does each achievement opportunity factor (e.g., difficulty of work) have a significant effect on job interest even when the effect of reward for achievement is discounted? (2) Does each achievement reward factor (e.g., praise from peers) have a significant effect on job interest, even when the effect of the opportunity factor is discounted? (3) Of particular interest, are there joint effects of (or interactions between) opportunity and reward which are different from merely the sum of their separate effects? Analyses aimed at helping to answer these questions were performed primarily for individuals, rather than for groups.[3]

Opportunity Factors and Overall Reward

The first set of analyses of variance concerns the joint effects on job interest of reward for achievement and each of several achievement opportunity factors—work difficulty, control over means, feedback on performance, and frequency of time limits. The results, shown in Appendix I, indicate that each of the opportunity factors has a strongly significant association with one or both job interest measures, independent of the effect of reward for achievement. The results indicate also that the reverse is true—i.e., achievement reward has a strongly significant association with job interest, independent of the effects of any achievement opportunity factor (or of the overall opportunity index).

These results also indicate that, for individuals, the interaction effects

---

[1]For this and other purposes, an overall reward for achievement index was computed for each individual according to the following formula: 8 (Achievement as a Means to Pride Index) + 2 (Achievement as a Means to Peer Approval Index) + 1 (Achievement as a Means to Promotion Index). The weights for the three component indices were derived from the approximate average relative size of their Beta weights in multiple correlations predicting to general job interest, interest in work innovation, and absence. A group score on the reward for achievement index was computed by taking the mean of individual scores for persons in that group.

[2]Absence was not used as a dependent variable in this analysis which is based on all TVA employees, because absence data are not strictly comparable across divisions.

[3]The primary analysis was for individuals because of the relatively small number of groups which would fall in the cells of any analysis of variance. Since the relationships among the variables are generally stronger for groups than for individuals, the use of individuals for these analyses probably result in somewhat weaker effects than would have been the case if we had enough groups to analyze in this way.

between the achievement opportunity factors and achievement reward are very small. Neither work difficulty, nor control over methods, nor frequency of time limits shows joint effects with achievement reward which even approach statistical significance. The one opportunity factor which comes close to having a statistically significant interaction with achievement reward is feedback on job performance. The data showing the joint effects of feedback and reward on general job interest are shown in Table 7-1. These data suggest that increased feedback on performance has an effect on general job interest when overall reward for achievement is high but not when it is low. Parallel results are found with respect to interest in work innovation (data not shown).[4]

Table 7-1 also indicates that overall reward for achievement brings a larger increase in general job interest among people who get high feedback on their work performance than among those who get little feedback.

TABLE 7-1 General Job Interest for Employees with Different Levels of Feedback on Performance and Different Levels of Overall Reward for Achievement

Feedback on Performance	Overall Reward for Performance		
	Low	*Medium*	*High*
Low	6.36 (126)	6.36 (67)	7.09 (34)
Medium	6.28 (68)	7.21 (82)	7.44 (89)
High	6.19 (52)	6.84 (79)	7.54 (95)

	F	df	p
Feedback	2.1	2,683	N.S.
Reward	29.2	2,683	.001
Feedback × Reward	2.2	4,683	.10

Note: Average scores; N in each cell in parentheses.

----

[4]These data for individuals are consistent with the results of the correlation analysis for groups (Tables 7-4), which show a much stronger correlation between feedback and job interest when achievement reward is high.

Again, the data for interest in work innovation show the same pattern of results as those for general job interest.

Reward Factors and Overall Opportunity

A second set of analyses of variance concerns the joint effects on individual job interest of each of several factors affecting reward for achievement, in combination with the overall opportunity for achievement. The reward factors considered are the major sources of reward: (1) overall rewards of personal pride for achievement; (2) approval from peers for achievement; (3) supervisory compliments for achievement; and (4) promotion rewards for achievement. In addition, the need for achievement (one factor relevant to pride in achievement) was considered because of its special theoretical interest.

The results of these analyses of variance, shown in Appendix J, indicate first that by far the largest effect on job interest is exerted by the overall opportunity for achievement, as compared with each of the separate reward factors. Secondly, the results show that several aspects of reward for achievement—personal pride rewards, peer approval, and supervisory compliments (though not promotion rewards)—have a significant effect on one or more aspects of job interest, independent of the effects of achievement opportunity; however, these separate reward effects are much smaller than the effect of overall achievement opportunity.[5]

Of particular interest are the results concerning interactions. The data show that there are no significant joint effects between each of the rewards for achievement[6] and achievement opportunity, as they relate to job interest. In other words, for individuals, the effect of each type of achievement reward on job interest is independent of the degree of the overall opportunity for achievement, and vice versa.

Achievement Need and Opportunity

There is, however, some indication of an interaction between opportunity for achievement and the personal trait of need for achievement.[7]

---

[5]The large effect of identification with one's occupation on job interest, included in the index of achievement as a means to personal pride, is somewhat masked in this particular analysis because identification with occupation is one of four equally weighted variables composing this index.

[6]An analysis of variance for supervisory rewards for achievement and achievement opportunity, as they relate to job interest, was not run. However, the correlational analysis suggests little interaction effect.

[7]This interaction is not statistically significant. However, this same pattern of results appears when job interest scores are compared for (1) those who differ in need for achievement and in job difficulty, and (2) those who differ in need for achievement and control over means.

Table 7-2 shows these data, which suggest that when opportunities for achievement are low, increases in need for achievement lead to a *decrease* in general job interest. It seems likely that when opportunities for achievement are poor, those with high need for achievement are more likely to be frustrated on the job and to turn their thoughts to situations outside the job (e.g., sports or home projects) which offer greater chances for accomplishment.

However, when opportunities for achievement are high, increases in need for achievement are not associated with greater job interest. Even among that one-eighth of the sample with the very highest achievement opportunity scores, stronger need for achievement does not bring stronger general job interest or stronger interest in innovation (data not shown). Other results, to be presented later (Table 7-5), show that when achievement opportunity is high, those with high need for achievement are somewhat less likely than others to be absent. However, these present data on job interest indicate that the positive impact of need for achievement on job motivation is not great even when opportunities for achievement are high.

TABLE 7-2 **General Job Interest Scores for Persons with Different Degrees of Need for Achievement and Different Levels of Opportunity for Achievement**

Opportunity for Achievement	Need for Achievement		
	Low	*Medium*	*High*
Low	6.64 (69)	6.23 (53)	5.83 (93)
Medium	7.07 (106)	6.61 (57)	6.77 (136)
High	7.47 (77)	7.51 (59)	7.50 (84)

	F	df	p
Need achievement	3.6	2,725	.05
Achievement opportunity	38.6	2,725	.001
Need × opportunity	1.8	4,725	N.S.

Note: Figures in parentheses indicate number of persons. Scores are means.

In trying to account for this unexpected result, several possible explanations present themselves. One possibility is that our measure of need for achievement is not adequate. Evidence from one experiment (Atkinson and O'Connor, 1966), based on a very small number of college subjects, suggests that the ARPS measure of need for achievement may not predict task performance as well as does the need for achievement measure which has been more commonly used in the past.[8] However, the evidence from work and school situations presented by Eckerman (1963), which shows ARPS scores related to performance under certain circumstances, plus the evidence on the construct validity of ARPS presented by Kasl (1966), plus the substantial correlations between the ARPS measure and the TAT measure of need for achievement (Atkinson and O'Connor, 1966), leads us to believe it is unlikely that the weak relation between need for achievement and our indicators of job motivation can be explained largely by any weakness in our measure of need for achievement.

Another possibility is that the level of achievement incentive represented by those jobs which we have called high in achievement opportunity is simply not high enough to arouse the interest of those high in need for substantial risk of gross, clearly defined failure which some salesmen's be that the risk of failure in these jobs is so small that there is little achievement incentive? It is true that none of the jobs studied here have the achievement," there are included engineers and craftsmen working on fresh jobs, some independent businessmen's positions, or some top executive jobs have. Yet, among those TVA employees who rank in the top one-eighth (or even one-third) of our sample with respect to "opportunity for achievement," there are included engineers and craftsmen working on fresh and nonroutine problems where there are substantial chances of making mistakes which, when detected by a "checker" or supervisor, represent failures. Thus, while a higher level of incentive might enhance the impact of need for achievement, it seems unlikely that the weak association between need for achievement and job interest is due primarily to a low incentive for achievement in the TVA jobs we studied.

The key to the understanding of these results may lie in noting that where opportunities for achievement are high, both those with high need for achievement and those with low need for achievement show a substantial increase in job interest. Thus, it is not, apparently, that those with high need for achievement fail to respond to challenging job situations but that others respond also.

Those who are low in need for achievement (relative to fear of failure)

---

[8]The more commonly used measure is a combination of the Thematic Apperception Test and a Test Anxiety Scale.

may be motivated to strive for success in challenging job situations for a variety of reasons. They may wish to maintain and enhance their self-esteem as capable members of their occupations; to win the approval and avoid the low opinion of supervisors or peers; to improve their promotion chances; etc.[9] If this is so, it would indicate that while the level of need for achievement (relative to fear of failure) may be an important predictor of *choice* among jobs of varying difficulty, its effect on performance in most jobs is modest because other motives may also influence the desire to perform successfully, once "caught" in the job.

We might expect, however, that when jobs are of moderate difficulty, those with high need for achievement will enjoy their work more and feel more zest in it. We do not have much direct evidence on this point at TVA. Where opportunities for achievement are high, those with strong need for achievement are no less likely than others to report symptoms of stress. However, in such situations, they are less likely to be absent (see below), which may be a reflection of the attractiveness of the job to such persons.

Importance of Challenge and Opportunity

Further data concerning the joint effects of achievement opportunity and personal needs relevant to achievement were obtained by categorizing people according to their responses to two questions. First, we asked people about the "chance . . . you get to feel at the end of the day that you have accomplished something" (five response categories from "very little or no chance" to "an excellent chance"). The second question asked people, "What are the things that are most important to you in a job?" Eight things were listed; among these was "having work that is a challenge to my ability."[10]

Each employee was placed into one of nine categories depending on (1) the importance to him of challenging work in a job, and (2) his self-judged opportunity for accomplishment on the job. For each of these nine categories, a mean score on job interest was computed.

Table 7-3 presents these data. It shows that among those who judge their chance to accomplish to be low, those to whom challenge in work is

---

[9]Eckerman (1963) suggests that the effect of need for achievement (ARPS measure) on performance may be masked by other motives for success, among securities salesmen in the earlier years of their activity. Atkinson and O'Connor (1966) also acknowledge, on the basis of unexpected results, that in moderate risk situations, persons may be motivated to do well by motives other than need for achievement.

[10]Other job characteristics mentioned concerned (1) pleasant working conditions, (2) chance to use skills, (3) chance to learn, (4) good wages, (5) friendly co-workers, (6) opportunities for promotion, (7) steady employment.

important are less interested in their work than are those for whom challenge is not important. On the other hand, among those who see a good chance for accomplishment on the job, those for whom challenging work is important are somewhat more interested in their work than are those for whom challenge is unimportant. The more chance people see to accomplish things on the job, the greater their job interest; but this effect is strongest for those to whom challenging work is important. Statistical tests indicate that the interaction effect between perceived chance to accomplish and judged importance of challenge is significant. It should be noted, however, that the overall impact of perceived opportunity for accomplishment is much greater than that of the felt importance of challenge on the job.

These data are similar to those of Table 7-2, which shows the joint effects of need for achievement and opportunity for achievement. In both cases, where there are poor chances for achievement, those who value achievement are more likely than others to be bored and apparently frustrated on the job. In both cases, when achievement chances are high,

TABLE 7-3   **Average General Job Interest Scores for Persons Differing in Perceived Chance to Accomplish Things and in Ranking of Importance on Job**

Perceived Chance to Accomplish Things	Ranking of Importance of Challenge on Job		
	Low (7 or 8)	*Medium* (4, 5, or 6)	*High* (1, 2, or 3)
Little or none	5.95 (41)	5.19 (31)	5.16 (49)
Some	6.52 (69)	6.54 (72)	6.62 (108)
Good or excellent	7.24 (116)	7.16 (134)	7.65 (140)

	F	df	p
Perceived chance to accomplish	79.6	2,751	.001
Ranking of challenge	0.6	2,751	N.S.
Chance × Ranking	2.9	4,751	.05

Note: Figures in parentheses indicate number of persons.

both those who are low and those who are high in achievement motivation show a substantial increase in job interest.

In general, the data indicate that the effect of personality needs on job motivation does vary as opportunities for achievement change. But differences in personal needs relevant to achievement have, at best, only a modest effect on job motivation. Differences in opportunity for achievement have a much greater effect. It is possible that these results are due in part to greater deficiencies in the measures of personal needs than in the measure of achievement opportunity. However, the data do suggest that, in many job situations, personal needs for achievement may be less important determinants of job motivation than are the incentives for achievement which the job situation provides.[11]

Overall Opportunity and Overall Reward for Achievement

Individual employees at TVA were also categorized according to their scores on both summary indices—the index of overall opportunity for achievement and the index of overall reward for achievement. Both overall opportunity and overall reward for achievement have large and significant effects on general job interest, independent of each other (see Appendix J).[12] The combined effect of both opportunity and reward is considerable. Thus, there is a difference of almost two points in average job interest score (on a scale having a range of eight points) between those low in both opportunity and reward for achievement and those high in both opportunity and reward.

The combined additive effect of opportunity and reward for achievement can be seen graphically in Figure 7-1. This figure shows that as the sum of opportunity and reward for achievement increases, job interest also increases sharply. The pattern of results (not shown) for scores on interest in work innovation is generally similar to those for general job interest, except that those who have high opportunity and low reward score almost as high as those high in both opportunity and reward. This

---

[11]In analyses related to those reported in this section, the joint effects on job interest of (1) perceived chance to accomplish things and overall reward for achievement and (2) ranking of the importance of challenge and overall opportunity for achievement, were studied. In neither case were there any significant interaction effects in predicting to general job interest or to interest in work innovation.

[12]The effect of overall achievement opportunity on general job interest is far larger than the effect of overall achievement reward. Note, however, that identification with occupation, which has the strongest relation to job interest of all reward-relevant factors, has only a modest weight in the index of overall achievement reward, whereas job difficulty and control over means (both strongly relating to job interest) are heavily weighted in the index of achievement opportunity. The modest weighting of identification with occupation in the overall reward index was due to its positive association with absence.

may be due to the fact that those who have personal responsibility for difficult work (i.e., high opportunity for achievement) are under pressure to find better ways of doing things even when their reward for achievement is low.

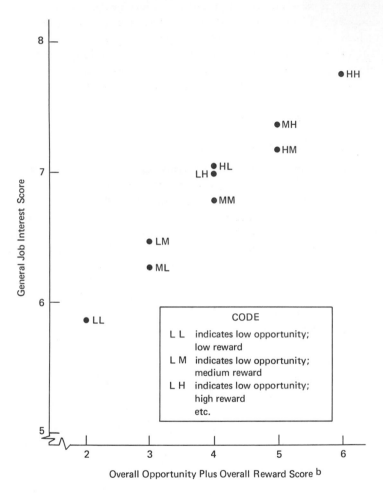

FIGURE 7-1 General job interest (mean scores) as related to scores on overall opportunity plus overall reward for achievement

Notes: 1. Each point on the graph represents a set of persons categorized according to their scores on the indices of overall opportunity for achievement and overall reward for achievement. Ns for each category are as follows: Low-Low, 99; Low-Medium, 91, Low-High, 38; Medium-Low, 59; Medium-Medium, 89; Medium-High, 71; High-Low, 27; High-Medium, 88; High-High, 93. See Appendix J for analysis of variance based on these data.

2. Overall opportunity plus overall reward score was assigned as follows: Low-Low=2; Low-Medium=3; Medium-Low=3; Medium-Medium=4; High-Low=4; Low-High=4; Medium-High=5; High-Medium=5; High-High=6.

While the additive effect of opportunity and reward are large, there is little evidence of an interaction effect between them—i.e., the effects of each is largely independent of the other (see Appendix J). An analysis of variance on parallel data for work groups, rather than for individuals, produces similar results (data not shown). Both overall reward for achievement and overall opportunity have a significant and positive effect on the average level of general job interest and of interest in work innovation. With respect to interest in innovation, the effect of overall achievement opportunity is especially strong. Examination of the data shows a tendency for both opportunity and reward to have greater effects on job interest when the other is high than when the other is low. This tendency is, however, a small one and there is no statistically significant interaction between opportunity and reward with respect to either measure of job interest; nor is there a significant interaction effect on average group absence.[13]

FURTHER EXAMINATION OF JOINT EFFECTS

We have been looking for possible joint effects on job motivation of opportunity for achievement and reward for achievement. Using the technique of analysis of variance, we have found some indications of such joint, or interaction, effects. In particular, there were indications that certain combinations of (1) feedback and high reward, and (2) desire for achievement and achievement opportunity produce effects on job interest that neither alone produces. However, these particular interaction effects were relatively small and the overall results of the analyses of variance provide only limited evidence that there are joint effects of achievement opportunity and achievement reward on job motivation, above and beyond their separate effects. However, there are other data to be considered.

For various practical reasons,[14] the analyses of the data presented so far were done primarily for individuals rather than for groups; used as dependent variables primarily the job interest measures (and not absence, pride, and stress symptoms); and did not include several job characteristics relevant to achievement opportunity and reward. Now we

---

[13]It may be that an index of overall achievement opportunity which gave equal weight to feedback on performance and to frequency of time limits would show greater evidence of interaction with the overall reward for achievement index.

[14]As noted above, the relatively small N of groups made two-way analysis of variance difficult in some cases. The lengthy and costly nature of this analysis also limited the number of independent variable combinations and dependent variables that it seemed feasible to use in the analysis.

will look at our data in a somewhat different way, using correlation analysis. While this approach does not permit the effects of specific combinations of opportunity and reward to be examined, it makes it easier to consider more job characteristics and more aspects of employee reactions to the job. It also permits us to examine more closely the results for groups, at which level associations between job characteristics and employee reactions are generally stronger than for individuals (see Chapter 5). In addition, the correlational analysis preserves more of the gradations in each aspect of achievement opportunity and reward, instead of categorizing each aspect as simply high, medium, or low.

OPPORTUNITY FOR ACHIEVEMENT
UNDER VARYING REWARD CONDITIONS

We ask now this general question : Do the job features that provide *opportunity* for achievement have different effects on people's reactions to their jobs depending on how much *reward* for achievement is present?

To throw light on this question, we correlated scores on each opportunity factor (work difficulty, control over means, etc.) with employee job reactions, separately for cases where achievement reward was relatively high, where reward was moderate, and where reward was relatively low. This type of analysis was done both for individuals and for work groups.

For individuals, the relation of achievement opportunity factors to job interest and to other employee reactions varies little as the reward for achievement varies. However, the results for groups, especially those concerning job interest, are more interesting. Results concerning average job interest for groups are shown in Table 7-4.

Feedback on Performance

The data show, first, that the relation between feedback on performance and interest in work innovation is greatly affected by the level of achievement reward. Feedback on performance has little relation to innovative interest among work groups where reward for achievement is low or medium. But among work groups where reward for achievement is high, the amount of feedback has a marked association ($r = .55$; $p < .01$) with innovative interest.[15] This result is in accord with our expectation that the increased achievement incentive due to feedback will have most effect on job motivation when the value of achievement is greatest. How-

---

[15]The correlation between feedback and interest in innovation is significantly higher when reward for achievement is high than when reward is low or medium.

TABLE 7-4   Relation of Job Interest to Job Characteristics Affecting the Opportunity for Achievement, for Different Levels of Overall Reward for Achievement

(Product-Moment Correlations for 89 Groups[a])

Job Characteristics Relevant to Opportunity for Achievement	General Job Interest			Interest in Work Innovation		
	Low Reward for Achievement (N = 31)	Medium Reward for Achievement (N = 30)	High Reward for Achievement (N = 28)	Low Reward for Achievement (N = 31)	Medium Reward for Achievement (N = 30)	High Reward for Achievement (N = 28)
Difficulty of work	.13	.36*	.25	.43*	.47**	.54**
Feedback on performance (Index B)	−.03	−.29	.36	−.02	−.04	.55**
Control over means (Index B)	.33	.28	.26	.34	.28	.13
Frequency of time limits	.17	−.33	−.08	.04	−.02	.52**
Chance to learn	.51**	.24	.56**	.19	.29	.21
Overall opportunity for achievement[b]	.21	.39*	.42*	.38*	.58**	.60**

* $p < .05$, two-tailed test
** $p < .01$, two-tailed test

a   Broken-line bracket joining two correlation coefficients indicates that they are significantly different from each other at the .05 level. Solid bracket indicates difference significant at .01 level.

b   The index of overall opportunity for achievement was derived as follows: 4 (difficulty of work score) + 4 (control over means score) + 1 (feedback on performance score).

ever, this "conditioning effect"[16] of achievement reward on the relation between feedback and reactions to the job does not operate consistently with respect to another indicator of job motivation, general job interest; nor does the conditioning effect show itself for absence.[17]

Time Limits

The relation between the frequency of time limits and interest in work innovation also is affected by the level of reward for achievement. Table 7-4 shows that among groups where reward for achievement is low or medium, frequency of time limits does not bring an increase in

---

[16]Variable A has a conditioning effect on the relation between variables B and C if the size of the relation between B and C differs for different levels of A.

[17]There is, in fact, a somewhat more positive relation between feedback and absence (more feedback, more absence) when achievement reward is high than when it is low.

innovative interest. But among groups where achievement reward is high, having frequent time limits is associated with greater innovative interest $(r = .52; p < .01)$.[18] This is consistent with our expectation that the greater achievement incentive associated with time limits will be most meaningful when the value of achievement is greatest.

However, the conditioning effect of achievement reward on the relation between time limits and reactions to the job is not found for general job interest, though there is a tendency in this direction with respect to absences. The relation between frequency of time limits and pride in work and between time limits and symptoms of stress is not affected by the level of reward for achievement.

Chance to Learn

The associations between chances to learn on the job and various employee reactions to the job do not change consistently as reward for achievement increases. In particular, the more chance people have to learn on the job, the greater their general job interest and the fewer their psychological symptoms of stress, regardless of the level of reward for achievement. That the effects of chance to learn do not vary as rewards for achievement vary may indicate that learning does not represent an achievement incentive; instead, learning chances may increase job interest for other reasons, such as the novelty of the work. Another possible explanation is that, although learning does represent an achievement incentive (i.e., success in mastering some skills or body of facts), the rewards relevant to this type of achievement (perhaps reassurance about one's capabilities) are somewhat different from the rewards relevant to successful accomplishment of specific tasks. Such rewards may not be affected by the factors included in our index of overall reward for achievement.

Job Difficulty and Control over Means

Two important aspects of the job, difficulty and control over work methods—both of which affect job motivation (see Chapter 5)—show about the same association with the indicators of job motivation regardless of the level of reward for achievement. Generally, these job characteristics also show similar associations with job pride and with symptoms of stress regardless of the level of reward for achievement.[19]

---

[18]The correlation between frequency of time limits and innovative interest is significantly higher when achievement reward is high than when it is low or medium.

[19]When reward for achievement is high, increases in job difficulty have a somewhat more negative association with symptoms of stress (more difficulty, fewer symptoms), and a smaller positive association with job pride, than when reward for achievement is low.

However, as we shall see next, the index of overall opportunity to achieve, which is based almost entirely on the measures of job difficulty and control over means,[20] shows a stronger association with job motivation as the reward for achievement increases.

Overall Opportunity to Achieve

As average reward for achievement increases from low to medium to high, there is no appreciable effect on the correlations between overall achievement opportunity and absence, job pride, or symptoms of stress. However, as reward for achievement increases, the correlation between overall achievement opportunity and interest in innovation also increases, from .38 to .58 to .60. There is a parallel increase in the correlation between overall achievement opportunity and general job interest as achievement reward increases, from .21 to .39 to .42. Although differences between these correlations fall short of statistical significance, the pattern is clearly consistent with our general expectation.

An index of overall achievement opportunity which included the frequency of time limits and which gave equal weight to feedback on performance (the impact of which increased as reward increased) would probably have given even stronger evidence that there is a greater association between achievement opportunity and job motivation when achievement reward is high than when it is low.[21]

In general, the results reported in this section indicate that the job features relevant to opportunity for achievement have a greater effect on job motivation when achievement reward (and thus presumably, the achievement motive) is high. Since there is evidence from previous work that achievement incentive has a greater effect on task motivation when achievement motive is high, these data are consistent with our expectation that these job features (difficulty, control over means, feedback, and standards of excellence) affect achievement incentive. The data are also consistent with the general theoretical expectation that achievement in-

---

[20]The achievement opportunity index was constructed for each individual according to the following formula: 4 (Control over Means Index B) + 4 (Work Difficulty Index) + 1 (Feedback Index A). The weights for the three component indices were derived from the approximate average relative size of their Beta weights in multiple correlations predicting to general job interest, interest in work innovation, and absence. A group score on the achievement opportunity index was computed by taking the mean of individual scores for persons in that group.

[21]Another factor relevant to achievement opportunity—chance to finish things—was also correlated with reactions to the job under varying levels of achievement reward. The lack of association between chance to finish and job motivation, found in Chapter 5, is still apparent regardless of the level of reward for achievement. As suggested in the previous chapter, the amount of variation in chances to finish things among jobs covered at TVA may be too limited to judge adequately the possible importance of this factor.

centive will raise job motivation most when the motivation for achievement is highest.

REWARD FOR ACHIEVEMENT UNDER
VARYING OPPORTUNITY FOR ACHIEVEMENT

The general question asked next is as follows : Does the presence of various rewards for good performance on the job have different effects on job motivation depending on the amount of achievement which is possible in the work situation?

To throw light on this question, we separated individuals, and groups, in our sample into three categories : the third for whom opportunities for achievement were lowest; the third for whom such opportunities were medium; and the third for whom achievement opportunities were best. Within each of these achievement opportunity categories, correlations were computed between (1) each job and personal characteristic relevant to the amount of reward which job achievement brings,[22] and (2) job interest, absence, and other employee reactions to the job. Does the association of each "reward factor" with employee reactions to the job vary as opportunity for achievement varies? Data concerning individual absences are shown in Table 7-5. Data concerning average job interest for groups are shown in Appendix K. (Other data are not shown.)

Need for Achievement

The data show that when achievement opportunity is low, increases in individual need for achievement lead to somewhat lower general job interest ($r = -.15$; $p<.05$) and have no association with absence. But when achievement opportunity is high, increased need for achievement has no association with general job interest and has a negative association ($r = -.19$; $p<.05$) with absence (higher need for achievement, fewer absences). In other words, higher need for achievement tends to have an *unfavorable* effect on job motivation when achievement opportunity is low and a *favorable* effect when achievement opportunity is high.[23] The

---

[22]Note that in this section the factors included in the index of pride in achievement are considered separately. In the earlier section of this chapter, which presented the results of analyses of variance, only the total index of pride in achievement was considered.

[23]For groups, this result tends to be reversed with respect to job interest. The most positive correlation between average need for achievement score and average interest in work innovation ($r = +.33$) occurs when opportunity for achievement is low. However, this association is not statistically significant. Moreover, for groups, the association between average need for achievement and absence becomes more negative (higher need, less absence) as opportunity for achievement increases, consistent with the results from individuals. The relation of need achievement to pride in work, to psychological symptoms of stress and to physical symptoms of stress does not change appreciably for groups as opportunities for achievement vary.

more favorable effect when achievement opportunity is high was expected on the basis of the general formulation that increases in the motive for achievement will have the greatest effect on job motivation when achievement incentive is high. In general, however, the positive effect of need for achievement on job motivation is a modest one when opportunities for achievement are high. (Possible explanations of this general finding are discussed earlier in this chapter.)

The tendency for achievement motivation to have a negative effect

TABLE 7-5   Relation of Number of Absences to Factors Which May Affect Rewards for Achievement, for Individuals with Different Levels of Opportunity for Achievement

(Product-Moment Correlations[a])

Factors which may affect rewards for achievement	Total Number of Absences		
	Low opportunity for achievement (N = 160)	*Medium opportunity for achievement (N = 200)*	*High opportunity for achievement (N = 130)*
1. Need for achievement	.02	.07	−.19*
2. Chance to use best abilities	.02	−.08	−.28**
3. Identification with occupation	.11	.12	.02
4. Influence on work goals	−.08	−.09	−.11
5. Achievement a means to pride[b]	.07	.00	−.27**
6. Achievement a means to peer reward	−.06	−.11	−.17
7. Achievement a means to promotion	−.04	.07	−.01
8. Achievement a means to supervisory reward	−.10	−.05	−.15
9. Overall reward for achievement[c]	.03	−.01	−.26**

* p <.05
** p <.01

a   Broken-line bracket joining two correlation coefficients indicates that difference between them is significant at .05 level; solid bracket indicates difference is significant at .01 level.

b   Scores on achievement as a means to pride are based on the sum of scores on need for achievement, identification with occupation, chance to use skills, and influence on work goals.

c   Scores on overall reward for achievement were computed as follows: 8 (achievement as means to pride) + 2 (achievement as means to peer reward) + 1 (achievement as means to promotion).

on job motivation when achievement opportunity is low, though not predicted, is consistent with results presented in Chapter 6, which show need for achievement to have an adverse effect on job motivation when other conditions affecting job motivation are unfavorable. When opportunities for achievement are poor, those with a high need for achievement evidently are more frustrated than are those with a lower need for achievement.

Influence on Goals

Employee influence on work goals has a more positive association with job interest when achievement opportunity is high than when opportunity is low. This effect is especially strong for groups (see Appendix K). Where there is good opportunity for achievement, the more influence over goals that employees have, the greater their general job interest ($r = .37$; $p < .05$) and the greater their interest in work innovation ($r = .38$; $p < .05$). But where opportunities for achievement are relatively poor, more influence over work goals is associated with lower general interest ($r = -.33$) and lower innovation interest ($r = -.32$). For both measures of job interest, these differences in the size of their correlations with influence on goals, as achievement opportunity varies, are statistically significant.

While we expected influence over goals to be more strongly associated with job interest when achievement opportunity was high, the negative association when opportunity was low is unexpected. The negative direction of the association under these circumstances may be solely a matter of chance (it is a little short of statistical significance). However, it suggests the possibility that the chance to influence work goals may be more frustrating than stimulating in a situation where opportunity for achievement is low. This latter possibility is strengthened by indications in the data for groups that influence on work goals has a negative association with symptoms of stress (greater influence, fewer symptoms) when achievement opportunity is high but a positive association (more influence, more symptoms) when achievement opportunity is low.[24]

Chance to Use Skills

The chance to do what one is best at also shows, as expected, a tendency to have more favorable effects on job reactions when achievement opportunity is high than when opportunity is low. These trends

---

[24]The correlations between group influence on work goals and physical symptoms of stress are .34, .13, and −.18 as achievement opportunities go from low to medium to high. The parallel correlations for psychological symptoms of stress are .50, −.44, and −.28.

are especially noticeable in the data for individuals. Most notably, when achievement opportunity is high, the more the chance to use one's best abilities, the fewer the absences (r=−.28; p<.01).[25] There is a similar tendency for greater chances to use one's skills to be associated with fewer physical and psychological symptoms of stress when achievement opportunities are high but not when achievement opportunity is low.[26]

Identification with Occupation

Identification with one's occupation has similar correlations with various reactions to the job, regardless of the level of achievement opportunity. This is true both when data for individuals and for groups are examined. Increases in the average level of occupational identification are associated with greater job interest and, paradoxically, with greater absence, regardless of the level of achievement opportunity.[27]

The fact that increases in occupational identification do not have a more favorable effect on indicators of job motivation—especially on absence—when achievement opportunity is high than when opportunity is low again raises questions about the meaning of occupational commitment. If commitment to one's occupation includes a desire for outstanding achievement in that occupation, should not those with strong occupational commitment have fewer absences (rather than somewhat more) when opportunities for achievement are high than when such opportunities are low? That this is not the case supports the suggestion advanced in Chapter 6 that, while commitment to one's occupation appears to reflect a genuine interest in the work role and in performing it effectively, such occupational commitment does not necessarily carry with it a drive for outstanding achievement on the job.

Achievement as a Means to Pride

For the overall index of achievement as a means to pride (based on need for achievement, influence over work goals, chance to use skills, and occupational identification), correlations with most reactions to the job are about the same, regardless of the level of achievement opportunity.

---

[25]The difference in the size of these correlations is statistically significant. Where achievement opportunity is intermediate, the association between chance to do one's best and absence is also intermediate (r = −.08).

[26]For low, medium, and high achievement opportunity, the correlations for individuals between chance to do what one is best at and physical symptoms of stress are −.07, −.12 and −.27, respectively. The parallel correlations for psychological symptoms of stress are −.13, −.17 and −.24.

[27]Although the positive association between occupational identification and absence does not rise continuously as achievement opportunity increases, it is noteworthy that the largest association between identification and absence (r = .73) occurs for those groups for which achievement opportunity is highest.

This probably reflects the somewhat different pattern of associations shown by the components of the index. However, the index of achievement as a means to pride shows, as expected, a more negative association with absence as opportunity for achievement increases. Where achievement opportunity is low, increases in the extent to which achievement is a means to pride are associated with a slight increase in absence (r = .07). But when the opportunity for achievement is high, increases in the extent to which the circumstances favor pride in achievement are associated with fewer absences (r = −.27; p < .01).[28]

Peer Rewards for Achievement

When achievement opportunity for groups is high, there is a somewhat more positive association (r = .26) between the level of peer reward for achievement and average interest in innovation than there is when achievement opportunity is low or medium (r = −.10 in each case).[29] However, the relation between peer rewards for achievement and other employee reactions to the job is not affected appreciably by the level of achievement opportunity. In particular, the overall tendency for average number of absences in a group to go down as peer rewards for achievement increase (see Chapter 6) is not heightened when opportunities for achievement are high.[30]

The finding that peer rewards have only a slightly greater impact on indicators of job motivation when achievement opportunity is high than when it is low may be due in part to our measure of peer rewards for achievement. This measure includes a question about mistakes being called to a person's attention by peers and a question about peers' attitudes toward "a fast, energetic worker," as well as a question about peer compliments for doing an "outstanding job on something."[31] Only the

---

[28]The difference in the size of these correlations is statistically significant.

[29]The difference in the size of the correlations between peer rewards and interest in innovation as achievement opportunity varies is statistically significant at the .05 level when the directionality of the difference is taken into account. However, the correlation of .26 between peer reward and interest in innovation, when achievement opportunity is high, is not significantly different from zero.

[30]For groups, the negative association previously found between absence and peer rewards for achievement is not found for each of the three "achievement opportunity" levels separately. This does not invalidate the finding of an overall negative relation between peer rewards and absence, since the correlation for all ninety groups was controlled for a large number of other variables including the components of the achievement opportunity measure. For individuals, there are small negative correlations between peer rewards and absence for each level of achievement opportunity and these correlations get somewhat more negative as opportunity increases.

[31]Questions about the closeness of relations with peers are also included in this measure. See Chapter 6.

third question is directly concerned with some kind of achievement. A "purer" measure of peer rewards for achievement might show more clearly a greater impact on job motivation when opportunities for achievement are high than when opportunities are low.

However, aside from possible deficiencies in our measure of peer rewards for achievement, there may be at least one other reason for these results. In most job situations, co-workers may be concerned primarily about whether a man "pulls his load" and whether he facilitates their own work, rather than whether he has succeeded on a particularly challenging assignment. If so, they would tend to compliment conscientious work and call attention to sloppy work regardless of the level of achievement involved. To the extent that this is true, peer sanctions would not really be for achievement and so would operate relatively independently of the level of achievement possible on this job.[32]

Supervisory Reward for Achievement

Like peer rewards for achievement, supervisory compliments for good work tend to be more highly associated with innovative interest when achievement opportunity is high than when opportunity is low. For groups which have a low opportunity for achievement, increases in the likelihood that good work will be complimented are not associated with greater innovative interest ($r = -.03$). But when achievement opportunity is high, an increased likelihood of supervisor compliments tends to be associated with higher innovative interest ($r = .29$).[33] Increases in supervisory compliments are also associated with fewer group absences ($r = -.23$) when achievement opportunity is high but not when achievement opportunity is low or medium ($r = .23$ and .11 respectively).[34] However, the relation of supervisory compliments to general job interest is not changed by the level of achievement opportunity.

In general, these data indicate that while supervisory reward for

---

[32]Atkinson and O'Connor (1966) found, contrary to their expectation, that the higher the level of individual need for affiliation (social approval), the greater the achievement-oriented behavior. On the basis of this evidence, they modify their previous theoretical assumptions and suggest that "the incentive value of any extrinsic reward that appears to S to be contingent upon the adequacy of his performance when skill and effort is demanded may be proportionate to the apparent difficulty of the task." (p. 317) While the recognition of the role of extrinsic rewards in affecting achievement-oriented behavior brings Atkinson's theoretical position closer to our own, we see social approval for achievement as affecting the motive for achievement, rather than being a direct incentive (see Chapter 2).

[33]The difference in the size of these correlations is just short of statistical significance. When achievement opportunity is intermediate, the correlation between supervisory compliments and innovative interest is intermediate ($r = .14$).

[34]The difference between the size of the correlations when opportunity is high and when opportunity is low (i.e., between $-.23$ and .23) is significant at beyond the .05 level.

achievement generally has little effect on job motivation (see Chapter 6), it has a somewhat more positive effect on motivation when the opportunity for achievement is high than when opportunity is low. While not dramatic in magnitude, these results are consistent with our expectation that approval for achievement will raise the motive for achievement.[35]

Other results concerning the effects of supervisory compliments for good work are also of interest. The relation of supervisory compliments to symptoms of stress does not vary much as achievement opportunity changes. However, there is a substantial association between the likelihood of supervisory compliments for good work and pride in one's performance ($r = .62$; $p < .01$) only when achievement opportunity is high. By contrast, close to zero associations are found between supervisory compliments and job pride when achievement opportunity is low or medium. The much stronger association between job pride and likelihood of compliments when achievement opportunities on the job are high may occur in part because such jobs provide more occasions for compliments by supervisors. It may be also that in situations where the individual himself knows that he has mastered a challenge, the compliment of a supervisor may be much more satisfying than it would be in situations where successful completion of a job is fairly routine.

Promotion Reward for Achievement

We have seen earlier (Chapter 6) that the extent to which achievement is a means to promotion for individuals has only very small associations with employee reactions to the job. This remains true regardless of the level of achievement opportunity.[36] It seems likely that even when achievement opportunities are great and promotion is based on ability, promotion will not be linked to specific achievements. Moreover, promotion is usually a much-delayed reward. Thus, even when achievement opportunities are great, achievement would not be likely to bring a large or immediate reward in the form of promotion or the prospect of promotion.

Overall Reward for Achievement

Our index of overall reward for achievement has similar associations with most employee reactions to the job (general job interest, interest in innovation, pride, and symptoms of stress), regardless of the level of

---

[35]The motive for achievement should have the greatest impact on job motivation when the achievement incentive is high. Since supervisory approval for achievement has its greatest impact on job motivation when achievement incentive (opportunity) is high, these data are consistent with the notion that approval for achievement affects the achievement motive.

[36]This analysis was run only for individuals.

opportunity for achievement.[37] However, the index of overall reward does have a more negative association ($r = -.26$) with individual absence (higher reward, fewer absences) when achievement opportunities are high than when opportunities are low ($r = .03$) or medium ($r = -.01$). These differences are statistically significant.

In general, the magnitude of the effects shown in this section are modest. When opportunities for achievement are high, the impact of reward-relevant factors on job motivation are generally greater than when opportunities for achievement are low; but these differences are generally not large. Since there is evidence (e.g., Atkinson, 1958b) that increased motivation for achievement will have stronger effects on task motivation when achievement incentive is high than when it is low, these results suggest that the "reward-relevant" factors considered here, whatever their impact on job motivation, had only modest effects on the motivation for achievement. While a number of possible explanations could be offered, the most obvious and likely explanation is to recall that those job and personal characteristics discussed as relevant to rewards for achievement (e.g., chance to use skills, control over goals, identification with occupation, peer approval for good work) are only indirect indicators of the amount of reward for achievement which people get on the job. It is likely that variations in these "reward-relevant" characteristics do not lead consistently to comparable variations in the level of reward for achievement.

Yet, despite their generally modest magnitude, the results presented in this section do indicate that certain reward-relevant characteristics have their greatest effect on job motivation when achievement incentive is high. These results are consistent with our theoretical expectation that certain job features and personal characteristics will raise the motive for achievement on the job. Insofar as increases in reward for achievement do increase the motive for achievement, these results are also consistent with our general theoretical expectation that the motive for achievement will have the greatest effect on job motivation when the achievement incentive is high.

---

[37]This result is probably due in part to the particular make-up of the index of overall reward for achievement. The index of overall reward for achievement includes measures of identification with occupation and of achievement as a means to promotion, both of which do not show a greater association with indicators of motivation as opportunity for achievement increases. The index does not include the measure of achievement as a means to supervisory approval, which does show a stronger association with indicators of job motivation as achievement opportunity increases. The index of overall reward for achievement was constructed by weighting reward-relevant factors according to an approximate average of their Beta weights in multiple correlations predicting to general job interest, interest in innovation, and absence.

OVERALL EXPLANATION OF DIFFERENCES

In Chapters 5 and 6 we examined the relationship between employee reactions to their jobs (especially indicators of motivation) and each of a variety of factors which may affect achievement opportunity and reward for achievement. We have seen that each separate factor can explain only a relatively small amount of the differences in job motivation among individuals and among work groups, when all other factors are held constant.

Now we ask : How much of the total variance in each type of reaction to the job can be explained by all of the predictive factors together. To answer these questions, we look at results from multiple correlation analyses for the ninety work groups.[38] These data will also give some additional information (supplementing that of Chapters 5 and 6) about the relative importance of various job and personal characteristics in predicting to employee reactions on the job.

Results show first (see Appendix M) that about half of the variance among work groups with respect to general job interest is "explained" by the (eighteen) predictors included in our analysis.[39] Among the various job and personal characteristics considered, identification with occupation has the strongest association with general job interest (as indicated by its Beta weight).[40] Control over work methods (Index A) also has a strong association with general job interest.

With respect to interest in work innovation, 47 per cent of the variance among work groups is explained by all the predictors together. Of the single predictors taken separately, work difficulty, identification with occupation, and control over work methods—in that order—have the strongest associations (largest Beta weights) with innovative interest.

With respect to absence, 53 per cent of the variance among work groups in total number of absences is accounted for by all the job and personal characteristics which we have considered. By far the strongest predictor of absence is identification with occupation (stronger occupational identification, more frequent absence). Other factors which make a

---

[38]Data for individuals are generally similar to those for groups, but the amount of variance explained for individuals is considerably less than that explained for groups.

[39]The analysis shown in Appendix M indicates that 47 per cent of the variance in general job interest is explained by these predictors. A very similar analysis, differing primarily in that control over means index A is used rather than index B, "explains" 50 per cent of the variance in general job interest.

[40]The Beta weights indicate how much change in the dependent variable is produced by a standardized change in one of the independent variables when the others are controlled. Beta weights and partial correlation coefficients will usually rank variables in the same order of importance.

substantial contribution to predicting the level of absence are (in order of importance, as indicated by their Beta weights) chances to use one's best abilities, work difficulty, dependence of co-workers on each other, frequency of time limits, chance to learn, peer rewards for achievement, and concern about work overload. All of these factors predict to less absence with the exception of chance to use abilities[41] and concern about work overload, which are associated with greater absence.

All of the predictors together account for 42 per cent of the variance among work groups on the pride in work measure, for 47 per cent of the variance in psychological symptoms of stress, and for only 34 per cent of the variance in physical symptoms of stress (see Appendix N). The factor which is by far the most strongly associated with pride in work (as indicated by the Beta weights) is the frequency of time limits (more frequent time limits, less pride in work). The factors most strongly associated with psychological symptoms of stress are the chance to learn (more chance, fewer symptoms) and difficulty in getting needed resources to do the job (more difficulty, more symptoms). Physical symptoms of stress are predicted best by the clarity of instruction on the job (more clarity, fewer symptoms).

These results concerning the factors which predict best to indicators of motivation, to job pride, and to symptoms of stress are consistent with the results for work groups (in the form of partial correlations) presented in Chapters 5 and 6.

SUMMARY

This chapter has examined the joint effects on job motivation (and on other employee reactions to the job) of opportunity for achievement and reward for achievement. First, we used the technique of analysis of variance to determine whether there were joint effects of opportunity and reward on the job interest of individuals. This analysis showed a tendency for a combination of high feedback on performance and high reward for achievement to bring increases in general job interest greater than that due to either feedback or reward alone. Analyses of variance also showed a tendency for a combination of high personal need for achievement and poor opportunity for achievement to bring lower job interest than is due to the effect of either personal need or opportunity alone. However, in

---

[41]Note, however, the data of Table 6-3, which indicates that the chance to test one's best abilities tends to have a negative association with absence for individuals within each of the major sites.

general, the analyses of variance showed only small joint effects (inter-actions) between achievement opportunity factors and achievement reward factors.

A second type of analysis, correlation analysis, was then employed which permitted fuller use of the data for groups and in which a greater number of variables were included. First, job characteristics which were thought to be relevant to achievement incentive (notably difficulty, control over means, feedback, and time limits) were correlated with employee reactions to the job, separately for job situations in which achievement reward was low, medium, and high. When achievement reward was high, increases in feedback on performance and more frequent time limits were associated with greater interest in work innovation; these associations were not found when reward for achievement was low or intermediate. An index of overall achievement opportunity (based largely on the measures of job difficulty and control over means) showed stronger associations with both interest in innovation and general job interest (though not to attendance) as reward for achievement increased. In general, the results are consistent with our expectation that certain job characteristics (i.e., difficulty, control over means, feedback, and standards of excellence) affect the level of achievement incentive (i.e., the magnitude of achievement perceived to be possible). The results are also consistent with our expecta-tion that an increased achievement incentive will have the greatest effect on job motivation when the motivation for achievement (based on the rewards for achievement) is high.

We also examined the correlations between factors relevant to reward for achievement and employee reactions to the job, separately for different levels of achievement opportunity. The results give some support to our expectation that reward for achievement will have a stronger relation to job motivation when achievement opportunity is high than when it is low—though this effect is not large or consistent. Increases in personal need for achievement tend to have a favorable effect on job motivation (notably on attendance) when achievement opportunity is high but a negative effect (notably on job interest) when opportunity is low. Evidently, those with a high need for achievement find situations of low achievement opportunity more frustrating and boring than do others.

Two other factors relevant to personal pride in achievement—chance to do what one is best at and influence on work goals—also are more positively associated with indicators of job motivation as achievement opportunity increases. However, identification with occupation has about the same degree of positive association with job interest, and a consistent positive association with absence (higher identification, more absence) regardless of the level of achievement opportunity. This latter result, as well as results from Chapter 6, suggests that identification with one's occupation usually involves satisfaction with being a member of the occupation more than it does a drive for outstanding achievement in that occupation.

Rewards for achievement from peers and from supervisors both tend, as expected, to have stronger associations with job motivation as opportunity for achievement increases. Promotion rewards for achievement have a similar weak relation to indicators of job motivation regardless of the level of opportunity for achievement on the job. The results concerning promotion suggest that it is too long deferred and indirect a reward to have much effect on day-to-day job motivation, regardless of the amount of opportunity for achievement.

In general, the results are consistent with our expectation that certain job and personal characteristics, in addition to the so-called need for achievement, will increase the motivation for achievement on the job. The results are also consistent with the general theoretical expectation that increases in the motivation for achievement will have the strongest effect on task motivation when the achievement incentive is high.

Finally, this chapter also considered the total amount of variance in job interest (and other reactions to the job) which is explained by all the factors considered in the study—both those most relevant to achievement opportunity and those most relevant to achievement reward. Together, all the job and personal characteristics considered account for about half of the variance among groups with respect to general job interest and slightly less than half of the variance with respect to interest in innovation. Identification with occupation and control over work methods are the best predictors of general job interest. The same two factors, along with work difficulty, are the best predictors of interest in work innovation.

Pride in work is predicted best by the frequency of time limits (more frequent deadlines, less pride). The chance to learn, clarity of instructions, and lack of difficulty in getting needed resources contribute most to reducing symptoms of stress.

IDENTIFICATION WITH THE WORK ORGANIZATION

PART

8

ORGANIZATIONAL IDENTIFICATION

Its Meaning and Determinants

We have already discussed briefly (Chapter 2) the importance of the social identifications which the job provides. In this chapter we will examine more closely the phenomena which has been termed identification with a group or organization. Having considered these phenomena and their interrelations, we will discuss some of the factors which affect the extent to which a person identifies with his work organization.

THE CONCEPT OF IDENTIFICATION

The concept of identification has been used to refer to a variety of separate, though related, phenomena. As they apply to groups or organizations, these phenomena may be grouped for convenience under the headings of (1) feelings of solidarity with the organization; (2) support of the organization; and (3) perception of shared characteristics with other organizational members.

Feelings of Solidarity

Some who have talked about identification with a group or organization have pointed to the feelings of belonging to, of oneness with, of really being part of, some group (Sherif and Cantril, 1947; Sanford, 1955). Other writers have discussed, under the heading of identification, an apparently related but more precisely defined phenomenon—the process by which the individual makes his membership role in some group or organization an important part of his self-image (Daniel Miller, 1963; French and Sherwood, 1965). Identification in this sense is self-labeling behavior. Either covertly in his own thoughts, or overtly in words or actions (e.g., wearing an organization pin), the person declares, "I am a . . ." Still another phenomenon which has been discussed as identification (Kagan, 1958) and which may be included under the heading of feelings of solidarity is the reaction of an individual to events affecting another person or persons as though they had happened to himself. In a group or organizational context, individuals may react in this way to events affecting other organization members—e.g., to attacks on organization leaders.

Support of Organization

In addition to feelings of solidarity with a group or organization, identification has also been discussed and assessed in terms of attitudes and behavior which support the group or strengthen the individual's association with it (e.g., Lazerwitz, 1953; Geismer, 1954). In a work organization, employees may voluntarily work overtime without pay, turn down attractive outside offers, "talk up" and defend the organization to outsiders, express enthusiasm about organizational goals, and so on. These kinds of attitudes and behaviors represent what is commonly called "loyalty" to the organization.[1]

Another kind of behavior, which has been discussed under the heading of identification (Sanford, 1955; Bettelheim, 1943; Argyris, 1957), is that of persons copying the behavior of others whom they wish to be like. A Marine recruit may copy the behavior of "ideal" Marines (the Marine Corps Commandant, his platoon sergeant, etc.). A junior executive may try to copy the dress and mannerisms of the top executives. Such copying behavior is probably related to the adoption of a certain self-concept (e.g., as a rising company executive) and the wish to maintain this self-concept. While copying behavior does not necessarily have as its aim the helping of the organization, or of the models, the copying of prestigious models in an organization will usually result in organizationally helpful behavior.

---

[1]Data concerning the relationship between loyalty to the organization and the distribution of control among hierarchical levels have been presented by Arnold Tannenbaum and his associates (see Smith and Tannenbaum, 1963).

Perception of Shared Characteristics

Another relevant conception of identification has been proposed by Stotland and his associates (e.g., Stotland, 1962; Stotland, Zander and Natsoulas, 1961; Stotland and Dunn, 1962). They see identification as a cognitive process based on the perception of similarities between oneself and another person. Extending this conception from identification with an individual to identification with a group, they write : "The cognitive process whereby a person sees in himself qualities that are similar to those he perceives in his group is designated here as 'identification with the group.' " (Zander, Stotland, and Wolfe, 1960, p. 463).[2] In order for a person to see similarities between himself and a group there must be properties that are possessed by groups as well as by individuals. Zander, Stotland, and Wolfe mention goals, standards of conduct, and certain kinds of performance as examples of characteristics which may apply both to individuals and to the group. We may note, in addition, that the individual may perceive similarities between himself and other group members or between himself and the "typical" group member.[3] Such perceived similarities may include many characteristics including demographic attributes like race, sex, age, education, religion, and national origin. Of special importance in organizations is the perception of shared interests and shared goals.

RELATION BETWEEN SOLIDARITY, LOYALTY, AND PERCEPTION OF SIMILARITY

Common experience suggests that the three general kinds of phenomena discussed above—i.e., sense of solidarity, loyal behavior, and perceptions of having things in common—tend to go together. Indeed, the fact that all of these phenomena have been called by the same term, "identification," suggests that they are likely to be closely interwoven. We would suggest, however, that there are logical and causal priorities among these phenomena.

The perception of similarities between oneself and other organization members is, we would suggest, often crucial for the occurrence of other

---

[2]In other places, Stotland uses the term "identification" to refer to the "process of generalizing similarity between oneself and a model" (e.g., 1962, p. 2). We will be concerned with the perception of similarities per se rather than with the generalizations of these perceived similarities.

[3]Stotland notes elsewhere in discussing identification with another person, termed a "model," that "a model can be an abstract type based on a generalization from the perception of a number of different persons" (1962, p. 3).

"identification" phenomena. When a person has similar social characteristics, similar status, similar goals, etc., with other organization members,[4]
he is likely to feel at home, to feel that he belongs—i.e., to have a sense
of solidarity with the organization.[5] Perceptions of interdependence[6] and
of proximity may also contribute to the sense of solidarity.[7] Such a sense
of solidarity with the organization should, in turn, contribute to the individual's motivation to defend and support—i.e., be loyal to—the organization. If he really feels a part of this organization, then he is helping his
own group, his own people.

There may be, in addition, some pragmatic motives for loyalty to an
organization. A person may support and defend an organization of which
he is a member because he derives, and expects to continue to derive,
various satisfactions from his organization membership (e.g., money, status,
friendships, feelings of pride in accomplishment). Perceptions that the
organization is, or is likely to be, a source of such satisfactions depend
in part upon the kinds of resources the organization has and how it
distributes them (e.g., the wages it pays). They depend also on the
prestige which the organization enjoys in the larger society (TVA as an

---

[4]As Stotland has pointed out (personal communication), certain similarities among
organization members may entail competition, however. Thus, those who are similar in
type of skill and seniority may compete for promotion. We would expect that, in this
example, the similarities of skill and seniority would contribute to a sense of solidarity with
the group while the nonsimilarity of goals with respect to promotion (i.e., each prefers
that he and not the others be promoted first) would diminish the sense of solidarity.

[5]Zander, Stotland, and Wolfe (1960), extending Wertheimer (1950), suggest that similarity among group members contributes, along with proximity and movement in the same
direction (shared task or interdependency), to perceptions of the group as a unified whole.
Zander, Stotland, and Wolfe also argue that where persons perceive themselves as belonging
to groups which have high unity, they will be more likely to see similarities between themselves and the group. However, it is not clear that their conceptualization or their experimental manipulation of perceived group unity is entirely separate from that of perceived
similarity between oneself and the group as a whole. Similarity among *members* is seen
conceptually as one determinant of perceived unity and the experimental manipulation of
group unity includes differential information about the similarity of members. It may be
that there is a reciprocal influence between perceptions of similarity with the group and
perceptions of the unity of the group.

[6]The principles of perceptual grouping stated by Wertheimer (1950) are applied by
Zander, Stotland, and Wolfe (1960) to perceptions of group unity. They suggest that
Wertheimer's principle that components moving in the same direction are more likely
than others to be seen as unified may be extended to the presence of a shared task or an
interdependent relationship with a group. Perhaps a more exact extension of Wertheimer's
principle would be that persons moving toward the same goal are likely to be perceived as
a unit. An interdependent relationship will usually be associated with movement toward
the same goal but this is not necessarily the case.

[7]The sense of solidarity with a group or organization may be looked on as the perception of oneself and the others forming a unified whole. Thus, discussions of the determinants of the perception of unity would seem to be relevant in considering the determinants of what we have termed solidarity.

organization is quite prestigious within the Tennessee Valley because of the widely publicized and visible benefits that it has brought to the Valley). A member's expectation of getting various satisfactions from his membership may also depend in part on his sense of having things in common with other organization members. If he feels he is with people like himself, the individual is more likely to feel he can count on other organization members to give him help when he needs it.

In general, we would expect that those who derive satisfactions from their membership roles will be likely to support and defend the organization for fairly pragmatic reasons. However, it may also be, as suggested by Brown (1964), that getting certain kinds of satisfactions from one's organizational role will also lead to a greater importance of that role in one's self-image. This is likely to be true where the satisfactions—like pride in achievement or in high status—are ones which enhance one's self-esteem and are seen as connected specifically to one's organizational role and not just to an occupational role which could be practiced anywhere.

Our Use of the Term "Identification"

In this volume, we will not attempt to decide which of the various uses of the term "identification" is most appropriate or useful. We will instead use the term as a broad, inclusive, somewhat loose concept, embracing a number of the various interrelated phenomena discussed above—especially perceptions of similarity with other organization members, sense of solidarity with the organization, and attitudes and behavior supporting the organization and one's ties to it.

However, for many purposes, it will be useful to keep separate the phenomena of perceived similarity, sense of solidarity, and loyalty. While these tend to go together, there are times when they may vary separately.

DETERMINANTS OF ORGANIZATIONAL IDENTIFICATION

We have suggested that the perception of certain things in common, especially shared goals, plays an important part in creating a sense of solidarity with an organization and loyalty to it. In addition we have noted that the perception of getting important satisfactions as a result of organizational membership may promote loyalty to that organization. Next we turn our attention to those features of the organization and the environment which are likely to affect such perceptions.

There are many factors which may help to determine members' perceptions about how much they have in common with other members and what satisfactions they derive from membership. Without attempting to be exhaustive, we will discuss next a number of factors which may be important in these respects. We will pay particular attention to those which may contribute to feelings by lower-level members of some common interest with management.

Congruence of Individual and Organization Goals

In some organizations the official goals, as espoused by its leaders, are shared, sometimes passionately, by the rank-and-file members. This is likely to be the case in many voluntary organizations devoted to religion, politics, or public service. Certain armies, whose ordinary soldiers have been devoted to some national cause, have had this characteristic. Likewise some government agencies devoted to a cause like fighting poverty or helping underdeveloped nations have goals which are accepted with some degree of enthusiasm by their members. This also appears to be the case for the Tennessee Valley Authority—though the urgency of the goal of building up the Valley has diminished over time. In all of these cases the objective congruence of at least some goals held by those throughout the organization is likely to be perceived by the members and contribute to a sense of solidarity with the organization.

Where explicit or implicit official goals of an organization—e.g., making a large profit to be distributed to stockholders—are not important ones to its rank-and-file members, they will perceive less in common with the organizational leaders and thus feel less sense of solidarity with the organization.

Participation in Decisions

Being given an opportunity to participate in decision making—e.g., in setting time deadlines for the work, in deciding on changes in work equipment or work methods—may create several kinds of important perceived similarities with management. There is likely to be, first, a greater sense of approximate similarity of status with management. There is no longer a wide gulf between two kinds of people—those who give orders and those who take them. To the extent that decision making is shared, all are on a level where they can contribute ideas, have them heard, and perhaps make an impact. A second kind of perceived similarity likely to arise from joint decision making is a similarity of values and goals. Through the process of mutual influence which comes with sustained interaction (Likert, 1961) and through the process of actual agreement on decisions, the perception of shared values and shared goals is likely to emerge.

Participation in decision making is also likely to be satisfying to many organizational members, as the work of Vroom (1960) indicates. The association of such satisfactions with organizational membership may further increase loyalty to the organization.

Reward System

The system of allocating rewards in an organization can exert great effect on perceptions of shared interest. Where the pay-off to all rises and falls together (e.g., in profit-sharing plans, bonus plans, commission plans), there will be a sense of sharing in the same economic fortunes. There will also be a sense of common material interest in having the organization do well. Where, on the other hand, the material fortunes of organization members do not rise and fall together (as where management gets a raise while some workers are laid off), there will be less overall sense of common interests within the organization. Besides money, rewards may also include promotions, better office space, or more appealing work. The more widely such rewards are shared, the greater the sense of common interest.

In addition to the sharing of rewards, the absolute level of formal rewards dispensed by an organization may affect members' reactions to it. Where organizational membership brings important pragmatic rewards, members will tend to value the organization and thus defend and support it.

Promotion Chances

Related to the topic of organizational rewards is that of promotion opportunities. Where an employee has the opportunity to rise high in status (and rewards) within an organization, he may be expected to see greater similarity—at least potentially—between himself and important organization members. He may also see his own interests as being intertwined with those of the organization, since the organization must survive and prosper if it is to promote him into a desirable position. Thus we would expect those with good prospects for promotion to feel a greater sense of solidarity with and loyalty toward the organization than those who are stuck at a low place in the hierarchy. Much may depend, however, on how high up in the organization the individual can reasonably expect to go. If he sees as his "ceiling" an unimportant position, the fact that his promotion chances are good may not contribute much to organizational identification.

Opportunities for Achievement

In addition to distributing pragmatic rewards, like money, an organization also creates opportunities for its members to derive other kinds of satisfaction from their organizational roles. In particular, we may note the satisfaction of pride in accomplishment which people may get on the job. We have already discussed at length in earlier chapters some of the job features—e.g., control over work methods, chance to use one's best abilities—which may make achievement more possible and more meaningful on the job.

Opportunities for deriving pride from performance on the job may be expected to affect a person's orientation toward the organization in several ways. First, the fact that his organizational role brings important satisfactions should, in itself, make the individual more ready to defend and support this organization. Secondly, to the extent that feelings (like pride), which are ego-enhancing, are associated with his organizational role, this role may become an important part of his self-image. Finally, where pursuing work goals provides important personal satisfactions, the individual may come to see greater congruence between his own goals and those of the organization leaders.

Nature of Interpersonal Relationships

A person's orientations toward an organization may be affected by the warmth of his interpersonal relations with other members. Friendly, co-operative, supportive relationships may lead a person to perceive things in common with, perhaps also a sense of interdependence with, and thus a sense of solidarity with, co-workers. Positive interpersonal relations should also lead the individual to associate important social satisfactions with organizational membership. Aspects of the work situation which foster positive interpersonal relations—e.g., good channels for communication, smooth-working functional interdependencies—may therefore contribute to a sense of organizational identification.

However, it is important to note that this should be true only when the individual's network of personal associates within the organization is not sharply distinguished from the rest of the organization. If a person has warm interpersonal relationships within his immediate work group (perhaps including the supervisor), he may come to identify with that group. Whether such identification generalizes to the larger organization depends in part on whether the interests of the immediate group are seen as congruent with or opposed to those of the larger organization.

Relative Status of Members

One important dimension on which organizational members will perceive similarities or differences is the dimension of status. In work organizations, the existence of such distinctions as separate eating areas, separate parking areas, different styles of dress, and formal titles, will emphasize differences between people at different levels of, and perhaps in different parts of, the organization. Aside from such symbols of status, more basic factors such as occupational level and salary level will also help to create perceptions of important similarities or differences among organization members. We would expect that, other things being equal, members of organizations where status differences are small will be more likely to identify with the organization than will members of organizations where status differences are large.

Demographic Similarities

In some organizations the presence or absence of common demographic characteristics may lead to perceptions of common interest or the lack thereof. For example, the predominantly Irish character of the Catholic Church hierarchy in the United States probably has given the Irish clergy an additional sense of similarity with other Catholic churchmen than they might otherwise have had. A company management which is predominantly of a particular demographic cast—white, Negro, young, old, Italian, male, Texan, etc.—may be expected to evoke perceptions of similarity from those of like characteristics. Such similarity may contribute to feelings of solidarity and the expectation of mutual help from those of like background.

Other Memberships

The extent of perceived similarity, especially with regard to shared goals, may depend in part on the extent to which memberships outside the organization are shared. An engineer who belongs to the same professional organization as does the management of his division has an important point of similarity with the management men. They are all engineers, with the shared values and goals of engineers. But an engineer (as at TVA) may also belong to an employee association which bargains with management. This membership is a point of dissimilarity with the management men and one which may cause the perception of common interest to be somewhat less (or, alternatively, may reflect areas of lack of common interest). Of course, the extent to which membership in an outside organization, like a union or a management association, is seen as an important dissimilarity will differ from one organization to another. Where union and management have had violent conflict, people may be regarded as being on either one side or the other, with little common interest. Where union-management relations have been amicable, labor or management memberships may little affect the sense of basic similarity and common interest.

A related question concerns the relation between identification with an occupation and identification with the organization in which one is practicing that occupation. Will high occupational identification contribute to or detract from identification with a work organization? On the one hand, one might expect that those who identify strongly with their occupations would share with organizational management a high valuation of work goals. If members perceive such a similarity, their sense of solidarity with the organization might on this count be increased. On the other hand, occupational identification may be an alternative to, or even compete with, organizational identification. Feelings of solidarity with an occupational group (which cuts across organizations) may not be completely compatible with feelings of solidarity with a particular organization. A self-image of oneself in terms of an occupational role may reduce the importance of a self-image in terms of one's organizational role. Also, at times (e.g., in completing a rush job) a choice may have to be made between organizational and occupational norms. In sum, the effects of occupational identification on organizational identification may be mixed.

Possibility of Leaving the Organization

One important similarity among organization members is the mere fact of their common membership. To the extent that a person has an option about whether he will stay with the organization next year, his common interest with other organization members is less strong than if, as a practical matter, he must remain indefinitely. We would therefore expect, other things being equal, that those who can leave a group or organization will identify with it less strongly than those who realistically cannot choose to leave—e.g., because there are no other good jobs available to them.[8]

What we are saying here applies, however, to those who have the prospect, or future possibility, of a realistic opportunity to move outside their own group or organization. For those who have already been presented with such opportunities (e.g., the offer of an equal or better job elsewhere) and turned these opportunities down, the fact that they have chosen to remain with the organization may be an indication of their having a sense of identification with that organization.

---

[8] This situation is similar to that of ethnic or racial group identification. For example, other things equal, we would expect a dark-skinned Negro, who cannot change the fact of his being a Negro, to have a greater sense of solidarity with Negroes as a group than would an extremely light-skinned "Negro," who may have an opportunity to "pass" as white, and, in effect, to leave the racial group to which he had been assigned previously.

Treatment by Outsiders

The extent to which organization members will see themselves as similar and "in the same boat" may also depend in part on how they are treated by those outside the organization. The soldier in uniform may be reacted to by civilians in terms of his uniform ("Want a lift, soldier?"). People who work for organizations which are well known—as TVA is in its area—will sometimes be treated by others a little more graciously or less so on the basis of their organizational membership. Such attention by outsiders to his membership in a particular organization will make such membership more salient to the individual himself.

The discussion in this section, concerning the various aspects of organizational identification and the determinants of identification, is summarized in Figure 8-1.

IDENTIFICATION WITH PART OF AN ORGANIZATION

It may be noted that, in discussing organizational identification, we have not distinguished between identification with a total organization (e.g., TVA) and identification with a subpart of the total organization (e.g., a division or branch). As Katz and Kahn (1966) point out, it is often easier for people to become attached to their own immediate part of the organization than to the larger whole. Sometimes, the subpart—a division, branch, department, etc.—may not be sharply distinguished from the whole; the subpart may, in the eyes of its members, represent the whole. (Thus, most TVA people do not appear to distinguish between their attitudes towards their division and their attitudes toward TVA.) However, in other circumstances (e.g., where subparts of an organization are more autonomous, more distinct or conflicting) members may have rather different degrees of identification with different levels of the organization. The present conceptual scheme is intended to be applicable either to an organization as a whole or to a smaller organizational unit.

THE PRESENT STUDY

From our study of TVA, we have data about variations in many, though not all, of the organizational and environmental factors shown on the left of Figure 8-1. Since the program of employee participation at TVA is one of the most outstanding features of the organization, we will look most intensively at the association between variations in organizational identification and variations in participation in the cooperative program.

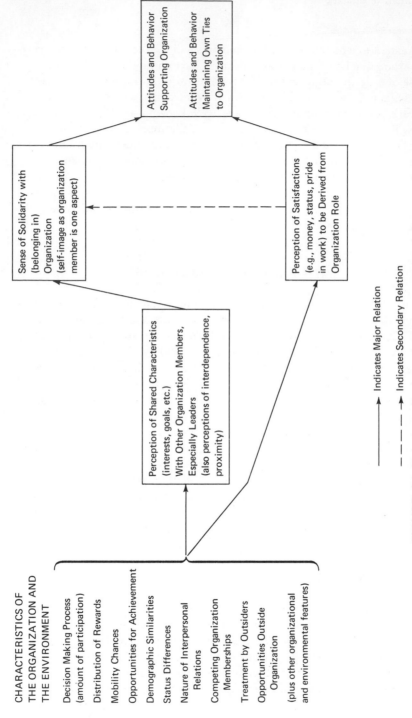

FIGURE 8-1 Hypothesized relation between organizational factors and reactions toward the work organization

We will also examine the relation between identification and a variety of other factors discussed above, including job opportunities outside TVA, commitment to occupational groups, opportunities for personal achievement, and relationships with co-workers. In addition, we will consider the ways in which several other job and personal characteristics —including length of service and certain personality differences—are related to organizational identification.

We will not be able to test rigorously for the causal relations hypothesized, as shown in Figure 8-1—e.g., that the perception of shared characteristics with other organization members is a prerequisite for a sense of solidarity with the organization. In large part, this is because our data provide only limited information about each of the separate orientations to the organization shown in Figure 8-1 (see Chapter 9 for description of data). However, we will be able to say something about which aspects of identification are most directly affected by various aspects of the work situation. We will also try, where this seems feasible, to examine evidence bearing on our expectation that the perception of having things in common with other organization members (especially management) serves as an important intervening variable between certain features of the work situation and attitudes and behavior supportive of the organization.

SUMMARY

The concept of identification has been used by various writers to refer to a variety of separate, though related, phenomena. As these phenomena apply to groups or organizations, they may be grouped under three headings : feelings of solidarity with the organization; support of the organization (loyalty); and perception of shared characteristics with other organization members.

We have suggested that a person's perception of similarities between himself and other organization members, particularly similarities of interest and of goals with the leadership of the organization, is crucial for the occurrence of feelings of solidarity with the organization. The sense of solidarity should contribute to the person's motivation to be loyal to the organization. Loyalty may also stem from more pragmatic motives. We will use the term "identification" as a broad inclusive term to cover the three separate orientations toward the organization which we have discussed : perception of similarity, sense of solidarity, and loyalty. However, for some purposes we will consider each of these aspects of identification separately.

If, as we have suggested, the perception of shared characteristics (espcially goals) is a key aspect of identification, it becomes important to consider features of the organization and the environment which may affect members' perceptions of having things in common with other organization members (especially the leadership). Features of the organization which affect the satisfactions derived from organization membership are also relevant to consider. We discussed a number of factors which may affect perceptions of having things in common and/or of deriving satisfactions from membership roles. These are (1) the congruence between individual and organization goals; (2) participation in decisions; (3) reward systems; (4) mobility chances; (5) opportunities for achievement; (6) the nature of interpersonal relations; (7) the relative status of members; (8) demographic similarities; (9) other organizational memberships; (10) the possibility of leaving the organization; and (11) treatment by outsiders.

Some of the major relationships we have hypothesized in this chapter are shown in Figure 8-1. In the present study we will not be able to test for the presence of all of these relationships in a rigorous way. The theoretical ideas presented will, however, serve as a general guide for examining relationships between features of the organization, on the one hand, and organizational identification among employees, on the other hand. Before proceeding to examine such relationships, however, we turn first to a look at the kinds of feelings toward their organization which TVA employees express and to the measures of identification which were used in the study.

9

ORGANIZATIONAL
IDENTIFICATION
AT TVA

In the previous chapter we discussed in fairly abstract terms the perceptions, attitudes, and behaviors toward an organization which have been labeled by various writers as "identification." In this chapter we look at some of the variations in the reactions toward TVA as an organization which are found within those parts of TVA which we studied. First, some comments by TVA employees about their feelings toward TVA will be reported. Next, the questionnaire measures used to systematically assess "identification with TVA" will be presented, along with some data about their validity. Finally, we will compare several types of work units with respect to their scores on the measures of organizational identification.

SOME COMMENTS BY TVA EMPLOYEES

In exploratory interviews, we questioned employees (most of them non-supervisory) about their feelings toward TVA.[1] The great majority of

[1]Specific questions included ones about (1) whether there were any things about TVA they felt especially proud of; (2) whether bad publicity about TVA bothered them much; (3) whether there were any things different about TVA as compared to other work places they knew about; and (4) what they did when someone criticized TVA.

those questioned expressed positive feelings toward TVA. Many spoke with enthusiasm of TVA's accomplishments. Typical is this statement by an unskilled laborer in a steam plant :

> *TVA is one of the wonderful things for the Tennessee Valley. It's improved the Tennessee Valley, oh, I'd say one hundred per cent. Because when TVA started, this was nothing but a flood state. The dams and plants made it one of the most outstanding places in the world. People from all over the world are living here now, that didn't live here before.*

Some employees spoke in terms of having a feeling of belonging at TVA. An electrician in a steam plant remarked :

> *There is a more pleasant feeling here than in private industry. You feel as if you're part of a big organization. Only the executives feel like they're a part in private industry.*

Asked about his reaction to any bad publicity about TVA, an engineering associate said :

> *I'm concerned about it. I like to be proud of any organization in which I work. It makes me a little uncomfortable for TVA to be put in an uncomfortable position. It's like someone in my own family were in an embarrassing position. I sort of feel like I'm akin to it.*

An electrical engineer commented :

> *I worked in the welfare department of the state. TVA, in comparison, has a well-organized program in informing employees concerning what the organization is doing and in getting employees to participate. You feel a part of the organization.*

Concern by the organization for employees was mentioned by some employees. For example, a payroll clerk said :

> *You don't find many concerns that give the benefits that TVA gives. Other firms are not interested in your general welfare like TVA. Your health and safety, they're interested in both. If you're sick and you need to get home, they'll see you get home. They have a nice first aid station with a full time nurse and a doctor who comes in two times a week.*

Some employees made it clear that they are prepared to defend TVA against verbal attack. For example, asked about his reaction to criticism of TVA, an electrical engineer launched into a vigorous defense of TVA's use of tax money and said concerning his reaction to criticism by others :

> *I rebuff them. I try not to get angry, but a person could get angry. I always point out to them what I think is true. I feel I should—it's my duty to give them the truth.*

A few employees indicated that their strong positive feelings toward TVA had been important in causing them to remain with the organization. An architect said :

> *I've stayed with TVA because I'm proud of lots of things they've done. Being a native of the valley, I felt that I'm doing something for my own area. I've stayed at a big loss of money. I could have accepted partnerships outside of TVA, but I'm proud of the whole thing.*

While many employees speak in strongly positive terms about the organization for which they work, there are some whose feelings toward TVA are less favorable and a few who are even somewhat hostile.

A civil engineer previously in the interview had criticized his division for not paying for work-related courses which employees wished to take and had criticized other management actions, such as the allocation of overtime. Asked how he feels when he hears criticism of TVA, he answered:

> *It doesn't make much difference to me what they say. A lot of waste goes on but it would cost more to eliminate than what it is worth. The biggest criticism is about taxes. Private power versus public power. I used to answer—I just let it go now.*

A unit operator in a steam plant appeared to reflect a fundamental sense of the separateness of management and labor in making this comment on the differences between TVA and other places :

> *Practically everywhere I have worked there were good relations between management and labor people. You can't strike at TVA. L & N Railroad struck recently. We don't have that privilege, or you might call it a liability. We talk about our problems rather than walking a picket line. We have to settle them by arbitration or something like that. As far as the way we are treated, I've found that if you do a job right, management would not bother you no matter where you're at. (Q: Would you prefer to have the right to strike?) That is hard to answer. We depend on people outside of TVA. Our wages and conditions are based on what they have. Those boys, by having the right to strike, have a bearing on what we get. Which I prefer, I don't know. I'd rather negotiate than strike, but sometimes a strike might be necessary.*

A rather extreme and very rare lack of support for TVA as an organization was expressed by an engineering aide at a steam plant, who identified himself as a Republican. Asked his reaction to bad publicity about TVA, he said :

> *You're talking to the wrong person now because a lot of things about TVA, I can't agree with. I don't think so much concentrating on the steam plant is good. They should be privately run . . . Actually I dassent say this around here. People are prejudiced because it's done so much for them, but I don't think the whole county should pay for it.*

The ideological position expressed by this employee was accompanied by a number of personal dissatisfactions with TVA. He went on to express dissatisfaction with the TVA health insurance plan, and especially about the fact that he had been "passed up" by management for someone with a college degree.

QUESTIONS RELEVANT TO IDENTIFICATION

To systematically assess organizational identification at TVA, data from a number of relevant questionnaire items are available.

Perception of Common Interest

The first question is relevant to one of the major aspects of identification discussed above, the perception of similarity—especially common goals and common interests—with other organization members :

1. Following are two somewhat different statements about the relations between management and employees at TVA:

    A. The relations between management and employees at TVA are much different than in private industry, because in TVA both are working together toward the same goal of building the Valley.

    B. Relations between management and employees at TVA are not really very different than in private industry; management is looking out for the organization's interests, and employees have to look out for their own interests.

    Which of the two statements above comes closer to *your* own opinion?

    (5) _____ Agree completely with A
    (4) _____ Agree more with A than with B
    (2) _____ Agree more with B than with A
    (1) _____ Agree completely with B

For TVA as a whole, 55 per cent answering the questionnaire agreed completely or mostly with statement A—that management and employees are working toward the same goals. Forty-three per cent agreed completely or mostly with statement B—that employees have to look out for their own interests. (Two per cent gave no answer.) Agreement with statement A was somewhat more frequent (64 per cent) in the engineering divisions than in the steam plants (48 per cent). Within the steam plants, men in the operating sections showed a consistently greater readiness than the craftsmen and laboratory people to agree with statement B—that stressing conflict of interest.

Self-Image

A second question is relevant to the second aspect of identification discussed above—i.e., the extent to which the individual has a sense of solidarity with, or belonging to, the organization. We suggested that closely related to such a sense of solidarity is the extent to which organizational membership is an important part of the individual's self-image. The question asked is as follows :

2. If someone asked you to describe yourself, and you could tell only one thing about yourself, which of the following answers would you be most likely to give? (Put a *number 1* next to that item.)

      ——————— I come from (my home state)
      ——————— I work for TVA
      ——————— I am a (my occupation or type of work)
      ——————— I am a (my church membership or preference)
      ——————— I am a graduate of (my school)

If you could give two answers, which one of the items above would you choose second? (Put a *number 2* next to that item.)

If you could give three answers, which one of the items would you choose third? (Put a *number 3* next to that item.)

For the sample as a whole, 32 per cent chose "I work for TVA" as the first attribute with which they would describe themselves. Thirty-six per cent chose this organizational membership second, and 18 per cent chose it third. People in the power plants were slightly more likely to choose the "TVA" response first than were those in the engineering divisions (35 per cent to 28 per cent), a difference which is undoubtedly accounted for by the fact that engineering division employees (mostly professionals) were more than twice as likely as power plant employees (45 per cent to 21 per cent) to choose their occupation as the first characteristic with which to describe themselves. Within the power plants, it is interesting to note that the operations personnel, though as highly skilled as the craftsmen, were much more likely to name their TVA membership as the first trait with which to describe themselves.[2]

———————

[2]This difference is probably due in part to the fact that the occupations of the operators are much more tied to TVA than are those of the craftsmen; within their geographic area at least, the operating men's skills are of use only at TVA. This finding is, therefore, consistent with our argument that the lack of opportunity to leave the organization contributes to organizational identification. An additional reason for this result may be that an occupational identity as a steam plant operator does not provide the clearly recognized social identity in the larger society as does, say, being an electrician, while identity as a TVA employee is clearly recognized in the larger society (see Slater, 1959).

Association with and Support of Organization

A number of other questions asked of TVA employees are relevant to attitudes or behaviors directed toward close association with, or support of, the organization. These questions are as follows:

3.   If you could begin working over again, but in the same occupation as you're in now, how likely would you be to choose TVA as a place to work?

    (1) _____ Definitely would choose another place over TVA
    (2) _____ Probably would choose another place over TVA
    (3) _____ Wouldn't care much whether it was TVA or some other place
    (4) _____ Probably would choose TVA over another place
    (5) _____ Definitely would choose TVA over another place for my occupation

4.   How do you feel when you hear (or read about) someone criticizing the TVA method of public power or comparing it unfavorably to private power?

    (1) _____ I mostly agree with the criticism
    (2) _____ It doesn't bother me
    (4) _____ It gets me a little mad
    (5) _____ It gets me quite mad
    _____ I never hear or read such criticism

5.   In general, how often do you tell someone in your immediate family (wife, child, parent, brother, sister) about some project that TVA has done or is doing?

    (5) _____ Once a week or more
    (4) _____ Several times a month
    (3) _____ About once a month
    (2) _____ Once every few months
    (1) _____ About once a year
    _____ Don't have any immediate family to talk to

6.   In general, how often do you tell someone *outside* your immediate family (friend, neighbor, store clerk, etc.) about some project that TVA has done or is doing?

    (5) _____ Once a week or more
    (4) _____ Several times a month
    (3) _____ About once a month
    (2) _____ Once every few months
    (1) _____ About once a year

7.   During the past two years, how many times has your part of TVA had a
     dinner or picnic or other social event outside of office hours?

     (5) ——————— Five or more times
     (4) ——————— Four times
     (3) ——————— Three times
     (2) ——————— Two times
     (1) ——————— Once
     ——————— Never that I know of

7a. If any social events held: How many of these social events did you attend?

     (5) ——————— Five or more
     (4) ——————— Four
     (3) ——————— Three
     (2) ——————— Two
     (1) ——————— One
     (0) ——————— None

        (Score on Q7 was based on proportion of social events attended)

Of those who answered our questionnaire at TVA, the great majority
(77 per cent) said they would probably or definitely choose TVA again
as a place to work; but some said they "wouldn't care much" whether they
worked for TVA and some said they would be likely to choose another
place to work. Power plant and engineering employees do not differ appreciably on this question, but there are differences within each of these
major organizational categories. Most strikingly, 21 per cent of employees
in one engineering division (I) say that they would be likely to choose
another place over TVA while only 8 per cent in the second engineering
division (II) give this response. This difference is consistent with informal
comments we heard from employees and staff personnel about a difference
of morale in the two divisions.[3]

Concerning their reactions to criticisms of TVA, most TVA employees
(69 per cent) reported some degree of anger at such criticism while about
one-fourth said such criticism doesn't bother them and 4 per cent said
they mostly agree with such criticism. Responses to these questions do not
differ appreciably between power plant and engineering division employees but there are some differences among subunits within each of these
major types of installation. One of these differences, again, is between the
two engineering divisions, with 82 per cent of those in "high morale"

---

[3]There is a similar, though less marked, difference between the two engineering
divisions in their response to the previous questions about the organization. Those in
engineering division II are more likely to agree with the statement that management and
employees have common interests and more likely to choose first "I work for TVA" as a
description of themselves.

division II saying they get angry about criticism of TVA as compared to 62 per cent giving this kind of response at division I.

Regarding telling people about TVA projects, average responses to the questions on this subject do not differ greatly among the major organizational units studied—i.e., among the two engineering divisions and three power plants. There are, however, some variations among subunits of these major groupings. With respect to attendance at social events, the average attendance at such events varies considerably among work groups.

Correlations Among Questionnaire Items

In general, work groups which score high on one question bearing on organizational identification also score high on the other items. (See Appendix L.) Thus, members of a work group who generally perceive a strong common interest with management also tend to describe themselves as TVA members, to express willingness to choose TVA again, to express anger at criticism of TVA, and to attend TVA social events. Perceived common interest with management, describing oneself as a TVA man, willingness to choose TVA again, and anger at criticism of TVA form a cluster of items, all of which have moderate correlations (in the .30s, .40s or .50s) with each other. Attendance at social events has somewhat smaller associations with the other items and telling one's family about TVA projects has very small associations with the other items. However, the latter items, like the former, are related to behaviors like turnover and displaying a TVA car sticker, which appear to reflect identification with the organization. (See below and Patchen, Pelz, and Allen, 1965.)

INDEX OF IDENTIFICATION WITH TVA

For each individual who took the questionnaire, an index score of identification with TVA (the mean of his responses to the above seven questions)[4] was computed.

There is evidence that employees' scores on this index of identification with TVA are related to several kinds of relevant employee behavior—including leaving the organization and displaying a TVA sticker.[5]

In engineering division I, where most turnover occurred in the year following administration of the questionnaire, the identification scores

---

[4]For most of the questions listed, the score assigned to each response alternative is indicated to the left of that alternative.

[5]Each of the items in the index was included largely on the basis of its association with various behaviors relevant to organizational identification.

of fifteen persons who resigned were compared to the much larger number who remained with the organization. Those who left TVA had a significantly lower mean score on the index of identification with TVA (at the .001 level) than the mean score of those who remained.

The relation of scores on the identification index to displaying a TVA auto sticker is shown in Figure 9-1.

Index of
Identification
With TVA

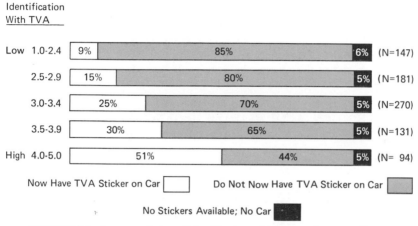

FIGURE 9-1   Scores on index of identification with TVA and report of having TVA sticker on car

These data show a marked relation between scores on the index of organizational identification and the likelihood of displaying a TVA sticker. Among those with the lowest identification scores, only 9 per cent reported the present display of a TVA sticker while 85 per cent said they did not show one now. As identification scores increase, the proportion displaying TVA auto stickers steadily increases also. Among those with the highest identification scores, 51 per cent report now displaying a TVA sticker as opposed to 44 per cent who do not.

More complete data bearing on the validity and reliability of indices of identification with a work organization are presented in another report.[6]

In addition to the scores for individuals, mean scores of identification with TVA were also computed for each of the ninety work groups in our sample. Average scores were also computed for each of eight cooperative

[6]See Patchen, M., D. Pelz, and C. Allen, *Some Measures of Employee Motivation and Morale: A Report on Their Reliability and Validity*, Ann Arbor, Michigan, Survey Research Center, monograph no. 41, 1965.

programs. (See Chapter 10 for a description of the cooperative programs.)

Scores on the index of identification with TVA vary widely among work groups and among larger organizational units. There is, most noticeably, a very striking difference between employees in the two engineering divisions. Comparing employees in all major units of our sample, those in engineering division I scored lowest on the identification index, while those in engineering division II, representing similar occupations, scored highest. The difference in mean scores between these two engineering divisions is highly significant statistically at beyond the .001 level.

Also relatively low on the overall index of identification are men in the operating sections of the steam plants. Craftsmen's units in the steam plants score moderate to high on organizational identification and laboratory employees in the steam plants tend to score fairly high.[7]

IDENTIFICATION WITH PRIVATE ORGANIZATIONS

There is a strong public service ideology which permeates TVA. Phrases like "building the valley," "serving the people of this area," and "contributing to the welfare of the nation" are often used by its management in discussing the goals and work of the organization. And in speaking to TVA employees about TVA, it is clear that their attitudes toward the organization are colored (favorably) by the public service nature of its aims and accomplishments. In fact, in measuring organizational identification, none of our questions (No. 1 above) is phrased in terms of the differences between private industry and the public nonprofit goal of TVA management to "build the valley."

This public character of TVA raises the question of whether identification of employees with their work organizations (such as is frequently found at TVA) is likely to be limited to public or nonprofit organizations or whether it may also be found among employees of private, profit-making firms. It may be of interest to digress from our consideration of identification at TVA to consider this question.

While we do not have general data about the comparative level of identification in public and private organizations, we do have data comparable to that at TVA from one private company. This company is located in a large midwestern city and manufactures electrical equipment. Unlike TVA employees, this company's employees are not unionized. However,

---

[7]The relative standing of units reported in this section are based on a short 4-item version of the index of organizational identification, based on the first four questions, as listed in the text.

the management of the company tries hard to keep its employees satisfied and well motivated, and to maintain good relations between management and employees; the keystone of this policy is a profit-sharing plan in which all employees participate and which pays very substantial benefits to employees when they retire.[8]

In January 1963, 223 employees at the electronics company answered a questionnaire similar to those answered by TVA employees. About half were in engineering units, about a fourth were in production jobs, and the rest were divided between finance, sales, marketing, and purchasing units. Most of these employees are men, with the exception of those in production units, most of whom are women.

On a number of key questions, employees at the private firm showed an even higher level of identification with their work organization than did those at TVA. First, in answer to a question similar to that asked at TVA, 78 per cent of the electronics firms employees agreed (completely or mostly) with the statement "the relations between management and employees at (company) are much different than in most other companies because in (company) both are working together for the same goals."

In answer to the "Who are you?" question, 57 per cent of the private company employees chose "I work for (company name)" as their first self-description. In answer to a question concerning their reactions to criticism of their work organization or its products, 65 per cent said this bothered them quite a bit. Asked if they would choose this company again (for a similar type of work), 86 per cent said they probably or definitely would. In each of these cases, the percentage of high-identification responses is somewhat higher than those for identical or highly similar questions at TVA.[9]

This comparison certainly does not indicate that most employees of private firms have a stronger sense of identification with their work organization than do those at TVA; nor that most private employees have a stronger sense of identification than most public employees. The private electronics firm in which these data were collected was atypical in its high level of good feeling between employees and management. Nor, for that matter, is TVA necessarily typical of governmental organizations in this respect. The point to be made here is, however, that there is no reason to think that the phenomenon of strong organizational identification is

---

[8] In answer to the question "How important to your personal welfare do you feel it is for (company) to make good profits?" 59 per cent of employees sampled in the private company said this was "of great importance to my own welfare" and 32 per cent said this was "of considerable importance."

[9] Variations in scores on the index of identification within the private company showed significant associations in the expected direction with actual turnover and with expectations about staying with the company.

limited to public, service-oriented organizations. Under appropriate conditions, strong identification of employees with private profit-making organizations is also possible.[10]

SUMMARY

Most TVA employees who were interviewed expressed positive feelings towards TVA as an organization. In particular, many nonsupervisory people who work for TVA are proud of its accomplishments, feel that management is concerned about employees, resent criticism of TVA, and feel "a part of" the organization. However, some persons appeared to see more of a fundamental split between the interests of management and those of other employees.

The questionnaire filled out by TVA employees asked a number of questions relevant to aspects of organizational identification. Relevant questions include those concerning perception of common interest between management and employees, self-image of oneself as a TVA employee, willingness to choose TVA again, reaction to criticism of TVA, telling people about TVA projects, and attendance at TVA social events. An overall index of identification with TVA was computed on the basis of responses to these questions. Employees' scores on this identification index are related to whether or not they left TVA following the study and to whether or not they display a TVA sticker on their car.

A generally high level of identification with the work organization, such as that found at TVA, is not restricted to public service, nonprofit organizations. Data from a private firm indicate that high levels of organizational identification exist among nonsupervisory employees in some private business organizations.

At TVA, there were substantial differences among different work groups and between larger organizational units (especially the two engineering divisions) with respect to the average level of identification with the organization. Why do these units differ in this way? In the following two chapters, we will examine some of the features of organizational life which may help to explain the differences in identification.

---

[10]The very high percentage of "high-identification" responses at the private company raises a suspicion that some employees, lacking union protection, may have distorted their answers. This possibility exists because employees were told that, while their questionnaires would not be seen by anyone at the company, there was an identifying code number (though not a name) on the questionnaire for the University's use. Some persons may have feared that their answers would be seen by company management. However, while it is possible that a few people may have been influenced by such a fear, our general impression of the company personnel policies, of employee morale at the company and of reactions of employees to the questionnaire administration (little concern about confidentiality was expressed) leads us to believe that the responses were, for the most part, candid.

10

PARTICIPATION IN DECISION MAKING AND IDENTIFICATION

We have suggested (Chapter 9) that employee participation in decision making for their work organization will lead to stronger perceptions of shared characteristics with management. These would include perceptions of common goals, common interests, common values, and more nearly common status. We suggested further that, because of its impact on feelings of shared characteristics (as well as the satisfaction which may result from participating), greater employee participation will lead to stronger feelings of solidarity with and loyalty to the organization.

One of the prominent features of TVA as an organization is a formal program of consultation and joint decision making between employee and management representatives, called the cooperative program. The TVA cooperative program is, in fact, probably the outstanding example in the United States today of this type of program. In this chapter we will briefly describe the cooperative programs and some of the variations found in their operations. Then we will examine the relation between the vigor of a cooperative program and the sense of organizational identification, as well as other reactions, of employees covered by that program.[1]

---

[1] Much of the material presented in this chapter concerning the effects of participation in the cooperative program has been presented in an earlier article (Patchen, 1965). The data in the earlier article are slightly different from those presented here, because of the use of a shorter index of identification in the earlier work and the fact that in the earlier analysis fewer persons were included in one of the cooperative programs.

Lastly, we will examine the relation between participation outside the co-operative program, in the more immediate job situation, and feelings of identification with TVA.

THE COOPERATIVE PROGRAM

The cooperative program sees the employees in their organized capacity as among the groups which have a vital interest in the TVA program. Indeed, what group conceivably might have the same intensity of interest—if that interest is properly motivated?

The above quotation is an excerpt from a talk given by Harry Case, former TVA Director of Personnel, at a valley-wide meeting of TVA union-management cooperative conferences in March 1956. It is fairly typical of the kind of sentiment which both management and employee representatives are likely to express at these annual meetings. The co-operative program meetings are likely to be the occasion for such sentiments because the cooperative program is the major formal mechanism through which employees can participate in decision making and thereby, it is hoped, develop a greater sense of involvement in TVA and its purposes.

A cooperative conference or committee is a continuing series of meetings between representatives of management and the unions which represent TVA employees.[2] The unit covered by a conference or committee is usually a fairly large one—like an engineering division or a power plant—although smaller units sometimes have their own conferences. The top executives of the units concerned represent management, while employees are represented about eight to ten employees chosen by men in various parts of the unit. The employee representatives are union members but usually do not hold official union positions. Formal meetings are generally held once a month for several hours. The agendas, especially in the power plants, are usually heavily concerned with im-provements of working methods. For example, reading from one agenda of one Power Plant Cooperative Committee, one notes the following sug-gestions which were being implemented through the cooperative pro-gram : "provisions for hanging hoist or chain-fall on soot blower steam regulating valves"; "completion of catwalk on units 1 and 2 coal trans-port gates"; "hangar rods be put up over pulverizer exhausters on unit

---

[2]Engineering employees are represented in negotiations with management by the TVA Engineers Association. This organization is, technically, a professional association rather than a union, but it performs most of the same functions as do unions at TVA.

1 and 2." There were fourteen other work improvements which were being implemented on the agenda of this one meeting. Work improvements of this kind save TVA a lot of money and often make the work safer or easier for employees. Employees do not get cash awards when their suggestions are adopted, though their accomplishments are usually publicized within the unit and sometimes more widely.

Cooperative meetings also cover many other topics of mutual interest, such as hospitalization plans, training, parking facilities, and community fund drives. Decisions are usually made by consensus rather than by voting; management retains final responsibility for accepting and executing decisions. Information about conference activities is supposed to be given to other employees by their representatives and through printed summaries. During the period between conference meetings, various committees work on projects initiated by the conference and report their progress back to the conference.

The vigor of the cooperative program differs from one unit to another. One variation is in the vigor of support from local management. Some conferences have the full support of local management; some have only half-hearted backing. The importance of a positive management attitude toward the program is indicated in this comment by a steam fitter in one of the steam plants :

> *There was more interest at (name of other unit). More interest in making suggestions and more interest in receiving them. Since it was a smaller installation, you got more recognition for your suggestions to the co-op committee. You really got credit—you received a letter from management everytime one of your suggestions was accepted. They have the same system here but there aren't as many suggestions and not as much notice since it's so big.*

In one engineering division, the management of the division appeared to assign the cooperative program low importance. A lower-level supervisor told us :

> *Now these cooperative conferences don't impress us much here at (division). The things they do don't seem to get to us as much as other parts of TVA. We don't seem to appreciate the benefits. We do get information, suggestions, and the committees are good, but there is no real enthusiasm for them here. Now prior to our present administrator, we felt that management wasn't particularly interested in these conferences and you need that for them to be important to the rest of us.*

There are differences among cooperative programs, too, in the extent to which employees exert real influence at the meetings.

In one steam plant, for example, employees who had been representatives to the cooperative committee, stressed their freedom to speak freely and their relative equality with management in the meetings.

A clerk who had represented the administrative section in that committee said :

> *It's hard to believe, but we all go in there and that's where we hash over our problems. Management has the final say and if something is unreasonable, they have to turn it down, but it is a cooperative, underline cooperative, conference and each side presents its ideas. On some important questions a committee is appointed to look into it. But the employee has as much to say as the employer in most things. If all labor unions take a lesson from TVA, they wouldn't have labor problems!*

An electrician in the same plant said :

> *As union steward, I go to the monthly co-op committee. All the crafts submit suggestions to management and it's discussed around the table. Usually after discussion, a committee is appointed to look into the matter . . . I feel absolutely free to express myself.*

A different picture of decision making in cooperative meetings in another division is given by an engineering associate who had been a representative to the cooperative conference in that division :

> *Any time employees and management get together is beneficial, but I felt that the division director had already set the policy on a lot of problems presented. He gave his answer and the question was promptly dropped.*

Perhaps related in part to the style of decision making within a cooperative program, there are variations in the extent to which employees appear to be interested in the cooperative program and see it as a channel for getting their own ideas seriously considered.

The generally high interest in the program in one steam plant was described by an assistant unit operator in that plant :

> *Yes, we have a cooperative committee here and if you have an idea you draw it up and submit it to the job steward who goes to the monthly meeting. Then they take it and have a committee survey it. And if they think it will work, they'll OK it. I could show you numerous changes around here suggested by employees. I've got three or four changes out there myself. Primarily, mine were safety precautions and making the job easier. I don't believe in doing things the hard way. Labor and management get along very good here. They have a joint cooperative conference once a year and they take ideas there to cover the whole valley. We took a 16 millimeter movie of our coal sampler to the cooperative conference. I worked on the movie and it was one of the big ideas and has been a big money saver for TVA. Labor and management get along very well on cooperation and things here. Anyone can give a suggestion and they'll look at it.*

In an engineering division, however, an electrical engineer told us :

I'm the secretary of the suggestion committee for (this division). At these meetings we read the suggestion and decide when to have a meeting and then at the meeting we talk about it . . . More interest should be taken in making suggestions. Supervisors should encourage people to turn in more. Some people feel their suggestions won't be accepted or don't want to spend the time thinking up or submitting suggestions . . . More people should become interested.

The varying level of interest by employees in different cooperative programs appears related also to variations in the extent to which employees participate in and are kept informed about them. The importance of getting employees directly or indirectly involved in conference activities was pointed out by a woman mathematician who served as a representative to the conference in her division. She remarked :

Most of the benefit comes when the representative comes back from the meeting and tells the people he represents just what happened at the meeting. But very few do . . . Representatives are elected and I served my two terms. The person who goes to the meeting gets the most benefit, so it's a good idea to move it around among different people.

Of course, attendance at meetings, discussion with representatives, and other cooperative program activities take time—even if a limited amount of time. Are the work improvements—as well as the other specific accomplishments of the cooperative program—its total result? If so, there are those—within TVA as well as elsewhere—who would argue that there might be more efficient mechanisms to achieve these results. Why spend top management as well as employee time in these meetings? Perhaps the same suggestions could be elicited through a more usual suggestion system and judged by some competent management group—probably with cash awards for money-saving suggestions.

To this kind of argument, the backers of the cooperative program would answer that the program is more than just a glorified suggestion system. As the quotation at the beginning of this section suggests, there has been the hope that the cooperative program, as a mechanism for employee participation in job decisions, can increase employees' enthusiasm for and dedication to their own work and to the larger purposes of TVA. This is, perhaps, quite a bit to expect from a program whose major meetings usually occur only about once a month. What do our research data have to say on the matter?

Relevant data are available from employees covered in eight administratively separate cooperative programs, in the five geographically separate units of our study. Two of these programs cover the two engineering divisions. Three other cooperative programs (A Programs) cover most employees in each of three power plants. Employees in these main (A) power plant cooperative programs fall into two major groupings : maintenance craftsmen and operating personnel.

Three additional cooperative programs (B Programs) are found in the same three power plants. Most employees covered by the B Programs are found in the laboratory section of each power plant. The B Programs cover a smaller number of employees (approximately 50 employees) than do the A Programs (about 150 employees) in each power plant.

Questions asked concerning the cooperative program were the following :

1. Have you ever served as a representative to the cooperative conference or committee in this unit?

2. Have you ever served on any committees which report to the cooperative conference or committee?

3. How many suggestions have you submitted to the cooperative conference or committee during the past three years?

4. How much do you usually hear about what goes on in the meetings of the cooperative conference or committee of your unit? (Five alternatives from "A full account of what goes on" to "Nothing of what goes on.")

5. How interested are the people you work with in the work of the cooperative conference or committee? (Four alternatives from "They pay little attention to it" to "They pay close attention to it and are very interested in its work.")

6. How much interest in the work of the conference or committee do you think the *management* of your division takes? (Four alternatives from "They pay very little attention to it" to "They pay very close attention to it and are very interested in its work.")

7. How much do you feel the work of the cooperative conference or committee in your unit helps to make TVA a better place to work? (Five alternatives from "Helps a great deal" to "Doesn't help at all.")

8. If you were to submit a good suggestion to the cooperative conference or committee in your unit, how seriously do you think it would be considered? (Three alternatives from "Very serious consideration" to "Little serious consideration; ideas are given only a quick look.")

Each employee was given a numerical score on each question, depending on which response he chose. Mean scores on each question were computed for employees covered by each of the eight cooperative programs. (Scores on most of these measures of interest and participation in the cooperative program differ significantly among programs. The differences are especially large between the two engineering divisions, but significant differences among power plant programs are also found.)

Mean scores were also computed for each work group consisting of employees who report to the same immediate supervisor. There are ninety such work groups in our sample, counting groups in all eight cooperative programs.

Each cooperative program (and each smaller group) was also scored on an index of participation through the cooperative program, based on average responses to four of the above questions (Questions 1, 2, 3, and 8). This index is intended to indicate the extent to which the cooperative program represents a channel for active participation in work decisions.

What is the relation between the vigor of a cooperative program and the attitudes of employees toward their work and toward the work organization?

We find first that, for the eight cooperative programs, there are positive but generally small and nonsignificant correlations between measures of the vigor of a cooperative program and the general job interest of people in that program. We find also generally *negative,* though nonsignificant, correlations between the vigor of the cooperative program and interest in work innovation—perhaps reflecting a tendency for employees to rely on the cooperative program as the main source of job innovations. These data are reported elsewhere (Patchen, 1965).

There are, however, stronger correlations between the vigor of a cooperative program and (1) identification with the work organization, and (2) acceptance of changes introduced into the work situation.[3]

These relations are shown in Table 10-1. The first column of Table 10-1 shows the correlations between scores on identification with TVA and aspects of participation in the cooperative program, for the eight cooperative programs. There is generally a fairly strong positive association between the vigor of a cooperative program and the overall index of identification with TVA. The strongest association is between identification and perception of the extent to which suggestions to the cooperative program are seriously considered ($r = .78$; $p < .05$). Employee identification with TVA is also related to the amount of information employees receive about the cooperative program; to perceived interest of employees and of management in the program; to overall employee evaluation of the cooperative program; to the percentage of employees who have served on a program committee; and to number of suggestions employees reported submitting through the program Despite the small number of cooperative groups, the association between the index of participation through the cooperative program and the index of identification is statistically signifi-

___

[3]The index of identification used for analyses done with the eight cooperative units is a six-item index; it omits the question concerning telling nonfamily members about TVA projects, which was a somewhat peripheral question in the seven-item index.

cant (r = .75; p<.05). Moreover, a scatter plot (see Figure 10-1) indicates that the association between participation and identification is general and is not due to the influence of one or two extreme groups. Further analysis shows also that the association between participation and identification is not an artifact of satisfaction with the job. An overall index of satisfaction shows no association with organizational identification (r = .03 for the eight cooperative programs). Several specific aspects of satisfaction (with pay, promotion, immediate supervisor, and co-workers) also have little or no positive associations with organizational identification. Moreover, neither the overall index of satisfaction nor specific aspects of satisfaction are positively associated with participation in and attitudes toward the cooperative program. In fact, the associations tend to be negative. Thus, the association found between identification with TVA and an active cooperative program cannot be a spurious one caused by the effect of general satisfaction.

TABLE 10-1   **Vigor of the Cooperative Program as Related to Attitudes Toward the Organization and to Acceptance of Changes Introduced on the Job**

(Product-Moment Correlations; N = 8 Cooperative Programs)

Vigor of Co-op Program	*Overall Identification with TVA*[a]	*Acceptance of Change*
1. Amount of information	.63	.89**
2. Perceived group interest in co-op program	.61	.66
3. Perceived interest of management	.68	.41
4. Perceived attention given suggestions	.78*	.78*
5. General evaluation of program	.62	.67
6. Percent who served on co-op committee	.63	.87**
7. Suggestions: No. Reported, 3 years	.43	.32
8. Index of program as channel for active participation (based on 4, 6, 7 above)	.75*	.86**

** p <.01, two-tailed test

* p <.05, two-tailed test

a   Index of identification used for this analysis is based on six items. It omits the item concerning telling nonfamily members about TVA projects, which was included in the seven-item index.

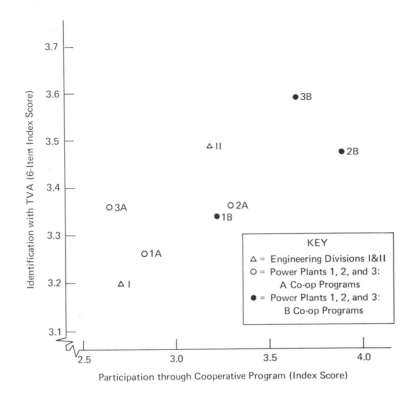

FIGURE 10-1 Identification with TVA as related to participation in the cooperative program (for eight co-op programs)

However, the overall association between participation and identification holds for some items of the identification index and not for others. There is a strong association (r=.79; p<.05) between the index of participation in the cooperative program and feelings of common purpose and goals with management. This is consistent with our expectation that employee participation in decision making will increase perceptions of having things in common with management. There is an even stronger association between participation in the cooperative program and attendance at TVA social events (r=.90; p<.01),[4] and a moderate association (r=.45) between participation and willingness to choose TVA again. How-

---

[4]This correlation is based on seven cooperative programs, since most of those in one program reported hearing of no social events. For the seven programs included, mean scores for attendance at social events are based on Ns smaller than the totals for those units, since some of those in each program reported not hearing of social events in their part of TVA.

ever, among the eight cooperative programs, there are no positive associations (in fact the associations are somewhat negative) between participation
and becoming angry at criticisms of TVA, describing oneself as someone
who works for TVA, or telling people about TVA projects. These
results may indicate that participation in decision making leads employees
to feel greater solidarity with others—especially higher-ups—in the organization but that some participation in an organization's affairs does not
necessarily make one's organizational membership a more important part
of one's life (at least within the narrow range of participation discussed
here).

A comment may also be made here about our suggestion that the
perception of shared characteristics with management may serve as an
intervening variable between participation and feelings of solidarity with
and support of the organization. For the eight cooperative programs the
overall set of correlations (not shown) gives little support to this idea.
Participation is strongly related to perceptions of common purpose with
management; but perceptions of common purpose are positively related
only to willingness to choose TVA again and attendance at social events,
and not to reaction to criticisms of TVA or self-image as a TVA member.
(Data for work groups, discussed below, are more in line with our expectation.)

Work Groups

Since the number of cooperative programs studied is small (eight),
it is of interest also to see how participation in the cooperative program
is related to organizational identification among the ninety immediate
work groups (i.e., subunits of the larger units having cooperative programs). In our analysis of the set of immediate work groups, we have
also examined the relation between participation and identification when
many other variables which may affect identification are held constant.[5]

For immediate work groups, there is a positive but modest association
between participation through the cooperative program and the overall
index of identification with TVA ($r=.31$; partial $r=.19$). Among the
separate items of the identification index, perceptions of a common purpose with management has the strongest association with participation
($r=.30$; partial $r=.28$; $p<.01$); this is consistent with the results for the
larger cooperative programs, where participation has a strong (and much
larger) association with perceptions of common purpose with management. For immediate work groups, participation through the cooperative
program also has positive though modest associations with almost all

---

[5]See Chapter 11 for variables included in partial correlation analysis.

other items of the overall identification index—i.e., with attendance at TVA social events, anger at criticism of TVA, self-image as a TVA person, and willingness to choose TVA again (though not with telling others about TVA projects).

For immediate work groups, the pattern of associations between the index of participation through the cooperative program and the various identification items tends to be consistent, though not completely so, with our expectation that perceptions of having things in common with management may serve as an intervening variable between participation and support of the organization. Participation is associated with percep-tions of common purpose with management; perceptions of common purpose are associated with indicators of solidarity with and support for the organization; and participation is associated with the indicators of solidarity and support but somewhat less strongly than to perceptions of common interest with management.[6]

In discussing the positive association between participation and identi-fication with TVA, we have been assuming that greater participation leads to greater identification—especially to greater perception of common purpose with management. However, another possibility is that prior differences in organizational identification among persons in the various cooperative programs have led to differences in perceptions about the efficacy of the programs and in actual participation in the programs. While this possibility cannot be ruled out completely, it seems very unlikely that the causal relation should go primarily in this direction. Such an interpretation would give us no explanation as to why there should be, initially, large differences in identification with TVA among the various cooperative programs. On the other hand, there are good reasons (as outlined in Chapter 9) why we would expect participation in decision making to lead to greater identification with the work organization. How-ever, it may be that once a sufficient level of identification is present (in part generated by participation) a reciprocal pattern of effects occurs such that more participation leads to greater identification which leads to more participation, etc.

---

[6]For example, participation on the job correlates .30 with perceptions of common purpose with management; perceptions of common purpose correlates .33 with anger at criticism of TVA; and participation correlates .20 with anger at criticism of TVA. For self-image as a TVA person, for willingness to choose TVA again, and for attendance at TVA social events, there is, also, a positive correlation between that item and percep-tions of common interest with management and a positive correlation with participation through the cooperative program that is smaller than the correlation between participa-tion and perceptions of common purpose with management. However, the correlations between each of these items and participation are almost as large as that between percep-tions of common purpose with management and participation. See Blalock (1961, Chapter 3) for a discussion of inferring causal chains from correlational data.

THE COOPERATIVE PROGRAM AND ACCEPTANCE OF CHANGE

A major concern of the cooperative program, as we have noted, is with the improvements of work facilities and methods to make them more efficient, and also with making things safer and more convenient. To what extent is high participation and interest in the cooperative program related to acceptance of changes introduced by management?

To assess acceptance versus resistance to change, the following four questions were asked :

1. Sometimes changes in the way a job is done are more trouble than they are worth because they create a lot of problems and confusion. How often do you feel that changes which have affected you and your job at TVA have been like this?

    (Five alternatives from "Fifty per cent or more of the changes have been more trouble than they're worth" to "Only five per cent or fewer have been more trouble than they're worth.")

2. From time to time changes in policies, procedures, and equipment are introduced by the management. How often do these changes lead to better ways of doing things?

    (Five alternatives from "Changes of this kind never improve things" to "Changes of this kind are always an improvement.")

3. How well do the various people in the plant or offices who are affected by these changes accept them?

    (Five alternatives from "Very few of the people involved accept the changes" to "Practically all of the people involved accept the changes.")

4. In general, how do you *now* feel about changes during the past year that affected the way your job is done?

    (Five alternatives from "Made things somewhat worse" to "Been a big improvement.")

For each individual, an index score of acceptance of change, based on his answers to these questions, was computed. There is evidence that responses to these questions are related to employees' actual behavior on the job. In nine out of ten units where acceptance of change scores were related to supervisors' ratings of willingness "to go along with changes management has made," there was a positive, though low, correlation between individual scores and supervisor ratings of the same individuals.[7] The index of acceptance of change has a marked positive relation to the (six-item) index of identification with TVA ($r = .66$ for the eight cooperative programs) though there is much less than complete overlap between these measures.

---

[7]See Patchen, Pelz, and Allen (1965), Chapter VI.

The data, presented in the second column of Table 10-1, show a strong association between the vigor of a cooperative program and the index of acceptance of change in that program. The association is strongest ($r=$ .89) between the amount of information employees get about the cooperative program and acceptance of change. Acceptance of change is also strongly related to the per cent of employees who served on any committee of the cooperative program ($r=.87$), to perceptions of the consideration given to suggestions ($r=.78$), and to the index of participation through the cooperative program ($r=.86$).

Figure 10-2 shows the scatter plot of the relation between participation in the cooperative program (index scores) and acceptance of change. This plot shows that the association holds separately for each of the three types of work units, i.e., for the two engineering divisions, for the three power plant A Programs, and for the three power plant B Programs— as well as for all eight cooperative programs combined.

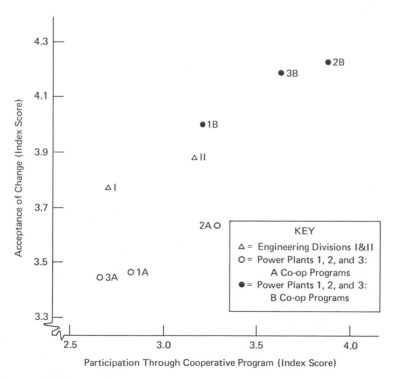

FIGURE 10-2 Acceptance of change as related to participation in the cooperative program (for eight co-op programs)

Why should high employee influence, especially through participation in the cooperative program, be related to increased acceptance of change? We can again rule out the possible explanation that general job satisfaction may be behind both greater participation in the cooperative program and more favorable attitudes. As noted above, there is no association between various aspects of job satisfaction (e.g., with wages, with promotion chances) and participation through the cooperative program. Nor is there any significant association between overall job satisfaction and acceptance of change ($r = .08$) for the eight cooperative programs.

Another possible explanation is that attitudes toward management may play a key role—perhaps as an intervening variable between participation and acceptance of change. Such an explanation would be consistent with the findings by Coch and French (1948) that employee participation resulted in much less hostility toward management.

In the present data, we also find a marked association in the eight cooperative programs between participation in the program and feelings of solidarity (common purpose) with management ($r = .79$). When feelings of solidarity with management are statistically held constant, the correlation between participation through the cooperative program and acceptance of change does drop (from .86 to .54), but a moderate association remains. Therefore, the effect of the cooperative program in fostering feelings of common goals with management appears to explain only part of the program's effect on acceptance of change.

Another part of the explanation may be related to the fact that the changes introduced are, at least in part, not arbitrarily imposed by management at all. Those employees who are well informed about the cooperative program and who participate in it (both actually and psychologically) should be more likely to see work changes as the product of joint consultation between management and employees. Thus, the changes introduced are "theirs" as well as management's, regardless of the extent to which management and employee goals are seen as consistent.

It should be noted that the differences among acceptance of change scores are generally greater among power plant units than between engineering divisions. Also differences in acceptance of change among immediate work groups are more strongly related to the cooperative program participation within power plants than within engineering divisions. It may be that engineering employees are more likely to judge proposed changes by objective professional standards, while the reaction to change of power plant employees is more affected by their participation in the change process.

The overall results are consistent with findings from earlier studies that employee participation in decisions affecting their jobs leads to greater acceptance of necessary job changes. The most notable of the previous studies is the now classic work of Coch and French (1948), already referred to.[8] However, participation in the pajama factory studied by Coch and French was much more direct than in the TVA sites. In the "representation" condition at the pajama factory, all of the operators were present at a meeting at which management explained the need for and nature of changes. Then several operators out of the total of thirteen participated in working out details of the change. Finally, another meeting was held with all operators to present details of the new job. In the TVA cooperative program, there is little direct participation at any given time by most employees. Moreover, in most cooperative programs, the proportion of employees serving as representatives at any one time is much lower than in the pajama factory.[9] The fact that such a less direct program, covering a large organizational unit, can have effects similar to the more intensive program in the pajama factory is especially noteworthy.

PARTICIPATION IN DECISIONS ON THE JOB

Participation through the cooperative program is one channel—reaching right up to division management—through which employees can have an influence on decisions. But there is, of course, a more immediate arena in which employees may have some influence—the work group under more immediate supervisors. To what extent is identification with TVA affected by the amount of control and influence which employees can exert within their own immediate group?

To throw light on this question we make use of a measure of direct participation on the job. This measure, which overlaps the measures of control over goals and control over means discussed earlier,[10] is based on answers to the following questions:

1. If you suggest to your immediate supervisor a way of doing some job, how often does he go along with your suggestion?

    He goes along with my suggestions: (Five alternatives from "About one-tenth of the time or less" to "Almost always.")

---

[8]There are also a number of other studies which indicate that coercive methods produce resistance to influence attempts. See Zipf (1958), Morrison and Levinger (1960).

[9]The ratio of employee representation in the programs covered here were estimated by the author to be roughly as follows: engineering division I, 1:40; engineering division II, 1:25; power plant A programs, 1:20; power plant B programs, 1:8.

[10]The direct participation measure focuses more on influence and on shared decisions with management than do the other measures which include items bearing on autonomy in the work situation.

2. Before your supervisors set deadlines, time limits, or target dates which involve your work, how often do they ask your opinion—either alone or as a member of a group—concerning how long the job will take?

They ask my opinion: (Five alternatives from "9 times out of 10 or more" to 1 time out of 10 or less.")

3. How much say or influence do you have (either alone or together with other people at about your level) when it comes to setting the time schedules for jobs that you work on?

(Five alternatives from "No influence at all" to "A great deal of influence."

Mean scores on the index of direct participation were computed for each of the ninety work groups, each of which is under a different immediate supervisor.[11]

The data show that, for work groups, the amount of direct participation in job decisions has a moderate association ($r = .39$ $p < .01$) with the index of identification with TVA. This association is reduced (partial $r = .20$) when other factors affecting identification are held constant[12] but remains statistically significant.[13]

Looking at the relations of participation to single items of the identification index, the measure of direct participation is most strongly associated with attendance at social events at TVA ($r = .45$; partial $r = .39$). Those in groups with high direct participation are also more likely to say that they would choose TVA again ($r = .48$; partial $r = .19$). There is only a slightly greater disposition in such groups to perceive common goals with TVA management ($r = .21$; partial $r = .13$). In view of our expectation that positive feelings toward the organization will be based, in part, on perceptions of shared characteristics with other organization members, especially management, the latter weak relation requires some explanation. It may be that joint decision making with the most immediate supervisors (which the measure of direct participation taps) creates perceptions of shared characteristics (goals, status, etc.) with immediate supervisors but not with "TVA management." The cooperative program,

---

[11]Work group scores on the index of direct participation correlated $-.44$ with a measure of the discrepancy between actual and desired influence "on what goes on in your present immediate work group" and $-.39$ with a measure of the reported discrepancy in influence between the supervisor and "the non-supervisory employees as a group."

[12]Fifteen other factors, including participation through the cooperative program were held constant in this partial correlation analysis. See Chapter 11 for discussion of other factors included in this analysis. For analyses involving immediate work groups, the seven-item index of identification with TVA was used.

[13]Influence on decisions in the immediate work group is more consistently related to organizational identification for professional than for non professional employees at TVA. See Patchen (1965) for further discussion of this point.

which involves a higher level of management does have a strong association, as we have seen, with perceptions of common purpose with "management."

PARTICIPATION AT TWO LEVELS

A question may be raised about the joint effects of participation in decision making through the cooperative program and in the immediate work situation. Do the effects of participation at one level depend on the level of participation at the other level?

To shed light on this question, work groups were divided into high, medium, and low with respect to (1) participation in the immediate work situation and (2) participation through the cooperative program. This yields nine sets of groups, and for each set, the mean score on the index of identification with TVA was computed.

TABLE 10-2   Identification with TVA (Mean Scores for Work Groups)[a] as Related to Participation in Decision Making Through Cooperative Program and in Immediate Work Group

Participation Through Co-op Program	Participation in Immediate Job Situation		
	Low	*Medium*	*High*
Low	2.86 (12)	3.19 (12)	2.97 (5)
Medium	2.98 (11)	3.21 (13)	3.35 (4)
High	2.89 (8)	3.24 (6)	3.40 (15)

	F	df	p
Participation through co-ops	1.4	2,77	N.S.
Participation immediate job	9.8	2,77	.001
Participation co-op × participation immediate	.9	4,77	N.S.

Note: Figures in parentheses indicate number of groups in each cell.

a   Seven-item index of identification with TVA was used for this analysis. Four work groups were omitted from this analysis because the number of persons answering all relevant questions was too small.

The results, shown in Table 10-2, indicate that when participation through the cooperative program is low, increased participation in the immediate job situation has little effect on identification. However, when participation through the co-op program is high, increased participation in decisions of the immediate work group is associated with higher identification with TVA. The converse also tends to be true. Increased participation through the cooperative program has a much greater effect on organizational identification when employees have high participation in decisions of the immediate work group. These data suggest (though the interaction effect is not statistically significant) that a combination of participation at both levels is most effective in creating a favorable orientation toward the organization. Supplementary analyses of the data (not shown here) show similar results when other measures of participation in the immediate job situation (e.g., perceived discrepancy in influence between employees and their immediate supervisor) are used in combination with the measure of participation through the cooperative program.

These data suggest that the effects of participation in decision making at one organizational level are not independent of participation at other levels. Employees' attitudes toward the work organization appear to be related to their total experience with regard to decision making at several organizational levels.

Finally, it may be noted that an overall index of participation, based primarily on items concerning direct participation and participation through the cooperative program,[14] has a fairly marked association with the index of identification ($r = .56$; $p < .01$ for ninety groups). In fact, among a wide variety of factors correlated with organizational identification in the ninety work groups, the measure of overall participation has the strongest association.

SUMMARY

A major formal program for eliciting employee participation in decision making at TVA is the cooperative program. In each of eight cooperative programs covered by our study, employee and management representatives meet regularly to discuss mutual problems outside the scope of ordinary collective bargaining. Systematic data gathered from

---

[14]The index of overall participation includes the three items composing the index of participation through the cooperative program, the three items composing the index of direct participation in the immediate work situation, two items concerning the free expression of opinions, and one general question concerning the amount of influence which employees exercise in the immediate work situation.

employees indicate that there is a fairly strong positive association between the vigor of a cooperative program (e.g., percentage of employees directly involved in program, attention given to employee suggestions) and the overall level of identification with the work organization. However, this association is not found for all aspects of identification. The results suggest that participation in decision making is likely to lead to a sense of solidarity with others in the organization but does not necessarily make organizational membership more important to the participants.

One of the aspects of identification which is strongly associated with participation in the cooperative program is the perception of common purpose with management. This finding is consistent with our expectation that one of the important effects of participation is on perceptions of things held in common with management. However, the overall results give only weak support to the notion that perceptions of common purpose with management may serve as an intervening variable between participation and other attitudes of solidarity with and support for the organization.

In addition to having stronger identification with TVA, employees in units with vigorous cooperative programs are also likely to accept work changes more readily than do employees in units with less active cooperative programs. The data indicate that this relationship is only partly due to the effect of greater participation on attitudes toward management. Greater acceptance of change in units with active cooperative programs may be due also to perceptions by employees in such units that many of the work changes introduced are the product of joint consultation and are thus "theirs" as much as management's. The significance of the fact that a labor-management consultation program which is based on a system of representation can have powerful effects on employee attitudes was pointed out.

The relationship between organizational identification and direct participation in the immediate job setting (e.g., in decisions about work methods and time limits) was also examined for ninety work groups. A moderate positive association was found between the average amount of participation which members of a work group enjoy and their average level of identification with TVA.

Finally, for the ninety work groups, a measure of overall participation in decision making has the strongest relation to organizational identification of any of a large number of factors examined. Our results suggest that a combination of participation in decision making at both the work group and higher (cooperative program) level may be necessary in order for sizable increases in organizational identification to occur.

11

OTHER
CORRELATES
OF IDENTIFICATION

In the previous chapter, we examined the relation between organizational identification and employee participation, especially through the formal channel for participation at TVA called the cooperative program. Now we ask: What other job and personal characteristics are related to identification with a work organization?

In this chapter we will examine a number of other aspects of the job situation and a number of personal characteristics which may affect identification with TVA. Some of these possible predictors of identification have been discussed in Chapter 9 as factors which would be expected, on theoretical grounds, to be related to identification. In addition, the relation between organizational identification and a number of other organizational and personal factors will be examined.

In trying to account for some of the differences in organizational identification, we will look primarily at differences among work groups— i.e., men working under the same immediate supervisor. Work group differences are studied more closely than individual differences because (1) identification tends to cluster among work groups,[1] (2) many of the variables which will be related to identification—e.g., participation in

---

[1] The F ratio for ninety groups is 1.94; p $<.05$.

immediate work decisions, frequency of time deadlines—are largely characteristic of work groups rather than individuals; and (3) correlations for individuals are generally smaller than correlations for work groups. However, some factors which are primarily individual—especially personality needs—are examined primarily at the individual level and correlations for individuals will be examined at other points as well.

It may be noted that in dealing with the work group ($N=90$) as the primary unit of analysis, the analysis differs from that concerning the cooperative program. That analysis centred primarily on differences among the eight cooperative programs and so the cooperative program was the most meaningful unit of analysis.

In the sections which follow we will examine in turn the relation between identification with TVA and (1) organizational rewards; (2) identification with occupation; (3) job opportunities elsewhere; (4) length of TVA service; (5) relation to co-workers; (6) opportunity for achievement on the job; (7) personality needs; (8) opportunity for achievement; (9) interpersonal relations with supervisors, and (10) free expression of opinion on the job. After examining the associations between each of these factors and identification with TVA, we will examine their relative impact and their total impact (together with participation in decision making) on identification with TVA.

SATISFACTION WITH PAY

The monetary reward system of an organization, we have noted, may affect employees' feelings in at least two ways. First, the way in which rewards are distributed may affect employees' perceptions about the extent to which management shares a concern for their welfare. In this way, the reward system can affect employees' feelings of solidarity with the organization and ultimately their loyalty to it. Secondly, and more pragmatically, the nature of the reward system may affect employees' loyalty to the organization by influencing their perception of the extent to which they are deriving benefits from their organizational membership.

At TVA, there are, to our knowledge, no dramatic differences among various units in the way that material rewards are distributed (e.g., no profit-sharing or bonus plans). There are, however, some differences in how employees feel about the pay they are receiving.

We asked employees, "How satisfied are you with (your) present salary?" Each person could check one of five alternatives from "not at all satisfied" to "completely satisfied."

Satisfaction with pay for one's present job varied considerably among employees. For all TVA employees covered, 43 per cent said they were "generally satisfied" or "completely satisfied"; 29 per cent said they were "fairly satisfied"; and 27 per cent said they were "not at all satisfied" or "not too satisfied." Various types of work units also varied considerably in their degree of satisfaction with pay. For example, in one drafting service unit, 53 per cent of employees were not at all or not too satisfied, while in an electrical maintenance unit, only 7 per cent gave these responses.

Now what is the relation between satisfaction with pay and identification with TVA? For the ninety work groups, there is a small positive correlation between average satisfaction with pay($r=.27$) and the index of identification with TVA,[2] but this association disappears (partial $r = -.01$) when other factors affecting identification are held constant.[3] Among the separate items of the identification index, there is some positive association ($r=.33$; partial $r=.17$) between pay satisfaction and feelings of common interest with management. However, satisfaction with pay has little or no association with other items of the identification index—e.g., labeling oneself as a TVA person, willingness to choose TVA again, attending TVA social events, and getting angry at criticism of TVA. Thus, while disssatisfaction with pay does tend to create feelings of estrangement from management, this tendency is not strong enough to affect overall attitudes toward the organization. It may be that in other work settings, where feelings about pay are stronger in intensity, satisfaction with pay will have a greater effect on organizational identification. However, in view of the frequent emphasis on wage rates as the key element in labor-management relations, the present data are noteworthy in suggesting the possibility that the issue of pay may frequently be less important than nonmaterial factors (e.g., participation in decision making) as a determinant of attitudes toward the work organization.

---

[2]For individuals the correlation between identification with TVA and satisfaction with pay is .22.

[3]The predictors used in the multiple and partial correlation analyses reported in this chapter are as follows: (1) compliments by supervisors for good work; (2) solidarity with co-workers; (3) opportunity to express complaints; (4) satisfaction with pay; (5) satisfaction with promotion; (6) identification with occupation; (7) participation through the co-op program; (8) participation in immediate work situation; (9) job opportunities elsewhere; (10) whether grew up in Tennessee; (11) chances for promotion; (12) perceived basis of promotion; (13) frequency of time limits for work; (14) chance to do what best at; (15) difficulties in getting needed resources for work; and (16) length of service.

PROMOTION CHANCES

Another important reward in an organization is promotion. What is the relation between organizational identification and chances for promotion?

We asked TVA employees these questions concerning their promotion chances:

1. In your opinion, about what percentage of people in TVA of your grade and seniority, doing your type of work, will be promoted to a higher grade in the next five years?

    (7) ——————— 90% or more
    (6) ——————— About 75 per cent
    (5) ——————— About 50 per cent
    (4) ——————— About 25 per cent
    (3) ——————— About 10 per cent
    (2) ——————— About 5 per cent
    (1) ——————— Less than 5 per cent

2. How many grades up can you expect to be promoted during the rest of the time you work for TVA?

    (0) ——————— None
    (1) ——————— One
    (2) ——————— Two
    (3) ——————— Three
    (4) ——————— Four or more grades up

Among steam plant employees, especially the craftsmen, the great majority (over 75 per cent) thought that only a very few people (10 per cent or less) in their job category would be promoted in the next five years. These perceptions reflect the fact that many men had reached the top nonsupervisory grade (e.g., journeyman craftsmen) and that very few supervisory slots become open. However, a few steam plant employees, like the assistant operators, could expect to be promoted at least one grade in the next few years. With regard to "the rest of the time you work for TVA," most steam plant employees were more optimistic, with about one-third expecting one promotion, and another one-third expecting two or more eventual promotions. (Five per cent said they expected to go up four or more grades.)

In the engineering divisions, where young engineers typically move up a number of grades before promotions slow down, perceptions of chances for people like themselves "in the next five years" were more optimistic than in the steam plants. Almost half of the engineering employees thought that half or more of the people in their category would be promoted during this five-year period. With regard to "the rest of the time you work for TVA," over half of the engineering personnel expected to go up two or more grades. However, about a third expected only one promotion and 13 per cent expected none.

In addition to the questions concerning promotion chances, we asked employees, "How satisfied are you with (your) chances for promotion?" Responses showed considerable discontent with promotion opportunities.

Almost half of all TVA employees said that they were "not at all" or "not too satisfied" with their promotion chances; however, one-fifth said they were "fairly satisfied," and one-third said they were "generally satisfied" or "completely satisfied." Satisfaction in the engineering divisions and steam plants is about the same, despite the differences in actual promotion chances for employees in the two types of sites. It is of interest to note that, for ninety TVA work groups, the likelihood of promotion has little relation to satisfaction with promotion chances ($r = -.07$). This result is consistent with the findings concerning promotion chances and satisfaction in the U.S. Army during World War II (Stouffer and others, 1949). The explanation suggested by these researchers was that the standard of reference concerning promotion was different for different Army units. This explanation seems quite applicable also to the TVA situation. Engineers are likely to compare themselves to other engineers, who are likely to be fairly mobile, while the "blue-collar" men in the steam plants are likely to compare themselves to other blue-collar men whose promotion chances are probably not generally great.

Now what effect do differences in promotion chances and in satisfaction with promotion chances have on identification with the organization?

Regarding perceived promotion chances, the data, both for individuals and for groups, show only a very weak positive association between such chances and the index of identification with TVA. For the ninety work groups, the correlation between average identification score and average probability of a promotion is exactly zero. The correlation between average identification and average number of promotions expected is $-.02$; the partial correlation, holding other things constant, is .14. Partial correlations between chances for promotion and the separate items of the identification index are very small, with the exception of a tendency among those employees who see good promotion chances to be more likely to label themselves as TVA members.

Why is the association between identification and perceived promotion chances generally a small one? We suggested earlier that the possibility of rising in the organization may make one feel more like, or at least potentially like, those in higher positions. In small and expanding organizations where an employee can hope to rise to top management, any such feelings of potential similarity would extend to top management. But for most employees in fairly big and nonexpanding organization like TVA, there is little possibility, even for those with the best promotion chances, to rise into top management or even close to it. Thus those with the better promotion chances at TVA could not be expected, on those grounds, to have greater feelings of shared characteristics with management.

It may be, too, that organizational identification is not affected as much by variations in the probability of promotion as by variations in the extent to which promotion is tied to the success of the organization or organizational units. Having one's own advancement tied to organizational success may create a perception of shared interest which would foster feelings of solidarity with and loyalty to the organization.

The association between identification and *satisfaction* with promotion chances is somewhat greater than that between identification and perceived amount of promotion possible.[4] This positive association is consistent with our expectation that people will feel more loyalty to an organization from which they derive, or expect to derive, important satisfactions. However, this association is still, both for individuals and for work groups, a modest one. For the ninety work groups, the correlation is .26 (p<.05); the partial r is .16, a nonsignificant association. Correlations and partial correlations between satisfaction with promotion and the separate items of the identification index are also modest. It is interesting that satisfaction with promotion has a smaller association with perceptions of common interest with management (r=.21) than does satisfaction with pay (r=.33). It may be that most employees see the amount of promotion opportunity as largely out of management's control; this would not be true of pay, which is negotiated directly with TVA management.

IDENTIFICATION WITH OCCUPATION

One factor which may conceivably affect organizational identification is the extent of identification with one's own occupation or occupational groups—i.e., unions or professional associations. Where there is hostility and conflict between management and occupational groups within a work organization, the employees may see themselves as sharply distinct from management and may be forced to choose between conflicting loyalties. At TVA, such union-management conflict is relatively slight, and so

---

[4]Sirota (1959) found a fairly small, but statistically significant, positive association between satisfaction with promotion and favorable attitude toward management in an electronics company.

it is not necessary for most TVA employees to make such a stark choice.[5] However, one may wonder whether a strong commitment to an occupation or an occupational group may not reduce feelings of identification with a particular work organization.

To assess a person's commitment to his occupation, we asked a number of questions concerning such matters as whether he would go into the same occupation again, whether he would wish to have his son enter the same occupation, time spent outside of work reading about occupation-connected things, and activities in unions or professional societies. (The seven relevant questions are given in Chapter 6.) For each individual, answers to these questions were combined to form an identification with occupation index. For each of the ninety work groups, mean scores were also computed. In general, work groups composed primarily of professional engineers (in the engineering divisions) scored higher on occupational identification than did other groups, although some power plant groups also scored high.

The data show only a negligible negative correlation ($r = -.04$; partial $r = -.05$) between identification with occupation and the overall index of identification with organization (TVA). There is, moreover, essentially no association between organizational identification and the most "behavioral" aspect of the occupational identification measure—attendance at occupational (i.e., union or professional association) meetings. Nor are there any notable associations between attendance at occupational meetings and responses to any of the single items of the index of identification with TVA.

There are, however, negative associations between overall occupational identification and several of the items composing the overall index of identification with TVA. Work groups which are more strongly identified with their occupations are less likely to assert that they would choose TVA again if given the chance ($r = -.40$; $p < .001$). This association decreases but remains statistically significant (partial $r = -.22$; $p < .05$) when other things—including job opportunities elsewhere—are held constant. This lesser attachment to TVA is probably related to the fact that work groups which feel more strongly identified with their occupations are also somewhat less likely to have a feeling of common purpose with management (partial $r = -.21$; $p < .05$). It probably reflects also a lesser sense among

---

[5]There were, however, some employees of one engineering division who reported that their division management preferred that engineers did not join the TVA Engineers Association and that therefore some employees felt they had to choose between joining this Association and retaining the favor of division management.

those with strong occupational identification that they are "getting things out of" their organizational association.[6]

On the other hand, groups with stronger occupational identification are no less likely to tell people about TVA projects or to label themselves as TVA men. They are only slightly less likely to attend TVA social events or to express anger when TVA is criticized. (That those who are strongly identified with their occupations are also more interested in their work is suggested by a correlation of .46 between occupational identification and the index of interest in work innovation.)

In general, these data suggest that identification with an occupational group tends to produce somewhat lesser feelings of solidarity with and loyalty to the work organization, but that this effect is weak. It may be that the lessened emphasis on things in common with other organization members, as opposed to occupational peers, is somewhat counterbalanced by the greater sharing of interest in work goals which occupational identification brings.

JOB OPPORTUNITIES ELSEWHERE

We have noted earlier that a person's sense of identification with a work organization may be affected by his probable chances to leave that organization at some future time. In the work situation, this becomes the question of how good the person's chances are to get a job elsewhere.

Job opportunities differ primarily because of variations in the demand for the skills and training of different occupational groups. To get a quantitative estimate of some of these differences, we asked personnel specialists at TVA[7] to rate independently the job opportunities of various occupational groups under their jurisdiction. The rating form gave these instructions :

For persons in each of the locations and occupations listed below, how good would you judge their chances of getting jobs outside TVA which pay an annual income as high or higher than what they make at TVA? Consider only opportunities for jobs which are likely to be known to employees and which represent real and practical alternatives for them. Jobs anywhere in the world are relevant, insofar as they are likely to be known to employees.

---

[6]Neither satisfaction with pay nor satisfaction with promotion can account for these results, since both of these satisfactions were controlled in the partial correlation analysis. However, the level of satisfaction with other aspects of the job may help account for the association between occupational identification and disinclination to choose TVA again.

[7]Four persons rated the job opportunites for steam plant occupational groups, and two persons rated the job chances of occupational groups in an engineering division. Ratings were not obtained for some occupational groups in the second engineering division.

For each occupational group listed (e.g., mechanical engineers, engineering aides, instrument mechanics, painters, machinists, etc.), each rater placed the group in one of the following categories: excellent chance, good chance, fair chance, poor chance, very poor chance, can't judge. In general, judges' ratings of the same occupational groups were closely similar for each group. A numerical score was assigned, representing the average rating of judges on the five-point scale of opportunities for jobs outside TVA.

There were wide differences in the scores assigned to various occupational groups. Among the highest occupational groups were engineering personnel who were rated as having between good and excellent chances for outside jobs, though there was some variation among the engineering specialties (civil, mechanical, electrical). Other occupational groups rated high included instrument mechanics, electricians, machinists, steam fitters, sheet-metal workers, and asbestos workers. As one personnel officer rater noted in a letter, "there are shortages in the country of engineers, chemists, and skilled craftsmen. Therefore these employees can, at the present time, get jobs nearly any place and any time they wish."

At the lower range of the ratings of outside job chances (between "poor" and "very poor") are such occupational groups as materials testers, auxiliary unit operators, clerks, and engineering aides, who are relatively unskilled. One personnel man commented: "There are no shortages in the lower skilled workers and their chances are poor of getting a job outside TVA that would pay as much as TVA."

Occupational groups whose outside job chances were intermediate (averaging close to "fair") included operators and assistant operators in the steam plants, painters, blacksmiths, and analytical chemists.

In addition to the scores which were assigned to members of each occupational group, a mean score on outside job chances was computed for the members of each work group (sometimes composed of several occupational specialties). These "outside job chance" scores were then correlated with scores on the measures of identification with TVA.

These data show that there is substantially no relation between chances for outside jobs and overall organizational identification. For ninety work groups, the correlation between outside job chances and the overall index of identification is $-.02$. This association remains essentially zero when other factors affecting identification are held constant and is close to zero for individuals as well as for work groups.

There is a tendency for those with better chances for outside jobs to show less commitment to their organizational membership—being slightly less likely to describe themselves in terms of their TVA membership ($r =$

—.20; partial r = —.13) or to say they would choose TVA again (r = —.34; partial r = —.07). But those with good outside job chances are as likely as others to see common goals with TVA management and to report anger when TVA is criticized; groups whose members have good job chances elsewhere also have significantly better attendance than others at TVA social events.

The net lack of association between outside job chances and overall organizational identification may be due, in part, to the fact of those with good outside chances and low organizational identification having already left TVA. This would tend to leave at TVA, among those who had good outside chances, only those with relatively high identification with TVA. While this mechanism may operate to some extent, there are still many people at TVA, especially young engineers, who have only a few years service and who have yet to make a long-range choice about staying with or leaving TVA. Thus, additional explanation of these results seems to be required.

It seems likely that, while the realistic possibility of leaving the organization may make less salient some similarities with other organization members—i.e., the fact of common membership and long-term sharing of fate—it does not necessarily affect other perceptions of shared interests and shared goals, such as those which derive from the work itself or from the cooperative program. And while outside job chances mean that many important satisfactions can be derived from other organization memberships as well as from this one (and may even reduce current satisfactions through making certain invidious comparisons salient), the pressure of outside opportunities does not change the fact that many important, and even fairly unique, satisfactions (e.g., through participation in the cooperative program) may be derived from one's present organizational ties. The present data suggest that outside job opportunities have a much less important effect on organizational identification than does the nature of a man's experiences in the organization to which he currently belongs.

LENGTH OF SERVICE

As in most organizations there is at TVA considerable variation among employees in the amount of time they have worked for this organization, although the great majority have worked for TVA for two or more years (see Appendix A). There is also variation among work groups in this respect, from some engineering units composed heavily of young engineers recently out of school to some steam plant maintenance units staffed by old-timers who have worked for TVA for many years.[8]

To what extent does the sheer length of time that men work for an organization lead them to feelings of identification with it? For the overall index of identification with TVA, the data show for ninety groups a small (.23) positive correlation between mean seniority and mean identification scores. However, when other factors affecting identification are held constant, this small association drops to close to zero (partial $r = .03$). (For individuals there is, likewise, very little association between length of service and scores on the overall index of identification ($r = .13$).)

There is, however, a stronger association between length of service and several items of the overall identification index—especially the readiness to respond to the question, "Who are you?" by saying, "I work for TVA" (for ninety groups, $r = .31$; partial $r = .24$; $p < .05$). In fact, among sixteen factors used in a multiple correlation analysis, length of service has one of the two strongest associations with readiness to label oneself as an organization member.[9] It appears, therefore, that men who have worked for TVA for a long time are more likely than others to incorporate this role into their personal identity. Such self-labeling for longer-service men may arise in part out of perceptions of certain shared characteristics with TVA men. One important shared characteristic is simply the fact of working for TVA. Those with greater length of service probably see themselves as more likely to remain at TVA and so the fact of working for TVA is an enduring characteristic which they will continue to share with other TVA men (along with a common fate in some respects). As the permanence of their association becomes clearer, so also, it seems, this organization membership begins to assume greater importance. Men in groups with longer average service are also somewhat more likely to say that they would choose TVA again over other places ($r = .35$; partial $r = .16$) and to report getting "mad" about criticisms of TVA ($r = .28$; partial $r = .17$).

However, greater length of service does not lead to stronger feelings of common purpose with TVA management, nor to greater attendance at TVA social events. Men in groups with longer average service are also somewhat less likely than others to tell people about TVA projects, perhaps indicating some loss of interest in the work among those with greater service. In general these data suggest that while greater length of service is likely to make stronger the self-image as an organization member, it

---

[8]For work groups, the mean length of employees' service is from five to nine years. Two-thirds of work groups fall within one response category on either side—i.e., within the range from "three to four years" to "ten to fourteen years."

[9]For individuals, the correlation between length of service and choice of the "I work for TVA" response is .23.

will not necessarily bring a heightened sense of common interest with management or of active involvement in the organization's activities.

RELATIONS TO CO-WORKERS

The relation of the individual to an organization is in large part a matter of his relation to other organization members. Some of these other people are his supervisors and higher management. But other contacts and work relationships are with people at about his own level. He may work in physical proximity to some co-workers and have various levels of technical and functional interdependence with others. Thus, for example, the mechanical engineer at TVA may have to check his "drawings" with electrical and civil engineers working on the same installation in order to see that his drawings are compatible with theirs; he may also have to work closely with people in the drafting service. In the power plant, the materials tester may have to talk things over with the chemical lab analyst to make sure that the coal samples brought for analysis are being prepared correctly. The auxiliary operator may have to consult with the operator of a power unit to see that he is checking the proper valves.

Individuals and units may be more or less interdependent with others in their work. Moreover, their relations with others may be more or less cooperative and friendly. One might expect that individuals who experience cooperative, friendly relations with co-workers would come to feel more of a sense of common interest and solidarity with these co-workers than would individuals whose relationships within the organization were strained and even hostile. To the extent that one's network of co-workers symbolizes the larger work organization (and is not sharply distinguished from "the bosses"), the nature of the relations with co-workers might be expected to affect identification with the larger work organization.

To assess the positiveness of relations with co-workers, the following questions were asked :

1.   Compared to people you've worked with elsewhere (other firms, other parts of TVA, the Armed Forces, etc.), how much do the people you work with in your present job help each other out?
     People I work with now help each other out:

     (1) —————— Much less than other people I've worked with
     (2) —————— A little less
     (3) —————— About the same
     (4) —————— A little more
     (5) —————— Much more than other people I've worked with
     —————— Never worked with any other groups

2.   Compared to people you've worked with elsewhere (other firms, other parts of TVA, the Armed Forces, etc.), how close do you feel to the people you work with in your present job?

    (5) _____ Much closer now than to other people I've worked with
    (4) _____ A little closer now
    (3) _____ About the same as other places
    (2) _____ A little less close
    (1) _____ Much less close than to other people I've worked with
    _____ Never worked with any other group

3.   Following are some kinds of people with whom you may now have or have previously had contact. Rank them according to *how close you feel to them personally*. Put a *number 1* next to the kind of group which, in general, you feel closest to; put a *number 2* next to the group you feel second closest to; put a *number 3* next to the group you feel least close to.

    _____ Your neighbors
    _____ Your relatives, other than your immediate family
    _____ People you work with at TVA

It may be noted that while the term "people you work with" does not exclude TVA management, this phrase and the context of the questions concerns mainly nonmanagement co-workers.

For each employee an index of solidarity with co-workers was computed, by averaging his scores on each of the three questions.[10] A mean score for each group of employees under the same immediate supervisor was also computed.

To assess the interdependence among employees, the following questions were asked:

1.   If the other people you have contact with on the job don't do *their* jobs right or on time, how often would this create problems for *your own* work?

If this happened, it would create problems for my work:

    (5) _____ Almost always
    (4) _____ Usually
    (3) _____ About half the time
    (2) _____ Occasionally
    (1) _____ Very rarely or never

---

[10]While mean scores on the index of solidarity with co-workers were computed for employees under the same immediate supervisor, the index does not necessarily represent only solidarity within this group, since each individual may have working relations with persons under other supervisors.

2. *How many* people with whom you have contact on the job could create problems for *your* work if they didn't do *their* jobs right or on time?

     (0) ⸻⸻ None of them could create problems for me
     (1) ⸻⸻ One
     (2) ⸻⸻ Two
     (3) ⸻⸻ Three
     (4) ⸻⸻ Four
     (5) ⸻⸻ Five to ten
     (6) ⸻⸻ More than ten could create problems for me

3. If *you* didn't do a good job on something or didn't do it fast enough, how often would this create problems for someone you have contact with on the job?
If this happened, it would create problems for someone I have contact with:

     (5) ⸻⸻ Almost always
     (4) ⸻⸻ Usually
     (3) ⸻⸻ About half the time
     (2) ⸻⸻ Occasionally
     (1) ⸻⸻ Very rarely or never

4. If *you* didn't do your own job right, for *how many* other people with whom you have contact on the job would this create problems?

     (0) ⸻⸻ None of them would have problems
     (1) ⸻⸻ One
     (2) ⸻⸻ Two
     (3) ⸻⸻ Three
     (4) ⸻⸻ Four
     (5) ⸻⸻ Five to ten
     (6) ⸻⸻ More than ten of them would have problems

Two indices were computed for each individual and for each work group based on these data. The first index, representing the product of scores on the first two questions, is the index of dependence upon others. The second index representing the product of the latter two questions, is the index of dependence of others upon oneself. For ninety work groups, the two measures of dependence are strongly correlated ($r = .66$).

What, then, is the association between organizational identification and the nature of the relations among co-workers?

The data show, first, that the more the members of a work group feel solidarity with their co-workers, the higher they score on the index of identification with TVA ($r = .45$; $p < .01$).[11] When other factors affect-

---

[11]Using our TVA data, Brown (1964) reports a nonsignificant but negative correlation ($-.21$) for twenty-six major units between a slightly different identification measure and the measure which we are calling solidarity with co-workers. However, the measure of interpersonal solidarity is probably less appropriate to the large units in Brown's analysis. Also, Brown did not control this correlation by other factors which may affect identification.

ing identification are controlled, this association is reduced (partial $r = .24$), but is still statistically significant ($p < .05$). Among the items making up the identification index, those which are most strongly related to solidarity with co-workers are (1) feeling of common purpose with management ($r = .40$; partial $r = .28$); and (2) attendance at TVA social events ($r = .34$; partial $r = .25$).

The first of these findings indicates that it is possible for feelings of solidarity with management to be part of a broader pattern of, and perhaps even a generalization of, feelings of solidarity with co-workers. However, it seems probable that this will not be the case in all organizations. Where there are sharp lines of cleavage between management and lower-level employees, close ties to people at the same level may bring no increase (or even a decrease) in sense of identification with the organization as a whole.

At TVA, the perception of common purpose with management which accompanies feelings of solidarity with co-workers may contribute to certain attitudes and behavior showing solidarity with TVA—i.e., to self-description as a TVA man, and to attendance at TVA social events. However, the pattern of correlations indicates that perceptions of common purpose with management cannot be the sole intervening variable between solidarity with co-workers and such pro-organizational attitudes and behavior.[12] Undoubtedly, those who feel solidarity with their co-workers tend to show more "loyal" attitudes and behavior—especially attendance at social events—in part because the work organization is a source of social satisfaction for them.

Another issue on which the data cast some light is that of the relation between interdependence of co-workers and organizational identification. One might suppose, as we have already suggested, that when the work of each employee is tied to that of co-workers by strong functional interdependence, these employees might also feel a heightened sense of psychological bonds to their co-workers and perhaps also to the organization of which they are all a part. However, the data do not support such an expectation. Neither dependence of employees on others in the organization nor the closely related phenomenon of having others dependent on them is associated with identification with TVA; there are, in fact, small negative associations.[13]

---

[12]The zero-order correlations between solidarity with co-workers and the items reflecting pro-organization attitudes and behavior are about equal to the correlations between perceptions of common purpose with management and the other pro-organization items.

[13]Using our TVA data, but a different index of task interdependence, Brown (1964) found a more marked negative correlation between task interdependence and organizational identification ($r = -.57$), for twenty-six major TVA units (larger units than those studied here).

The lack of positive association between task interdependence and organizational identification appears to be due in part to the fact that interdependence does not necessarily bring feelings of solidarity with co-workers. (The correlations between solidarity with co-workers and the two measures of dependence are −.07 and −.06.) Moreover, there is a tendency for those who are more interdependent with co-workers to experience more frustration in doing their jobs. Work groups which score high on their dependence on others, and on dependence of others on them, tend to report more often that they are not "able to get information, tools, or materials needed to carry out my job properly" (r=.17 and .20). It may be that any positive effects of interdependence with others (e.g., in fostering perceptions of forming an organic whole) are counterbalanced by the frustrations and occasional resentments which come from interdependence.

PERSONALITY NEEDS

To what extent are feelings of identification with the work organization a function of personality? While our information on the personalities of people in our sample is limited, we do have measures of two important personality characteristics which are relevant to the work situation. The first is an eight-item measure of need for affiliation which is adapted from Murray (1938). In the adaptation of the items for this study, a person indicates whether each of seven statements describes him well or not. Examples of the items are:

1. The statement: "I make a point of keeping in close touch with the doings and interest of my friends"

    _____ describes me pretty well
    _____ does not describe me very well

2. The statement: "I generally would accept a social invitation rather than do something by myself"

    _____ describes me pretty well
    _____ does not describe me very well

Individual scores on the measure of need for affiliation show only tiny and nonsignificant associations with the overall index of organizational identification and with the component items of the identification index. The correlation between need affiliation scores and scores on the overall index of identification with TVA is .08. These data indicate, then, no substantial association between the need for affiliation and organizational identification.[14]

A second personality characteristic on which we have some data is the strength of the need for achievement (relative to the strength of fear of failure). The measure used was a shortened, eleven-item version of a scale developed by O'Connor and Atkinson (see Chapter 6). As with need for affiliation, there is no noticeable relation between the strength of need for achievement and the amount of identification with TVA. For individuals, the correlation between scores on the need achievement measure and scores on the overall index of identification is $-.05$. Correlations between need achievement scores and single items composing the identification index are also very small and not statistically significant.

The lack of association found in our data between personality needs and organizational identification does not, of course, mean that no such association exists. First, it may be that certain personality characteristics will help to produce identification only in certain situations. For example, need for affiliation may be related to organizational identification only in situations of strong group cohesiveness or warm interpersonal relations with supervisors. (Unfortunately, because of the need to delimit our analysis, we could not pursue such possibilities further.) Secondly, it may be that personality characteristics not considered in this anlysis are associated with organizational identification. For example, there is some data from other work (G. Allport, 1954) which suggest that persons who score high on a measure of "authoritarian personality" may show a stronger attachment to organizations than do low authoritarians. Also, a personality dimension directly relevant to our theoretical conception of identification (see Chapter 9) would be the propensity to perceive similarities between oneself and others—a possible trait which we have not attempted to measure.

Yet, despite these necessary reservations about the limitations of these findings, it is noteworthy that the personality differences we did measure —especially need for affiliation—show so little overall relation to identification with TVA, as compared to situational variables like participation in decision making and solidarity with co-workers. These data suggest, at least tentatively, that personality variables may be of lesser impor-

---

[14]Using our TVA data, Brown (1964) reports a correlation of $-.38$ (p $<.05$) for twenty-six major organizational units between average need for affiliation and a measure of organizational identification. However, there is no evidence presented to show that the average level of need for achievement differs significantly among these organizational units. Moreover, since the association found was not examined when other variables affecting identification were controlled, it may well be a spurious one.

tance in determining organizational identification than are the features of the job situation.

OPPORTUNITY FOR ACHIEVEMENT ON JOB

In previous chapters we have examined the relation between job motivation and the extent to which the job provides opportunities for achievement. Now we ask : What is the relation between opportunities for achievement on the job and feelings of identification with the work organization.

To shed light on this question, we computed correlations for ninety work groups, between scores on the index of identification with TVA and scores on job characteristics which may affect the opportunity, and reward, for achievement on the job.

One such job characteristic is the level of work difficulty, which, as we have seen in previous chapters, has marked associations with measures of job motivation. However, job difficulty has only a very small and nonsignificant correlation $(r = .08)$ with the identification measure. It may be that while challenging work evokes interest in the work itself, it makes little contribution to the sense of shared goals and interest which, we have suggested, are important for organizational identification.

Other achievement-relevant factors which show little relation to organizational identification are feedback on work performance and fre quency of time limits. There are statistically significant but fairly small associations between identification and chance to finish things $(r = .21;$ $p < .05)$, control over job methods $(r = .29; p < .01)$,[15] and difficulty in getting information, tools, or materials $(r = -.24; p < .05)$.

The achievement-related factor which shows the strongest association with the identification index is the chance to do what one is best at $(r = .42;$ partial $r = .19)$. Among the various items of the identification index, chance to do what one is best at is most strongly related to feelings of common goals with TVA management $(r = .38;$ partial $r = .23)$. It appears, therefore, that when men are doing the kind of work they want to do, they see more in common between their own goals (e.g., doing a job well, or on time) and the goals of the organization. Under such circumstances, they are less likely to feel a conflict between the work goals of the organization and their own personal desires, including the desire for self-expression.

---

[15]Brown (1964), using our TVA data, reports sizable positive correlations between an index of identification with TVA and a measure of "autonomy of means" $(r = .60)$ and "autonomy of ends" $(r = .61)$. These correlations are for twenty-six major TVA units.

The pattern of correlations between perceived chance to use one's abilities and the various identification items is consistent with the possibility that perceptions of common goals with management act as an intervening variable between the chance to use one's best abilities and self-image as a TVA member.[16] The pattern of correlations also suggests that perceptions of common interest with management is not the only intervening variable between chance to use one's abilities and (1) willingness to choose TVA again, and (2) anger at criticism of TVA. The chance to use one's best abilities may also affect these indicators of "loyalty" to TVA by increasing the extent to which important personal satisfactions are derived from organizational membership. Consistent with this latter possibility, there are significant positive associations between average chance for people to use their best skills and pride in work ($r = .29$) and between pride in work and overall identification with TVA ($r = .33$). Pride in work is related especially to telling family members about TVA projects and expressed willingness to choose TVA again, and is also related significantly to anger at criticism of TVA.

INTERPERSONAL RELATIONS WITH SUPERVISORS

A question of some interest is the extent to which employees' feelings of solidarity with the larger oganization are affected by their interpersonal relations with the supervisor or supervisors with whom they have contact. In this study we have relatively little information concerning the interpersonal relations between employees and their supervisors. There is, however, data from answers to one question which may indicate something about the warmth of these relations. The question is:

> If you do an outstanding job on something, how likely are you to be complimented by one of your supervisors?
> (Six response categories from "almost always" to "almost never")

We noted in Chapter 6 that TVA employees whose supervisors show appreciation of their efforts seem quite pleased about this and that employees who feel that their supervisors do not recognize their efforts are often angry about this. We noted also in the earlier chapter that employees' responses about the likelihood of supervisor compliments for

---

[16]The correlation between chance to use one's skills and perception of common interest with management is .38; between perception of common interest and self-description as a TVA member, .34; between chance to use one's best abilities and self-description as a TVA member, .13. See Blalock (1961, Chapter 3) for a discussion of inferring causal sequences from correlations among variables.

good work differ greatly among the various work units. Do such differences make a difference for employee identification with TVA?

For the ninety work groups, we find a moderate positive correlation ($r = .36$) between the likelihood of supervisory praise for good work and the overall index of identification with TVA. However, when other factors affecting identification are held constant, this association goes down to approximately zero (partial $r = -.01$). The likelihood of supervisory compliments even has a somewhat negative association with perceptions of common purpose with TVA management, when other factors affecting such perceptions are held constant.

These data, while not covering the entire range of interpersonal relations between employees and supervisors, do suggest that identification with the organization owes little to warm, friendly, interpersonal relations with supervisors. It should be remembered, however, that the data of Chapter 10 strongly indicate that the sharing of work-relevant decisions between employees and supervisors has a marked effect on identification with the organization. Evidently, while employee participation (along with supervisors) in decision making leads to feelings of common purpose with management, the mere presence of friendly relations does not. We might expect too that participation in decision making will cause employees to see a leveling of the status differences between management and worker, whereas pleasant supervisor-employee interaction may not affect the basic boss-subordinate dichotomy.

FREE EXPRESSION OF OPINION

Another aspect of the relation between rank-and-file employees and supervisors in an organization is the extent to which employees feel free to voice their opinions and complaints. Does employees' freedom of expression have any relation to their identification with the work organization?

To assess the extent to which employees feel free to express opinions and disagreement on the job, the following questions were asked:

1. How free do you feel to *disagree* with your immediate supervisor to his face?

   (*1*) _____ It's better not to disagree
   (*2*) _____ I'd hesitate some before disagreeing
   (*4*) _____ I'd hesitate only a little
   (*5*) _____ I wouldn't hesitate at all to disagree to his face

2.   When you don't like some policy or procedure on the job, how often do
      you tell your opinion to one of your supervisors?

      (1) _____ Very rarely or never
      (2) _____ About a tenth of the time
      (3) _____ About a quarter of the time
      (4) _____ About half of the time
      (5) _____ About three-quarters of the time
      (6) _____ Almost always

An index of freedom to disagree with supervisors was computed for
each individual and for each work group.[17] The data show no positive
correlation between group scores on the index of freedom to disagree and
scores on the index of identification with TVA (partial $r = -.07$). There
is, in fact, a significant negative relation between freedom to disagree
and that item of the identification index which concerns employees'
readiness to label themselves as TVA members (partial $r = -.27$; $p < .05$).
The explanation of this tendency toward a negative relation is not
readily apparent. It may be that the index of freedom to disagree measures
in part the propensity of employees to voice complaints as well as the
freedom which the work situation allows for such expression. Such a
greater desire to complain may be based on feelings of injustice and
opposed goals, which would contribute to a lesser sense of solidarity with
the organization. Another possibility is that those who are reluctant to
voice disagreement are compliant people and that compliant people are
more likely to have prominent in their self-image their roles in hierarchical work organizations.

OVERALL PREDICTION OF IDENTIFICATION WITH TVA

So far in this chapter we have discussed the relationship between
identification with TVA and each of a number of job and personal characteristics. (The major relationships for work groups are summarized in
Figure 11-1.) Now we examine further the *relative* impact of these factors
on identification, as well as the total impact of all of these factors, taken
together, on organizational identification.

To do this, we have performed several multiple correlation analyses of
our data for the ninety work groups at TVA. These analyses permit us
to assess how much of the variation among work groups in identification
with TVA can be accounted for by all of the job and personal character-

---

[17]A longer four-item index of willingness to disagree with supervisors is reported in
Patchen, Pelz, and Allen, 1965.

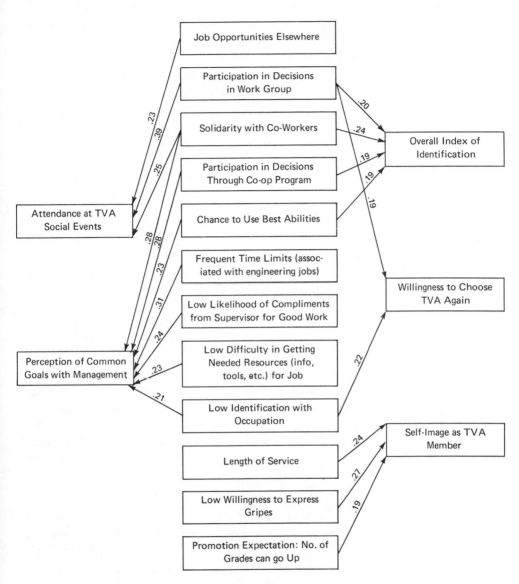

Note: Numbers are partial coefficients showing the strength of each association independent of other relevant variables. See footnote 3 in this chapter for a list of variables held constant.

FIGURE 11-1 Job and personal characteristics most strongly associated with overall index of identification with TVA and with selected aspects of identification (for ninety work groups)

istics together. They also indicate the relative importance of each characteristic in predicting to organizational identification. (In this respect, these
results are supplementary to the partial correlations presented earlier.)[18]

Sixteen job and personal characteristics (listed in Appendix P) were
included in this analysis. These characteristics include most of the factors
discussed in this chapter, plus participation in decision making on the job
and participation through the cooperative conference (discussed in
Chapter 10), plus several other variables which showed sizeable correlations with organizational identification.[19] This roster of job and personal
characteristics was related both to the overall index of identification with
TVA and to separate aspects of identification which compose the index.

Overall Index of Identification

Appendix P shows the results of the analyses which relate various job
and personal characteristics to the overall index of identification with
TVA. This analysis shows that the average group level of identification
with TVA is affected most by the extent of solidarity among co-workers,
followed by the degree of participation in decisions on the job and the
chance for employees to use their best abilities. Satisfaction with promotion chances, participation through the cooperative program, and number
of future promotions expected make smaller contributions to the level
of overall identification. The multiple correlation coefficient for all sixteen predictors (most of which contribute little to the overall prediction)
is .614; this indicates that 38 per cent ($.614^2$) of the variance among the
ninety groups on the overall index of identification is "explained" by
these predictors together. It may be noted that the proportion of variance
among work groups accounted for by these predictors is less than the
amount of variance in identification among the eight cooperative programs (56 per cent) which is accounted for by differences in the extent

---

[18]The relative importance of each predictor is indicated in the multiple correlation
analysis by the size of its Beta weight. A Beta weight indicates how much change in the
dependent variable is produced by a standardized change in one of the independent
variables when the other independent variables are controlled. The partial correlation is
a measure of the amount of variation explained by one independent variable after the
others have explained all they could. Note that the relative order of importance of the
predictors, as indicated by their Beta weights, is approximately the same as the order
indicated by the partial correlation coefficients; this is usually the case.

[19]Variables were chosen for inclusion in these analyses because of their theoretical or
practical interest or because they showed relatively strong zero-order correlations with
identification items; where predictor variables were overlapping, the one with the
stronger zero-order correlation was usually included.

of participation by employees in these cooperative programs.[20] Also, as we shall see next, the predictors used explain somewhat more of the variance among work groups on certain aspects of identification than they do on the overall identification index (see below).

Perception of Common Goals

Looking at the relation of various factors to employees' perceptions of common goals with management[21] (see Beta weights in Appendix P), we find that of the five factors which are most strongly related to the overall index of identification with TVA, three of these factors (solidarity with co-workers, participation through the cooperative program, and chance to use one's best abilities) are even more strongly associated with perceptions of common interest with management. The two other factors which are most strongly related to the overall index of identification— participation in decisions on the job and satisfaction with promotion— have lesser, though still positive, associations with the perception of common goals with management. In general, these data are consistent with our expectation that organizational differences which affect their members' overall pattern of attitudes toward the organization will have some of their most direct effects on perceptions of common goals with the organization leaders.

Several other job factors also have a substantial association with the perception of common interest with management. The more frequently groups work under time limits, the stronger their identification with the organization; frequency of time limits turns out, in fact, to have the strongest relation of any factor to perception of common goals (though it is little related to the overall index of identification). The relation, an unexpected one, may be due to the types of work and occupations with which frequent time limits are most likely to be associated. Among the TVA units studied, time deadlines are most frequently found among those engineering units which are contributing to the building of new installations—e.g., new power plants, new substations, new transmission lines— within the TVA system. Time limits are less likely to be found in work units (primarily those in the power plants) whose jobs are concerned with efficient running of an already created system. Thus, those in jobs with more frequent time limits are in more intimate contact with the "goal of

---

[20]The lesser predictability of average organizational identification in the immediate work group, as opposed to the much larger cooperative program, may be due, at least in part, to a greater effect of idiosyncratic factors in relatively small groups than in larger units, where such factors may tend more to cancel out.

[21]See Chapter 9 for the question concerning common goals with management.

building the Valley" which our question about common goals with management asks about. In addition, the fact that the units with frequent time goals are more likely to have a heavy representation of professional engineers probably helps to account for the finding. By virtue of their social origins, training, and professional ideology, engineers are somewhat less likely to perceive a "class" split between workers and management than are nonprofessional, especially blue-collar, workers.

Another factor which has an appreciable, but surprisingly negative, association with perceptions of common interest with management, when other things are held constant, is the likelihood that supervisors will praise good work. We see no reason why a *greater* likelihood of supervisory praise should lead to *lower* identification with TVA. It seems likely that this is a spurious association, caused by the association of these variables with other factors which were not included in this analysis.

Finally, several other factors have fairly substantial associations, either positive or negative, with perceptions of common interest with management. These are (1) difficulty in getting the information, tools, or materials needed to carry out the work properly (more difficulty, less perceived common interest); (2) identification with occupation (more occupational identification, less perceived common interest); and (3) satisfaction with pay (greater satisfaction, more perceived common interest). The last two of these factors have already been discussed. The fact that difficulty in getting necessary resources is associated with lower perceived common interest may indicate that such difficulties are attributed in part to a conflict of priorities with organization management.

Overall, the sixteen factors listed in Appendix P, taken together, have a multiple correlation of .662 with perception of common goals with management. This indicates that these factors account for 44 per cent ($.662^2$) of the variance among work groups in their average perception of common interests and goals with management.

Willingness to Choose TVA Again

Next we look at the associations between various job and personal characteristics and answers to the question "If you could begin working over again, but in the same occupation as you're in, how likely would you be to choose TVA as a place to work?" The factors which are most strongly associated with willingness to choose TVA again (as indicated by their Beta weights) are (1) identification with occupation (more occupational identification, less willingness to choose TVA again) and (2) participation in decisions on the job (more participation, more willingness to choose TVA). A number of other job and personal characteristics also contribute to the prediction of willingness to choose TVA again, but the relation of each factor to choice of TVA is fairly small.

For all sixteen factors included in the analysis, taken together, the multiple correlation with willingness to choose TVA again is .684; this indicates that 47 per cent ($.684^2$) of the variance among work groups in willingness to choose TVA again is accounted for by these factors.

Self-Image as TVA Member

Description by employees of themselves in terms of their working for TVA (as opposed to other social characteristics) is predicted best by length of service, followed by reluctance to voice disagreement with supervisors. Two other factors which predict most strongly to self-image as a TVA member concern promotion chances—both the number of grades up which employees expect to rise and their present satisfaction with their promotion chances. However, all of the predictors together "explain" only 30 per cent of the variance among groups in the average extent to which their members label themselves as TVA members.

Other Aspects of Identification

By far the best predictor of attendance at TVA social events is the extent to which employees participate in decisions in the immediate job situation. Solidarity with co-workers also has a marked positive association with attendance at social events, as does (surprisingly) job opportunities elsewhere.

Telling family members about TVA projects is predicted best by the likelihood that supervisors will compliment good work while anger at criticism of TVA is related most strongly to having been raised in Tennessee.

All the predictors together account for 34 per cent of the variance among groups in attendance at social events, 24 per cent of the variance in anger at criticism of TVA, and 29 per cent of the variance in telling family members about TVA projects.

SUMMARY

The previous chapter examined the effects on employees' identification with TVA of their participation in decision making; it concentrated in large part on differences in identification among the large organizational units represented by the cooperative programs. The present chapter has examined additional job and personal characteristics which may affect identification with the work organization; it has focused primarily on differences among immediate work groups, though giving some attention also to differences among individuals.

Several factors, in addition to participation in decision making, stand out as most strongly related to the overall index of identification with TVA. The foremost of these is solidarity within the work group—the extent to which co-workers feel close to each other and help each other out. Solidarity with co-workers is linked especially to perceptions of common purpose with management and to attendance at TVA social events. Although feelings of closeness to co-workers at one's own level and to management may not go together in many organizations, it appears that both can be part of a single pattern of felt closeness to others in the organization. It was suggested that at TVA solidarity with co-workers contributes to a total pattern of favorable attitudes and behavior toward the organization by (1) its positive association with perceptions of common purpose with management and (2) by making the organization a source of important social satisfactions.

The overall level of identification in work groups also has a relatively strong association with the extent to which people get a chance to do what they feel they are best at. Among the specific indicators of identification, the chance to use one's abilities is most strongly related to perceptions of common goals with management. Evidently, men who feel they are doing the kind of work they are best at see more in common between their own goals and those of management. Such perceptions of common goals appears to be one link between the chance for employees to use their best abilities and other favorable attitudes toward the organization. Increased personal satisfactions from organizational membership may be another link between chance to use one's abilities and favorable attitudes toward the work organization.

Satisfaction with promotion chances and expectation of promotion each has only a modest positive association with the overall index of identification with TVA. A variety of other job and personal characteristics—including occupational identification, job opportunities elsewhere, length of service, and satisfaction with pay—all show little association with overall organizational identification, especially when other things are held constant.

A number of factors which are not much related to the overall index of identification do, however, show marked associations with particular aspects of organizational identification. The more men identify with their particular occupations, the less likely they are to say that they would choose TVA again and the less likely they are to see common goals with management. These results suggest that identification with an occupational group tends to produce lesser feelings of solidarity with and commitment to the work organization, though not lesser involvement in its activities.

Several additional factors contribute to differences in the extent to which employees and management are seen as having common goals. The more frequently men at TVA work under time limits (a circumstance associated with engineering work), the more likely they are to see common goals with management (though they are also somewhat less likely to say they would choose TVA again). And the more difficulty they have in getting the things needed to carry out their jobs properly, the less common interest with management they perceive.

Length of service, though it is not related to the overall index of identification with TVA, is one of the few factors which has a fairly marked association with the readiness to describe oneself in terms of working for TVA. Evidently, long service makes organizational membership more central in one's self-image.

In general, the factors which are most strongly related to the overall index of identification are even more strongly associated with the item of the identification index which concerns perceptions of common goals with management. These results are consistent with our expectation that perceptions of having things in common with organizational leaders is one of the key variables which links organizational and personal characteristics to attitudes and behavior favorable to the organization. It is likely that organizational and personal factors which are associated with a high level of overall organizational identification also have these associations because of their effect in enabling people to derive important satisfactions from organizational membership.

CONCLUSION

PART **IV**

12

SUMMARY
AND
IMPLICATIONS

This book has been concerned with the involvement or noninvolvement of people in their jobs. When are people apathetic or bored and when do they seek personal achievement at work? When do people feel estranged and apart from the work organization and when do they feel a part of that organization?

SITE OF THE STUDY

A study of these and related questions was conducted in selected units of the Tennessee Valley Authority, a semiautonomous agency of the United States government. Management at TVA has long been dedicated to the goal of encouraging among all TVA employees a sense of pride and enthusiasm in their work and a sense of being truly a part of the organization. TVA has taken a variety of actions to encourage such employee feelings of involvement in their jobs—especially through a network of "cooperative programs" which permit employees to participate in work-related decisions outside the scope of normal collective bargaining. However, at the time of this study it seemed clear to many people that there were considerable variations among TVA units in the extent to which the ideal of high job involvement among employees was being realized. The object of our study was to assess some of the differences in job involvement which existed among certain TVA units and to try to see how these were related to differences in the job situations and personal characteristics of employees in these units.

Five geographically separate units at TVA—two engineering divisions and three steam (power) plants—were selected for study. These units have a wide range of different job settings and different occupations; employees include engineers, draftsmen, operators of automated equipment, craftsmen like boilermakers and machinists, chemical laboratory analysts, clerks, and a variety of other occupational groups.

DATA OBTAINED

To assess various aspects of job involvement, especially job motivation and identification with the work organization—we relied primarily on responses which employees made to relevant questions asked on a questionnaire. Previous work on this project had established that the responses which employees gave on selected questionnaire items could be treated as valid indicators of various aspects of job involvement; the questionnaire measures had been shown to be associated with supervisors' ratings of employees' behavior and with such behavior as absence, submitting suggestions, and leaving TVA. In addition to the questionnaire measures, attendance data were also used to help assess job involvement.

Information about the work situation was also obtained primarily from employees themselves, by questionnaire. Finally, information was obtained by questionnaire concerning personal characteristics of employees—e.g., length of TVA service, union or professional activities, and personality characteristics.

From all the data collected, we hoped to shed light on two main questions : First, under what conditions are people highly motivated for achievement on the job? Secondly, when do people come to have a sense of identification with the work organization?

ACHIEVEMENT MOTIVATION ON THE JOB

In studying motivation on the job, we looked at three indicators of motivation—general job interest, interest in innovation, and attendance as well as at pride in work and symptoms of stress.

In trying to account for differences in job motivation, as such motivation relates to achievement on the job, we began with the theoretical approach of Atkinson. He sees aroused motivation as a function of the motive for achievement, the achievement incentive (amount of achievement possible), and the probability that one's efforts will lead to successful achievement. We wished to pinpoint those features of the job situation which will affect the amount of achievement incentive (and also the probability of success) and which thus may be said to provide opportunities for achievement. We wished also to study those job and personal characteristics which might affect the motive for achievement by providing rewards for achievement. For each factor which might be related to motivation, we considered its impact on motivation when other relevant factors are held constant, and also its joint effects with other factors.

INCENTIVE FOR ACHIEVEMENT

In considering features of the job situation which may affect achievement incentive, we focused on four job features : (1) difficulty of the work; (2) personal responsibility for success—i.e., control over work methods; (3) feedback on the amount of success in performance; and (4) the existence of standards of excellence against which success in performance of the task can be judged (our most relevant data concerned time standards). The first of these features—task difficulty (or probability of success)—has received considerably study in the experimental literature on achievement motivation. The other job features have tended to be treated as conditions necessary for achievement incentive, but the way in which variation in these features may affect achievement motivation has received little attention in the past.

Work Difficulty

Results of our study at TVA indicate that jobs of moderate difficulty, as compared with jobs of lesser challenge, lead to stronger motivation—as reflected by stronger interest in work innovation and by fewer absences. These results are consistent with laboratory studies which have shown motivation to increase in situations of moderate task difficulty. They suggest that there are important motivational advantages to be gained by trying to structure job content in a way that introduces some elements of problem solving and challenge into what might tend to be routine work. Our results also indicate that the higher motivation of those in moderately difficult jobs is *not* accompanied by greater symptoms of stress. This may not be the case in all work situations. For example, where individuals feel that their abilities are not adequate to meet the difficulties posed by the work, they may become tense, angry, or depressed. How-ever, the present findings do suggest that, in a fairly wide range of job situations, the motivational advantages that come with the challenge of some difficulty are not bought at the expense of greater psychological stress.

Control over Methods

Results concerning job features relevant to achievement incentive also indicate the great importance of employees' control over work methods as a determinant of work motivation. The more control employees have over work methods, the greater their general job interest and their interest in work innovation, and the fewer their absences. These results are consis-tent with the general trend of results from other studies which usually show a positive association between employee influence on work methods and work performance. What is particularly impressive and noteworthy in the present results is that, when the effects of a large number of factors affecting job motivation are compared (each controlled for the effect of other factors), control over work methods emerges as the one factor which has sizeable associations with all indicators of job motivation. These results emphasize the advantages of designing job specifications and assigning responsibilities, insofar as technology allows, in such a way that employees are not greatly constrained by procedural rules or by supervisory instruc-tions. Where, instead, employees are encouraged, within the limits of their training and abilities, to decide themselves (or in consultation with others) how their work shall be done, their motivation to do the work well is likely to be considerably enchanced.

Expected Feedback on Performance

The amount of feedback which people get on their work performance showed, in itself, little association with motivation on the job. However, when other circumstances also favor a high achievement incentive (i.e., when the work is fairly difficult or when employees have considerable control over work methods) or when reward for achievement is high, feedback shows a more positive association with indicators of job motiva-tion. These results suggest that the prospect of feedback on performance, by itself, contributes little to motivation on the job unless other conditions make a considerable amount of personal achievement possible, and/or provide rewards for achievement. Thus, for example, a program where supervisors meet regularly with employees to review their performance may not have much effect on employees' job motivation unless it is possible for them to make personal achievements and/or there are rewards of some kind for achievement.

Time Limits

With regard to standards of excellence in performance, our data are somewhat limited. The most salient data concern the frequency of time limits on the work (which may be one kind of standard of excellence). When time limits are more frequent, people are absent somewhat less often. However, the presence of frequent time limits does not, in itself, bring greater general interest in the job. Nor do frequent time limits bring greater interest in work innovation—except where overall rewards for achievement are high. On the other hand, the more frequently there are time limits, the *less* pride people take in their work.

Overall, frequent time limits appear to contribute only a little to job motivation, at the cost of reduced pride in work. It may be that time limits are not actually viewed by many employees as a standard of excellence, or that the attention which they focus on the speed of work diverts attention from the possibility of doing work which is creative or innovative, thereby reducing achievement incentive. These results suggest that time limits should be used very cautiously, and probably not alone, as a standard of excellence at work. Where it is necessary to establish time limits, their function as a standard against which achievement can be measured and rewards distributed, rather than merely as a noxious pressure, should probably be emphasized.

Chance to Learn

In discussing achievement incentive on the job, we have considered mainly job features which may affect the amount of success a person can have in mastering work problems. Another type of accomplishment possible on the job is improvement of oneself through learning. The chance to learn new things on the job has a substantial association with our indicators of job motivation—though the size of these associations is greatly reduced when other factors affecting job motivation are held constant. The strongest association of the chance to learn is with reported symptoms of stress; the more the chance to learn, the fewer symptoms of stress such as depression, fatigue, or nervousness. Just why the chance to learn new things should lead to greater happiness—one might say better mental health—on the job is not certain. Learning opportunities may prevent monotony and may provide positive satisfactions through improving one's knowledge and skills. These results suggest that organizations should pay greater attention to the psychological and motivational effects of learning opportunities as well as to their effects on improving skills. In job situations, opportunities to learn new things generally cease after an initial breaking-in or training period on the job. In many organizations it may be possible to provide additional learning chances throughout employees' work careers—through such techniques as job rotation, providing on-the-job experience with new techniques, and formal courses. To the extent that such programs are feasible, they may help to maintain some of the enthusiasm which tends to accompany the period of initial learning on the job.

Combinations of Incentive-Relevant Factors

In addition to examining the separate impact of each job characteristic which might contribute to achievement incentive, we also examined their effects in combination. People whose jobs combine moderate difficulty, high control over work methods, and high feedback on performance show stronger interest in their work than might be predicted from the simple addition of each of these separate job features. In other words, the data indicate that there is an extra boost in job motivation which comes from the *combination* of these job characteristics. However, the results also indicate that these combination (or interaction) effects are small in comparison with the effects of the separate job features, especially job difficulty and control over work methods. The relatively small interaction effects between those job features which we have seen as relevant to achievement incentive are not too consistent with our expectation that the effects of these job features on motivation will be multiplicative. It may be that only some minimum of all the requisites for achievement is necessary in order for increases in a single relevant factor—especially in difficulty of the job or in control over means of doing the job—to bring substantial increases in job motivation. From a practical point of view, this would mean that where it is hard to change greatly one job feature relevant to achievement incentive (e.g., difficulty of the job), it may still be possible to get a sizable increase in job motivation by increasing another relevant job feature—e.g., by giving employees greater influence over means of doing the job.

The job characteristics which we expected to affect achievement incentive have their greatest effect on job motivation when reward for achievement is high. This is consistent with the supposition that these job features —i.e., difficulty, control over means, feedback, and time limits—do in fact affect achievement incentive. This is because, according to Atkinson's general formula, increases in achievement incentive should have their strongest effect on aroused motivation when the motive for achievement is high. If these job features do affect achievement incentive, they should also have their greatest effect on job motivation when rewards (and thus motivation) for achievement are high. And this is what, in general, we found.

Job Features and Stress

With respect to symptoms of stress, the greatest number of stress symptoms was shown by people in difficult jobs which have frequent time limits but who have low control over work methods and low feedback on performance. Where there are frequent time limits and work is difficult but employees have more control over work methods and more feedback on performance, anxiety and other symptoms of stress are much less frequent. Even lower in reported symptoms of stress are those who have fairly difficult jobs but have only infrequent time deadlines as well as high control over means and high feedback on performance. The implication appears to be that if one wants to reduce psychological and physical symptoms of stress among employees (which may affect efficiency as well as health), it is best to reduce time pressures as much as possible. If time deadlines are necessary, giving those who must meet them as much control over and information about the situation as possible may reduce their stressful effects.

THE MOTIVE FOR ACHIEVEMENT

In thinking about the motive for achievement on the job, we have argued that the emphasis of much of the work on the achievement motive, which focuses on personality characteristics based on early life experiences, is not wholly adequate. In addition to paying attention to personality differences among people on the job, we have also examined features of the present job situation which may affect the value of achievement. We have looked on achievement as not only a possible goal in itself but also as a means to other rewards, such as peer approval and supervisory approval. Moreover, we have seen the intrinsic value of achievement (i.e., as a source of personal pride) as depending in part on features of the present job situation (e.g., the chance to use one's best abilities).

Need for Achievement

First, we looked at the relation between motivation on the job and the personality characteristic of need for achievement, as measured by the Achievement Risk Preference Scale. In general, differences in the need for achievement appear to have little impact on job motivation. When other things making achievement a source of pride (e.g., chance to use one's best abilities) are low, those with the highest need for achievement have the *lowest* job interest and the lowest amount of pride in their work.

Similarly, when opportunities for achievement are low, increased need for achievement brings lower job interest. It appears that when the job situation is not conducive to achievement, those with high need for achievement are more likely than others to be frustrated and bored and to turn their thoughts elsewhere. These findings suggest, therefore, that an employee's need for achievement is a blessing neither for the employee himself nor for the management if there is little chance of real accomplishment on the job.

On the other hand, when opportunities for achievement are high, we expected to find that high need for achievement would contribute to stronger motivation on the job. There is only limited evidence that this is so. Under conditions of high opportunity for achievement, those high in need for achievement are somewhat less likely to be absent; but they do not show greater general job interest or greater interest in innovation than do others. Further examination of the data show that, when opportunities for achievement are high, both those high in need for achievement and those low in need for achievement respond with greater job interest and greater tendency to innovate. One possible explanation of these results is that, while personality differences in need for achievement may be an important determinant of *choice* among jobs, its effect on motivation once in a job may be modest because other motives (e.g. for the supervisory or peer approval which may follow achievement) also influence the desire for achievement on the job.

Identification with Occupation

Identification with occupation is another personal characteristic which was expected to contribute to the intrinsic satisfaction of achievement on the job, and thus to the overall motive for achievement. Those with stronger occupational identification did, in fact, show greater general job interest and greater interest in work innovation than people who were less strongly identified with their occupations. However, those with stronger occupational identification were also more likely than others to be absent from work. This mixed relation of occupational identification to the indicators of job motivation stayed about the same regardless of the level of opportunity for achievement on the job. These results suggest that though commitment to an occupation increases interest in the work, it does not contribute much to a stronger motive for achievement. Occupational commitment may reflect a satisfaction with being a member of the particular occupation rather than a drive for outstanding achievement in that type of work.

Influence on Goals

Two other aspects of the job situation which may affect the intrinsic satisfaction to be derived from achievement were also examined. These are the amount of influence which employees have over work goals and the extent to which they have a chance to do what they are best at. Greater employee influence on work goals has, in general, only a small positive impact on job motivation. However, among those with good opportunity for achievement, influence on goals has a somewhat greater impact on job motivation. These results are consistent with our expectation that people will value more highly goals which they help to set for themselves—though they lead us to add that this is likely to be so particularly when attainment of the goal has significance as a personal achievement.

Chance to Use Abilities

The chance to do what one is best at on the job was also expected to increase the amount of pride to be derived from achievement and thus increase the motive for achievement on the job. In general, only a small positive association is found between employees' chances to use their best abilities and our indicators of job motivation. However, this association becomes stronger when opportunities for achievement (achievement incentive) are high. Since, according to Atkinson's formulation, increases in achievement motive should have their greatest effect on aroused motivation when achievement incentive is high, these results are consistent with our expectation that having the chance to use one's most valued abilities will raise the motive for achievement.

Peer Rewards for Good Work

In addition to factors which may affect the intrinsic value of achievement on the job, we have also been concerned with factors which may increase the value of achievement as a means to other rewards.

One possible reward for achievement on the job is praise from co-workers whose good opinion is valued. We found that the more people belong to a cohesive group who are concerned about each other's work (e.g., complimenting good work), the less likely they are to be absent. Also, the more effect their work has on that of their co-workers, the less likely they are to be absent. However, rewards from co-workers contributed little to increased interest in or pride on the job. These results are consistent with previous research which shows attendance and turnover on the job to be related to the existence of cohesive, mutually supportive work units. However, the results suggest that the better attendance in such groups is due more to a sensitivity to others' opinions and to the social attractions of work than to any increase in the motivation for achievement on the job. This may be because the praise of peers is directed primarily to conscientiousness—i.e., to not creating problems for one's fellows—rather than to creative accomplishment. An exception to this possible rule is suggested by the finding that when opportunity for achievement is high, interest in innovation tends to be higher in groups whose members reward each other for good work. It is likely that many innovations at work would be helpful to one's peers and so would draw their praise.

Reward from Supervisors

Although some employees appear to have strong feelings about lack of appreciation by supervisors, we found that, in general, the likelihood that supervisors will compliment good work had little association with any of our indicators of job motivation, pride, or stress on the job. These results suggest the possibility that in many job situations praise (and perhaps negative criticism) by supervisors is not greatly valued. It may be incorrect to assume that a supervisor—just by virtue of his position—is a person whose evaluations constitute important rewards or punishments. Just how important his compliments or criticisms are may depend on such things as the extent to which he is admired and respected and the amount of influence he has over pragmatic rewards like promotion.

However, compliments from supervisors did tend to have a positive association with job motivation when opportunities for achievement were high. Also, where opportunities for achievement were high, a greater likelihood of supervisory compliments for good work appears to bring a considerably greater pride in work. The readiness of supervisors to praise in such situations may be more meaningful than where work is relatively routine.

Promotion Rewards

At TVA, the extent to which good work is seen as a means to promotion has little effect on job motivation, regardless of the level of achievement opportunity. It may be that only reasonable competence and not outstanding performance may often be required for promotion and that promotion may be too far distant a reward to greatly affect motivation in the present. Promotion as a reward for achievement may serve to increase the motive for achievement only when substantial achievement (and not merely adequate performance) is required for promotion and where the time lag between achievement and promotion is not too long.

Combinations of Rewards

The effects of each of the rewards for achievement were found to be generally additive—i.e., the effect of each reward on motivation was, in general, not much dependent on the level of other rewards. However, there were indications of certain joint effects of different rewards. A notable instance is that increases in peer rewards for good work tend to be associated with interest in work innovation only when circumstances favor people also getting pride from work achievement; the reverse is also true— i.e., pride rewards tend to be more strongly associated with innovative interest when peer rewards for achievement are high. These results suggest that while each type of reward for achievement may have important effects in itself, it may sometimes be necessary to combine several types of rewards in order to activate the motive for achievement.

Overall, the results concerning external rewards for achievement tend toward consistency with our theoretical expectation that the presence of such rewards in the job situation can affect the motive for achievement. Both peer rewards for achievement and supervisory rewards for achievement tend to be more strongly related to job motivation when achievement opportunity (reflecting achievement incentive) is high. Since, under the Atkinson formulation, increases in the achievement motive should have the greatest impact on aroused motivation when achievement incentive is high, factors which affect the achievement motive should also have a stronger effect when incentive is high. And this is what we tend to find.

Overall, the results of the study which concern job motivation suggest that interest, pride, and enthusiasm on the job are much affected by the extent to which the job provides both opportunities and rewards for achievement. They suggest that administrators who want their employees to be motivated to achieve on the job should not rely only, or even primarily, on finding people with the right personal qualities; they should turn their attention also to creating a work environment which will create and elicit such motivation.

IDENTIFICATION WITH THE WORK ORGANIZATION

After considering achievement-related motivation on the job, we turned to the second major focus of the study—identification with the work organization. The concept of identification has been used to refer to a variety of different, although related, phenomena. At least three major kinds of individual orientations toward an organization may be distinguished : (1) perception of shared characteristics with other members; (2) feelings of solidarity with, or being part of, the organization; and (3) support of the organization. (We have used "identification" as a global term to cover all of these phenomena.)

We have suggested that the perception of similarities between oneself and other organization members, especially of shared goals and interest with organization leaders, may be crucial for the occurrence of a sense of solidarity with the organization. Such a sense of solidarity should, in turn, contribute to the individual's motivation to defend and support— i.e., be loyal to—the organization. However, in addition to the organizational loyalty which may derive from feelings of solidarity or oneness with the organization, there may be pragmatic motives for loyalty. A person may support and defend an organization of which he is a member because he derives various satisfactions from his membership role (e.g., money, status, pride in accomplishment). We have hypothesized, then, two major mechanisms leading to loyal attitudes and behavior—one based on a nonpragmatic sense of solidarity with the organization (stemming largely from perceptions of things in common with other members) and the other based more pragmatically on the benefits from memberships. This conceptual scheme, shown diagrammatically in Figure 8-1, could not be tested fully in the present study because of limitations in our data. However, it has served as a framework for discussing and interpreting the results of the study and for limited tests of certain relationships.

In informal interviews with some TVA employees, we asked them about TVA as an organization and about their feelings toward TVA. Most of those interviewed expressed positive feelings toward TVA—some speaking with pride of TVA's accomplishments, some indicating anger at criticism of TVA, and some saying that they felt "a part of" the organization. However, other employees appear to be more indifferent to the organization or to focus on the differences in interest between "management and labor."

Answers from a number of questionnaire items are available to more systematically assess employee orientations toward TVA. One question concerns the perception of similar goals and interests between management and other employees. A second question attempts to get at the salience of the individual's organizational role to his self-image by asking him to choose among alternative ways in which to describe himself. Other questions, which appear to reflect support of or desire for close association with TVA, include questions concerning willingness to choose TVA again, reaction to hearing criticism of TVA, telling others about TVA projects, and attendance at TVA social events. For each individual, an index score of "identification with TVA," based on responses to these questions, was computed. There is evidence that employees' scores on this index are related to several kinds of relevant behavior—including leaving the organization and displaying a TVA sticker.

We found that average scores on the index of identification with TVA varied widely among immediate work groups and among larger organizational units. For example, there was a sizeable difference in the average level of identification with TVA found in the two engineering divisions. Our aim was to try to see what characteristics of the organization, of the larger environment, and of the employees themselves might be associated with differences in overall identification with TVA. In addition, we wanted to see what factors were associated with differences in the separate aspects of identification—e.g., with differences in perceptions of common interest with management.

Participation in Decision Making

One organizational characteristic which we expected to be related to employee identification with the organization is the extent of employee participation in decisions affecting the work. One of the prominent features of TVA as an organization is a formal program of consultation and joint decision making between employee and management representatives called the cooperative program. There are eight cooperative programs in units covered by our study—one in each of the engineering divisions and two in each of the power plants. These cooperative programs consider a wide variety of mutual problems but tend to concentrate on improvements in work methods and equipment. While generally similar in their operation, these programs differ with respect to the vigor of support from local management, the interest of employees, the influence which employees exert, and the actual amount of participation by employees, as reflected by the percentage of employees who have served on a program committee or who have submitted suggestions to the cooperative program. Systematic information about the degree of employee participation, interest, and faith in the cooperative program was obtained from the questionnaire which employees filled out.

The strength of overall identification with TVA among employees covered by a given cooperative program turned out to have a positive association with the vigor of that cooperative program. The more information employees got about the program, the larger the proportion who served on a program committee, and especially the more employees believed their suggestions would get serious consideration, the higher their overall level of identification with TVA. Participation through the cooperative program did not affect positively all aspects of identification with TVA. However, high participation was likely to greatly increase the likelihood that employees would perceive common interests and goals with management. These results indicate that involving employees in decisions concerning such things as work methods and equipment, even where management retains the final say (as it does at TVA), can be a powerful tool for reducing the psychological cleavage between management and other employees. The results also suggest, however, that merely having the formality of a participation program—but one in which the actual involvement and influence of employees is small—is not likely to have a great effect on employee feelings toward management and the organization.

It should be noted too that at TVA both the unions and many management people believe that the fact that employee representatives are union members (or members of an independent employee association) is important to the success of the joint decision-making program. Although employee representatives to the cooperative program do not serve as representatives of their union, the general belief is that these representatives could not speak to management with complete freedom if they did not have the job security and other protections that come from union membership. Of course, regardless of the status of employee representatives could not speak to management wtih complete freedom if they did management to take into account the knowledge, judgment, and preferences of nonsupervisory employees in making what are often considered exclusively management's decisions.

Our results also showed a strong association between participation in the cooperative program and acceptance of changes (in equipment, work procedures, records, etc.) introduced into the work situation. This greater acceptance of change appears to be due only partly to the greater sense of shared interest between management and employees shown by those in more vigorous cooperative programs. In addition, changes may be more readily accepted by those with greater participation in a joint decision-making program because they see the changes as being "theirs" as well as management's. Some well-known earlier research relating employee participation to acceptance of change involved fairly small groups and some direct participation by all employees in those groups (at least in receiving relevant information). The present findings are noteworthy in indicating that a system of employee representation covering groups of several hundred people can, if it is handled effectively, have effects similar to those demonstrated for the more intensive programs in smaller groups.

In addition to studying the effects of employee participation at the division or branch level through a system of representation, we have also looked at the effects of participation in decisions in the immediate work group. The more nonsupervisory employees have influence over such matters as ways of doing the job and time schedules for the work, the higher their overall level of identification with TVA—although this association is a modest one. With regard to specific items of the overall identification index, participation in the immediate work group has only a slight effect on perceptions of common purpose with management—perhaps because participation in the immediate work situation does not involve the men whom employees are likely to think of as "management." Participation in decision making in the immediate work group has its greatest impact on attendance at TVA social events—indicating perhaps that participation makes men feel more a part of their own work groups, even if not necessarily close to higher TVA management.

Participation at both levels—at the larger division or branch level and in the immediate work group—each has an independent positive effect on the overall index of identification with TVA. However, the impact of participation at each level is greatest when participation at the other level is high. Evidently, low participation at one level tends to *reduce* the favorable effects of high participation at the other level, while high participation at one level tends to *augment* the favorable effects of participation at the other level. One of the implications of this finding is that organizations which plan a joint decision-making program for a large unit should try to see that the style of decision making in the day-to-day operations of work groups under lower-level supervisors is consistent with the philosophy of decision making represented by the higher-level program.

Solidarity with Co-Workers

In addition to participation in decision making, several other features of the work situation also have substantial associations with work group scores on the overall index of identification with TVA. The foremost of these features is the extent of solidarity with co-workers—i.e., the extent to which co-workers feel close to each other and help each other out. Work groups whose members feel a high degree of solidarity with co-workers are especially likely to perceive common goals with management and to attend TVA social events. Thus, at TVA cohesiveness among co-workers appears to form part of a single pattern of feelings of solidarity with the entire organization. We have noted that this will not necessarily always be the case, that closely knit work groups can have norms and attitudes hostile to the larger work organization. However, the present results suggest that those who wish to promote member identification with the total organization would be wise to attend to conditions (e.g., noncompetitive relations) which are likely to promote solidarity at the level of the employee's most immediate organizational experiences. A further requirement, of course, is that steps be taken (e.g., providing information about the larger organization and involving employees in decisions concerning the larger organization) which would cause the positive feelings generated at the lower level to extend to the larger organization.

Chance to Use Best Abilities

Another feature of the work situation which shows a substantial association with the overall level of identification is the extent to which people believe they have the chance "to do the things (they) are best at." Having the opportunity to use one's best abilities not only increases, presumably, the satisfactions derived from one's organizational role but also is associated with the perception of common purpose with management —perhaps through greater acceptance of work goals. The results indicate also that the satisfactions derived from achievement in one's organizational role may be somewhat more important in determining the level of organizational identification than are the more pragmatic satisfactions derived from promotion chances and pay (although each of the latter also makes some contribution). Perhaps managements, in trying to promote loyalty to organizations, have tended to pay too much attention to the pragmatic rewards of organizational membership and not enough to the rewards of achievement which are possible in an organizational role.

Perception of Common Goals

In general the factors which are most strongly related to the overall index of identification are even more strongly associated with that item of the identification index which concerns perceptions of common goals with management. These results are consistent with (though they do not prove) our hypothesis that perception of common goals with organization leaders is one of the key variables which links certain organizational and personal characteristics with attitudes and behavior favorable to the organization. Other results indicate, however, that perception of common purpose with management does not in itself account for many of the associations between organizational factors and loyalty to the organization. We continue to assume that the satisfaction derived from one's organizational role is another crucial intervening variable. We would judge the overall results—e.g., those showing an association between promotion chances and willingness to choose TVA again—to be consistent with this assumption although we have not been able to test it in a rigorous way.

Occupational Identification

A number of factors which have only small associations with scores on the overall index of identification with TVA have more marked associations with particular aspects of overall identification. One of these factors is the extent to which people identify with their occupations. While those who identify strongly with their occupations do not score appreciably lower than others on the overall index of identification, they are less likely than others to say they would choose TVA again and less likely to see common interests with management.

In part the negative relation between commitment to an occupation and commitment to a particular organization may be an inevitable one. An occupational community (or organization) may provide an alternative focus for feelings of solidarity. On the other hand, as we noted in discussing job motivation, those with strong commitment to their occupations are more interested than others in their work, which is also the organization's work; they are, in addition, just as likely as other employees to tell people about TVA projects. It may be that employees such as professionals, who are strongly committed to their occupations, may come to feel a strong sense of solidarity with a particular organization when they see the goals and work of that organization as being congruent with their own occupational goals. The management of organizations whose members are strongly identified with particular occupations would probably do well to try to learn more about the extent to which the personal professional goals of their members are consistent with (and are seen as consistent with) the goals and work of the organization.

Several other aspects of the work situation are also associated with employees' perceptions of common goals and interests with management. Most notably, men in work groups which have frequent time limits are more likely to see common goals between themselves and management. The meaning of this result is not entirely clear. Work groups with frequent time limits at TVA are found most often in the engineering divisions. It may be that the nature of the work in these divisions—which focuses on further "building of the Valley" rather than on maintaining an existing system—contributes to a sense of common goals with management. In addition, it seems very probable that the primarily professional men in the engineering divisions are less likely than "blue-collar" men in other parts of TVA to see a "class" split between themselves and management.

Problems on the Job

Another factor related to perceptions of common purpose with management is the amount of difficulty people report in getting the things they need to carry out their jobs properly (i.e., information, tools, or materials).

Those with the greatest difficulties of this kind are less likely than others to see common interest between themselves and TVA management. Men in such units may interpret their difficulties as reflecting a difference of priorities between themselves and management, or a lack of concern by management with their problems. Such a perception would be likely to lead to the feeling that management is not on their side or not interested in their problems—i.e., that the goals and interests of management are not congruent with their own. Anything management can do to demonstrate its genuine concern for the problems faced by employees may contribute to perceptions of common interests with management and to overall identification with the organization. In discussing their positive feelings toward TVA, some men commented about TVA's interest in their welfare, as shown by its health and safety programs. Management's concern for employees' welfare can also be expressed by an attempt to deal with problems they face on the job.

Length of Service

The longer people had worked for TVA, the more likely they were to describe themselves in terms of their TVA membership. Evidently those who have worked longest for TVA are most likely to have incorporated their organizational roles into their self-images. Men with longer service also tend to be more "loyal"—as reflected by saying they would choose TVA again and that they get angry about criticism of TVA. However, longer service is not associated with perception of common goals with TVA management, telling people about TVA projects, or attendance at social events (or with the overall index of identification). It appears that long service leads to a greater personal involvement in one's organizational role but not necessarily to greater dedication to the organization's goals and activities.

Finally, we may note that the phenomenon of strong identification with a work organization—which is found frequently among TVA employees—is not restricted to public, nonprofit organizations. Results from a similar questionnaire administered at a private electronics firm show that a high level of identification with private, profit-making organizations is possible. The specific means which promote such identification (e.g., a profit-sharing plan in this particular electronics firm) may differ in private companies but the basic social-psychological determinants of organizational identification may be expected to be essentially the same.

APPENDICES

APPENDIX A. Characteristics of Total Sample of Employees (N = 834)

Age	Per Cent	Education	Per Cent
Under 25	4	Grade 8 or below	7
25-29	13	Some high school	7
30-34	19	Some high school and business or	
35-39	24	trade school	5
40-44	15	Completed high school	21
45-49	10	Completed high school and business	
50-54	6	or trade school	12
55-59	5	Some college	18
60 and over	3	Completed college	17
Not ascertained	1	Some graduate school but no degree	9
		Graduate degree	3
	100%	Not ascertained	1
			100%

Length of Service	Per Cent	Region Where Grew Up	Per Cent
Less than 6 months	0	Tennessee	58
6-11 months	3	Tennessee & other state	11
1 Year (up to 2)	6	South (other than Tennessee)*	22
2 Years (up to 3)	5	New England or Middle	
3-4 Years	8	Atlantic	2
5-9 Years	27	Midwest	2
10-14 Years	29	Plains or mountains	1
15 Years or more	20	Far West	0
Not ascertained	2	Several non-Southern states	1
		Foreign country	1
	100%	Not ascertained	2
			100%

*Where a Southern state was mentioned, along with a non-Southern state, respondent was coded as having grown up in the South.

250

Salary (1961-62)		Sex	
	Per Cent		*Per Cent*
3,000-3,999	2	Men	92
4,000-4,999	6	Women	7
5,000-5,999	25	Not ascertained	1
6,000-6,999	43		—
7,000-7,999	8		100%
8,000-8,999	5		
9,000-9,999	4	Race*	
10,000-10,999	4		*Per Cent*
11,000 and above	2		
Not ascertained	1	White	98
	—	Negro	2
	100%		—
			100%

*Race was not asked on questionnaire, but an attempt was made to note those of Negro race when the questionnaires were turned in. It is possible that a few Negres were not recorded as such. It may be noted that some of the jobs in which a higher proportion of Negres were found were not included in this study.

Occupation

Steam Plants	*N*	*Engineering Divisions*	*N*
Mechanical engineers	4	Clerks	10
Analytical chemists	7	Clerk-typists	6
Engineering aides	16	Clerk-stenos	16
Engineering cooperative students	1	File clerks	9
Chemical lab analysts	11	Accounting clerks	2
Materials testers	22	Secretaries	11
Instrument mechanics	18	Cost engineer	1
Senior switchboard operators	13	Administration officer	3
Switchboard operators	8	Stores clerk	1
Unit operators	47	Engineering aides	17
Assistant unit operators	65	Trainees	6
Auxiliary unit operators	31	Draftsmen	31
Electricians	33	Mathematicians	7
Machinists	45	Design engineering associates	24
Boilermakers	45	Blueprint operators	4
Steam fitters	46	Civil engineers	81
Painters	16	Electrical engineers	82
Sheetmetal workers	6	Mechanical engineers	48
Asbestos workers	6	Power supply engineers	8
Truck drivers	4	Architects	10
Carpenters	7		
Structural iron workers	2		
Blacksmiths	4		
Total	457	Total	377

APPENDIX B.   Procedures for Data Collection

The following paragraph will describe the general procedures followed in the study, in roughly chronological order.

Obtaining approval for the study. Project personnel met separately with management representatives and with union officials to explain the purposes of the study. These purposes—to attempt to measure employee interest and enthusiasm for the job and to understand some of the factors that affect these reactions—were outlined. Both management and union officials gave their approval and backing to the study.

Informal interviews. Informal interviews were conducted with approximately twenty-five supervisory employees and approximately fifty nonsupervisory employees in various types of jobs. These interviews were conducted at the two engineering divisions covered by the main part of the study and at two steam plants which were not covered in the main study but which have exactly the same types of jobs and administrative structures as do the three plants later covered. The purposes of these informal exploratory interviews were to learn something about the work in the types of units to be covered in the study and to become familiar with what was on the minds of employees.

Pre-tests of questionnaires. Following the exploratory interviews, a tentative questionnaire was constructed for use in both steam plants and engineering divisions. This questionnaire asks about various aspects of the job situation and feelings about the job situation as well as some related topics. Most of the items used were written for the present study. Some were adapted from items used in previous Survey Research Center studies. This first tentative questionnaire was pre-tested with employees in one engineering division and one steam plant, totaling forty employees, some of whom were interviewed about their jobs at the same time. Questions which were inappropriate, misunderstood, or which had a poor "spread" of responses were revised or omitted. A revised but still tentative questionnaire was then pre-tested with sixty-six employees in the second engineering division and in a different steam plant. On the basis of this second pre-test, questions were again revised and a final version of the questionnaire was prepared.

Choice of respondents. Within the Division of Design, approximately half of the nonsupervisory employees stationed at Knoxville were asked to take the final questionnaire. In the larger work sections (seven persons or more), every other name on the organizational personnel list was chosen. In the smaller work sections (six or under), every other section doing similar work was chosen. This method of sampling was adopted in order to ensure that there would be enough employees from every section represented so that a mean score on certain variables could be computed. Of those chosen to take the questionnaire, 95 per cent actually filled it out.

In the Division of Power Planning and Engineering, a smaller division, all nonsupervisory employees stationed at Chattanooga were asked to take questionnaires. Ninety-eight per cent of those asked filled out questionnaires.

In each power plant, all nonsupervisory employees in the mechanical maintenance, laboratory, and electrical maintenance sections were asked to take the questionnaire. Those in a portion of the operating section— that portion which is responsible for the actual operation of the equipment —were also included. (A modification in this procedure was followed for the Johnsonville steam plant which has about twice as many operating personnel as the other two steam plants. For Johnsonville, one-half of the operating personnel were randomly selected.)

Persons in that part of the operating section who do work in the "yard" were omitted. These men are mostly unskilled or semiskilled, including janitors, heavy equipment operators, and laborers. One reason for their being omitted was that pre-tests indicated that these poorly schooled men had some trouble understanding the questionnaire. Persons in the administrative section of each steam plant were also omitted from the study.

Response rates to the questionnaire were 84 per cent at Gallatin Steam Plant, 87 per cent at John Sevier Steam Plant, and 88 per cent at Johnsonville Steam Plant. Nonrespondents included absentees, those on vacations and leave of absence, and those who missed a questionnaire administration session (usually because of their shift schedule) and then did not mail back the form left for them.

Conditions of questionnaire administration. Questionnaires were administered at TVA in April 1962. Employees had received, about a week before administration, individual letters from the University of Michigan staff explaining the purposes and procedures of the study. They were assembled in groups of 30 to 70. Usually this was during working hours— except for some operating employees in the steam plants who met after or before their work shift, but who were paid for their time. A University of Michigan representative again described the study and answered questions before employees filled out the questionnaire. Management persons were not present during these sessions.

Employees were assured of the complete confidentiality of their individual answers. They were informed prior to taking the questionnaire that a code number identifying them—in order to match their answers with other information about them—would be placed on their questionnaires when they were finished. They were assured, truthfully, that these code numbers would be seen only by the University people. With only a few isolated exceptions, the explanation of the code system and its confidentiality seemed to be accepted.

Mail-back questionnaires—to be completed either at work or at home —were left for the persons who were unable to attend the group sessions. Most of these were filled out and returned.

Non-questionnaire data. In some units we asked supervisors to rank employees they know on five qualities: (1) concern for doing a good job; (2) interest in innovation; (3) acceptance of changes introduced by management; (4) willingness to express disagreement to supervisors; and (5) sense of belonging to TVA. Each employee was then given a score on each of these characteristics, derived from supervisors' rankings. Data were also collected from organizational records concerning attendance, suggestions submitted to the cooperative program, and turnover. As noted above, the non-questionnaire data were used in part to help validate various questionnaire measures of employee reactions to their jobs.

APPENDIX C. General Job Interest for Persons Experiencing Various Combinations of Feedback on Performance, Frequency of Time Limits, and Job Difficulty

N	Feedback on Job Performance Index B	Frequency of Time Limits	Job Difficulty Index	Mean Score on General Job Interest
46	Low	Low	Low	6.50
33	Low	Low	Medium	6.70
30	Low	Low	High	6.27
25	Low	Medium	Low	6.80
23	Low	Medium	Medium	6.57
22	Low	Medium	High	6.41
13	Low	High	Low	5.08
24	Low	High	Medium	6.29
27	Low	High	High	7.11
39	Medium	Low	Low	6.77
24	Medium	Low	Medium	7.58
18	Medium	Low	High	6.94
23	Medium	Medium	Low	7.04
27	Medium	Medium	Medium	6.89
38	Medium	Medium	High	7.08
20	Medium	High	Low	7.40
23	Medium	High	Medium	6.57
42	Medium	High	High	7.17
20	High	Low	Low	6.45
19	High	Low	Medium	6.58
20	High	Low	High	7.95
15	High	Medium	Low	6.60
26	High	Medium	Medium	6.85
18	High	Medium	High	7.11
32	High	High	Low	6.44
39	High	High	Medium	7.10
50	High	High	High	7.20

APPENDIX D. Interest in Work Innovation, for Persons Experiencing Various Combinations of Control over Means, Feedback on Performance, and Job Difficulty

N	Control Over Means Index	Feedback on Performance Index B	Job Difficulty Index	Mean Score on Index of Interest in Work Innovation
34	Low	Low	Low	2.55
34	Low	Low	Medium	2.71
36	Low	Low	High	2.80
25	Low	Medium	Low	2.61
26	Low	Medium	Medium	2.97
23	Low	Medium	High	3.22
32	Low	High	Low	2.95
37	Low	High	Medium	2.68
24	Low	High	High	2.87
25	Medium	Low	Low	3.09
29	Medium	Low	Medium	2.91
28	Medium	Low	High	2.95
23	Medium	Medium	Low	2.77
24	Medium	Medium	Medium	3.05
34	Medium	Medium	High	3.51
18	Medium	High	Low	2.85
33	Medium	High	Medium	3.26
36	Medium	High	High	3.47
25	High	Low	Low	3.01
17	High	Low	Medium	3.00
15	High	Low	High	3.87
34	High	Medium	Low	3.08
24	High	Medium	Medium	3.46
41	High	Medium	High	3.74
17	High	High	Low	3.07
14	High	High	Medium	3.19
28	High	High	High	3.68

APPENDIX E.   Pride in Job, Psychological Symptoms of Stress, and Physical Symptoms of Stress, for Persons Experiencing Different Combinations of Job Factors Relevant to Achievement Incentive

CODE OF JOB FACTORS
A.   High control over means
B.   High Job difficulty
C.   High feedback on performance
D.   Frequent time limits

Job Factors		Pride in Job Performance		Psychological Symptoms of Stress		Physical Symptoms of Stress	
Category	N	Mean Score	Standard Error	Mean Score	Standard Error	Mean Score	Standard Error
ABCD	72	3.14	.11	2.03	.10	1.91	.10
ABCD̄	42	3.35	.17	1.97	.11	1.99	.11
ABDC̄	41	2.66	.15	2.27	.17	2.16	.16
ACDB̄	47	2.84	.15	2.04	.15	2.01	.13
BCDA̅	41	2.62	.16	2.44	.16	2.34	.16
AB̄C̄D̄	30	2.87	.17	2.11	.18	2.18	.20
AC̄B̄D	59	2.98	.14	1.97	.12	1.92	.11
ADB̄C̄	32	2.61	.20	2.13	.17	1.94	.17
BC̄A̅D̄	22	3.23	.23	2.53	.24	1.88	.19
BDA̅C̄	47	2.56	.16	2.70	.17	2.45	.18
C̄DA̅B̄	70	2.49	.12	2.37	.13	2.17	.11
A̅B̄C̄D̄	48	2.71	.15	1.83	.11	1.94	.11
B̄A̅C̄D	40	2.32	.18	2.20	.16	2.30	.16
C̄A̅B̄D	40	2.88	.18	2.08	.14	2.03	.17
D̄A̅B̄C̄	54	2.15	.14	2.35	.17	2.13	.15
A̅B̄C̄D̄	85	2.31	.12	2.33	.11	2.30	.11

APPENDIX F. General Job Interest Scores, for Selected Persons with Different Levels of Need for Achievement, and Different Levels on Other Variables Making Achievement a Means to Pride[a]

Other Variables Making Achievement a Means to Pride[a] Are All:	Need for Achievement	General Job Interest[b]	N
Low	Low	4.93	15
	Medium	4.67	6
	High	4.43	14
High	Low	7.68	22
	Medium	7.94	18
	High	7.46	26

a   Other variables relevant to job achievement as a means to pride are (1) identification with occupation; (2) influence on work goals; (3) chance to do the things one is best at. The small number of persons who scored medium on all of these variables are not shown.

b   Differences among the three mean scores in each section of the table are not statistically significant.

APPENDIX G.   Analysis of the Effects on Job Interest of Various Combinations of Factors Relevant to Making Achievement a Source of Personal Pride[a]

(Analyses of Variance)

Factors Relevant to Achievement as Means to Pride[b]	Predicting to General Job Interest	Predicting to Interest in Innovation
	F	F
A. Need for achievement	2.1	0.4
B. Control over job goals	9.4***	22.6***
C. Identification with own occupation	27.5***	19.3***
D. Chance to do what one is best at	62.3***	27.9***
A × B	0.2	1.2
A × C	0.8	0.8
A × D	2.0	0.5
B × C	0.3	0.6
B × D	4.2*	2.5
C × D	1.4	0.0
A × B × C	0.6	0.6
A × B × D	1.0	1.6
A × C × D	0.3	1.3
B × C × D	2.1	0.8
A × B × C × D	1.5	1.1

*p < .05
***p < .001

a   N = 686 individuals; each individual was scored as high, medium, or low on variables A, B, and C and either high or low on variable D.

b   Scores on each independent variable were trichotomized (high, medium, low) except for scores on chance to do what one is best at which were dichotomized (high, low).

APPENDIX H.   Analysis of the Effects on Job Interest of Various Combinations of Rewards for Achievement on the Job[a]

(Analyses of Variance)

Rewards for Achievement on the Job	Predicting to General Job Interest F	Predicting to Interest in Innovation F
A. Achievement leads to promotion	.01	.01
B. Supervisors compliment achievement	9.37***	4.27*
C. Peer rewards for achievement	6.67**	4.06*
D. Achievement a source of pride	36.12***	24.24***
A × B	0.89	0.38
A × C	0.56	0.43
A × D	0.83	0.33
B × C	0.61	1.42
B × D	1.58	0.69
C × D	0.65	1.89
A × B × C	2.29	1.11
A × B × D	2.89*	2.12
A × C × D	0.42	0.63
B × C × D	0.56	1.40
A × B × C × D	1.28	1.49

*p <.05
**p <.01
***p <.001

a   N = 694 individuals; each individual was scored as high, medium, or low on variables B, C, and D and as high or low on variable A.

APPENDIX I. Analysis of the Joint Effects on Individual Job Interest of Overall Reward for Achievement and Each of Four Job Characteristics Which Help to Provide Opportunity for Achievement

(Analyses of Variance[a])

	Predicting to General Job Interest F	Predicting to Interest in Work Innovation F
I. A. Control over means (Index B)	23.7***	23.0***
B. Overall reward for achievement	28.4***	24.9***
A × B	1.5	0.8
II. A. Difficulty of work	3.6*	27.7***
B. Overall reward for achievement	28.2***	29.4***
A × B	0.5	1.1
III. A. Feedback on performance (Index A)	2.1	5.1**
B. Overall reward for achievement	29.2***	27.5***
A × B	2.2	2.2
IV. A. Frequency of time limits	0.6	5.7**
B. Overall reward for achievement	26.6***	27.4***
A × B	1.0	0.8

*p <.05
**p <.01
***p <.001
a Degrees of freedom: $n_1 = 2$ for single variables; $n_1 = 4$ for interactions; n_2 = approximately 650 for each row of table.

APPENDIX J. Analysis of the Joint Effects on Individual Job Interest of Overall Opportunity for Achievement and of Factors Affecting the Reward for Achievement

(Analyses of Variance[a])

	Predicting to General Job Interest	Predicting to Interest in Work Innovation
	F	F
I. A. Need for achievement	3.6*	0.4
B. Overall opportunity for achievement	38.6***	71.0***
A × B	1.8	2.3
II. A. Achievement as a means to pride	14.4***	4.5*
B. Overall opportunity for achievement	37.9***	68.4***
A × B	0.6	1.2
III. A. Achievement as a means to promotion	2.9	0.8
B. Overall opportunity for achievement	36.7***	69.9***
A × B	0.3	0.2
IV. A. Achievement as a means to peer rewards	9.9***	4.2*
B. Overall opportunity for achievement	38.2***	73.2***
A × B	0.5	1.0
V. A. Overall reward for achievement[b]	14.0***	8.4***
B. Overall opportunity for achievement	34.6***	68.3***
A × B	0.4	1.7

*p <.05
***p <.001
a   Degrees of freedom: $n_1 = 2$ for single variables; $n_1 = 4$ for interactions. $n_2 =$ approximately 700 throughout table.
b   Overall reward for achievement index includes data on achievement as a means to pride, to peer approval, and to promotion. Pride rewards are weighted 8, peer rewards 2, and promotion rewards 1 in the overall index.

APPENDIX K. Relation of Job Interest to Factors Affecting the Reward for Achievement, for Different Levels of Opportunity for Achievement

(Product-Moment Correlations for 90 Work Groups[a])

Factors Relevant to Reward for Achievement	General Job Interest When Opportunity for Achievement is:			Interest in Work Innovation When Opportunity for Achievement is:		
	Low ($N=30$)	Medium ($N=30$)	High ($N=30$)	Low ($N=30$)	Medium ($N=30$)	High ($N=30$)
1. Achievement means to peer reward	.19	−.20	.15	−.10	−.10	.26
2. Achievement means to supervisory reward	.28	.14	.35	−.03	.14	.29
3. Achievement means to promotion[b]	.06	.06	−.09	.08	.08	.02
4. Need for achievement	.07	−.27	−.23	.33	.08	.03
5. Identification with occupation	.45*	−.14	.40*	.50**	.40*	.34
6. Chance to use skills	.35	.25	.38*	.26	−.07	.28
7. Influence on work goals	−.33	.49**	.37*	−.32	−.12	.38*
8. Achievement means to personal pride[c]	.26	.21	.40*	.35	.09	.48**
9. Overall reward for achievement[d]	.39*	.23	.27	.22	−.10	.27

*p <.05
**p <.01

a   Solid-line bracket joining two correlation coefficients indicates that the difference between them is significant at beyond the .01 level. Broken-line bracket indicates difference is significant at .10 level (.05 level in one-tail test).

b   Data on this line are for 834 individuals; group data not available for this part of table.

c   Scores on achievement as a means to personal pride are based on the sum of scores on need for achievement, identification with occupation, chance to use skills, and influence on work goals.

d   Scores on overall reward for achievement were computed as follows: 8 (achievement as means to pride) + 2 (achievement as means to peer reward) + 1 (achievement as means to promotion).

APPENDIX L. Associations Among Items Comprising the Index of Identification with TVA[a]

(Product-Moment Correlations for 90 Work Groups)

	(1) Perceived Common Interest with Management	(2) Describing Self as TVA Man	(3) Willingness to Choose TVA Again	(4) Anger at Criticism of TVA	(5) Tell Family About TVA Projects	(6) Attendance at TVA Social Events
(1)	×	.34	.33	.33	−.03	.34
(2)		×	.43	.36	.13	.07
(3)			×	.51	.09	.29
(4)				×	.16	.21
(5)					×	.01
(6)						×

a Data on the question concerning the frequency with which employees tell persons other than members of their family about TVA projects are not available for groups. For data on the intercorrelation among all seven items for individuals, see Patchen, Pelz, and Allen (1965).

264

APPENDIX M. Indicators of Job Motivation, as Related to Characteristics of Job and of Employees

(Multiple Correlation Analyses for 90 Work Groups)

Job and Personal Characteristics	General Job Interest		Interest in Work Innovation		Absences, Total No.	
	r	Beta	r	Beta	r	Beta
Work difficulty	.25	.06	.45	.38	−.06	−.30
Control over means[a] (Index B)	.33[a]	.12[a]	.31	.28	−.17	−.25
Feedback on performance (Index A)	.11	.03	.22	.11	.25	.03
Time limits, frequency	−.03	−.20	.21	.03	.17	−.28
Chance to learn	.50	.18	.28	−.10	−.08	−.26
Opportunity to compare performance	−.22	−.19	−.09	−.02	−.19	−.18
Clarity of instructions	.19	−.05	.10	.03	−.06	−.17
Need for achievement	−.16	−.08	.08	.08	.18	.12
Peer reward for achievement	.26	.18	.06	.11	−.21	−.26
Promotion reward for achievement	.04	.15	−.02	.03	.16	.14
Supervisor reward for achievement	.34	.12	.25	.06	.05	.16
Identification with occupation	.32	.32	.46	.30	.39	.71
Influence on work goals	.24	.04	.09	.01	−.09	.18
Chance to use abilities	.43	.15	.36	.13	.04	.33
Dependence of co-workers on you	.17	.13	.19	.06	−.22	−.30
Overload of work	−.08	−.06	−.04	−.07	.04	.25
Difficulty getting tools, information, materials	−.09	−.05	.11	−.04	.05	−.10
Chance to finish things	.15	−.14	.06	−.16	−.02	−.04
	$R = .69^b$		$R = .69$		$R = .73$	
	$R^2 = .47^b$		$R^2 = .47$		$R^2 = .53$	

a   For control over means index A, r with general job interest is .42, and Beta is .26 in a multiple correlation analysis very similar to the one presented here. Control over means index A differs from index B in that it includes the question "How often do you get chances to try out your own ideas on your job, either before or after checking with your supervisor?" This question was omitted from the control over means index in some analyses because the question also appears in the Interest in Work Innovation Index.

b   An R of .71 ($R_2 = .50$) was obtained in a multiple correlation analysis which used the same list of predictors with the exceptions that control over means index A and feedback index B were used and overload of work and difficulty getting resources were omitted.

APPENDIX N. Pride in Work and Symptoms of Stress, as Related to Characteristics of Job and of Employees

(Multiple Correlation Analyses for 90 Work Groups)

Job and Personal Characteristics	Pride in Work		Psychological Symptoms of Stress		Physical Symptoms of Stress	
	r	Beta	r	Beta	r	Beta
Need for achievement	−.30	−.11	.17	.07	.08	.12
Peer reward for achievement	.34	.08	−.15	−.07	−.07	−.14
Promotion reward for achievement	−.10	.16	.17	.12	−.06	.11
Supervisory reward for achievement	.27	.19	−.13	.15	−.08	.13
Clarity of instructions	−.08	−.14	−.27	−.23	−.26	−.44
Work difficulty	.24	.14	−.02	−.05	.02	−.19
Identification with occupation	−.03	.08	−.13	−.12	−.08	−.06
Dependence of co-workers on you	.02	.09	.05	.03	.24	.24
Opportunity to compare performance	.24	.18	.13	.08	.29	.26
Feedback on performance (Index A)	−.10	.07	.06	.07	−.19	−.05
Control over means (Index B)	.24	.17	−.33	−.21	−.01	.19
Influence on work goals	.18	−.04	−.05	.29	.06	.09
Time limits, frequency	−.33	−.39	.15	.06	−.04	−.02
Chance to use abilities	.29	.16	−.26	−.06	−.17	−.08
Chance to learn	.27	.07	−.43	−.38	−.15	.00
Chance to finish things	−.01	−.21	−.06	.27	−.11	.10
Overload of work	.13	.09	.28	.16	.32	.18
Difficulty getting tools, information, materials	−.11	−.08	.26	.31	.19	.12
	R = .651		R = .689		R = .585	
	R^2 = .42		R^2 = .47		R^2 = .34	

APPENDIX O. Correlations Among Group Scores on Measures of Motivation, Pride, and Stress, for Engineering Division I Groups, Power Plant Groups, and All Groups Combined

A. Engineering Division I Groups (N = 34)

	Absences Total (1)	Interest in Innovation (2)	Psychological Symptoms of Stress (3)	Pride in Work (4)	General Job Interest (5)
(1)	×	.16	−.05	−.06	.15
(2)		×	−.25	.19	.51
(3)			×	−.01	−.47
(4)				×	.30

B. Power Plant Nonoperating Groups (N = 29)

	(1)	(2)	(3)	(4)	(5)
(1)	×	−.21	.59	−.61	−.53
(2)		×	−.35	.54	.38
(3)			×	−.54	−.58
(4)				×	.60

C. All Work Groups Combined (Including Engineering Division II and Power Plant Operating; (N = 90)[a]

	(1)	(2)	(3)	(4)	(5)	Physical Symptoms of Stress (6)
(1)	×	.12	.21	−.27	−.06	.04
(2)		×	−.23	.25	.46	−.22
(3)			×	−.22	−.56	.51
(4)				×	.38	.02
(5)					×	−.25

a   For Section C of Table, N for correlations involving absence is 63, since absence data were not available for Engineering Division I.

APPENDIX P. Overall Index of Identification with TVA, and Selected Aspects of Identification, as Related to Characteristics of Job and of Employees

(Multiple Correlation Analyses for 90 Work Groups)

Job and Personal Characteristics	Overall Index of Identification (7 Item)		Perception of Common Goals with Management		Willingness to Choose TVA Again	
	r	Beta	r	Beta	r	Beta
Compliments from supervisor	.36	−.02	.26	−.32	.32	.10
Solidarity with co-workers	.45	.26	.40	.30	.32	.04
Free expression of gripes	.24	−.06	.09	−.15	.19	−.07
Satisfaction with pay	.27	−.01	.33	.20	.11	−.03
Satisfaction with promotion	.26	.19	.21	.14	.15	.12
Identification with occupation	−.04	−.05	−.06	−.22	−.40	−.22
Participation through co-ops	.31	.17	.30	.26	.26	.09
Participation in work groups	.39	.24	.21	.14	.48	.21
Job opportunities elsewhere	−.02	.02	.04	.08	−.34	−.08
Raised in Tennessee?	.10	−.04	.04	.02	.41	.13
Promotion chances	−.02	.16	.05	.06	−.16	.18
Promotion based on ability	.30	−.03	.29	−.03	.29	.05
Time limits, frequency	−.12	−.04	.11	.34	−.39	−.15
Chance to use abilities	.42	.21	.38	.24	.29	.14
Difficulty getting resources for job	−.24	−.01	−.32	−.23	−.34	.05
Length of service	.23	.04	.11	−.02	.35	.17
	$R = .614$		$R = .662$		$R = .684$	
	$R^2 = .38$		$R^2 = .44$		$R^2 = .47$	

Appendix P (continued)

Job and Personal Characteristics	Self-Image as TVA Member		Attendance at TVA Social Events	
	r	Beta	r	Beta
Compliments from Supervisor	.04	−.06	.18	−.08
Solidarity with co-workers	.23	.10	.34	.29
Free expression of gripes	−.14	−.29	.28	.00
Satisfaction with pay	.08	.00	.05	−.08
Satisfaction with promotion	.14	.20	.00	−.01
Identification with occupation	−.09	.04	−.05	−.06
Participation through co-ops	.23	.17	.27	.16
Participation in work groups	.10	.00	.45	.50
Job opportunities elsewhere	−.20	−.16	.05	.29
Raised in Tennessee?	.17	.03	.01	−.03
Promotion chances	−.05	.23	−.01	.15
Promotion based on ability	.04	−.08	.19	.01
Time limits, frequency	−.24	−.13	−.08	−.01
Chance to use abilities	.13	.14	.18	−.10
Difficulty getting resources for job	−.13	−.04	−.18	−.04
Length of service	.31	.31	.18	−.05
	$R = .544$		$R = .585$	
	$R^2 = .30$		$R^2 = .34$	

NOTE: The multiple correlation (R) of these same predictors with anger at criticism of TVA is .49; only being raised in Tennessee has a Beta over .20 (.24) in that analysis. The multiple correlation of the same predictors with telling family members about TVA projects is .54; the two strongest predictors are compliments for good work from supervisors (Beta = .25) and being raised outside Tennessee (Beta = .22).

REFERENCES

Adams, J. S., and W. B. Rosenbaum, "The Relationship of Worker Productivity to Cognitive Dissonance about Wage Inequities," *Journal of Applied Psychology*, 46 (1962), 161-164.

Allport, G., *The Nature of Prejudice*. Reading, Mass.: Addison-Wesley, 1954.

Alper, Thelma G., "Task-Orientation Versus Ego-Orientation in Learning and Retention," *American Journal of Psychology*, 59 (1946), 236-248.

Argyris, C., *Integrating the Individual and the Organization*. New York: John Wiley & Sons, Inc., 1964.

———, *Personality and Organization*. New York: Harper and Row, Publishers, 1957.

Arps, G. F., "Work with Knowledge of Results Versus Work without Knowledge of Results," *Psychological Monographs*, 28, No. 3 (1920).

Atkinson, J. W., *An Introduction to Motivation*. Princeton, N.J.: D. Van Nostrand Co., Inc., 1964.

———, "Motivational Determinants of Risk-Taking Behavior," in *Motives in Fantasy, Action and Society*, ed. J. W. Atkinson. Princeton, N.J.: D. Van Nostrand, Co., Inc., 1958b.

———, "Towards Experimental Analysis of Human Motivation in Terms of Motives, Expectancies, and Incentives," in *Motives in Fantasy, Action and Society*, ed. J. W. Atkinson. Princeton, N.J.: D. Van Nostrand Co., Inc., 1958a.

———, and N. T. Feather (eds.), *A Theory of Achievement Motivation*. New York: John Wiley & Sons, Inc., 1966.

———, and Patricia O'Connor, "Neglected Factors in Studies of Achievement-Oriented Performance," in *A Theory of Achievement Motivation*, ed. J. W. Atkinson and N. T. Feather. New York: John Wiley & Sons, Inc., 1966.

Baldamus, W., "Type of Work Motivation," *The British Journal of Sociology*, LL, No. 1 (March, 1951), 44-58.

Becker, H. S., and J. W. Casper, "Elements of Identification with an Occupation," *American Sociological Review*, 21 (1956a), 341-348.

———, ———, "The Development of Identification with an Occupation," *American Journal of Sociology*, 61 (1956b), 289-298.

Bettelheim, B., "Individual and Mass Behavior in Extreme Situations," *Journal of Abnormal and Social Psychology*, 38 (1943), 417-452.

Blalock, H. M., Jr., *Causal Inferences in Nonexperimental Research*. Chapel Hill: University of North Carolina Press, 1961.

Blauner, Robert, *Alienation and Freedom: The Factory Worker and His Identity*. Chicago: University of Chicago Press, 1964.

Brown, M. E., "Identification, Integration, and the Conditions of Organizational Involvement." Unpublished doctoral dissertation, University of Michigan, 1964.

Buros, O. K., ed., *The Fifth Mental Measurements Yearbook*. New Brunswick, N.J.: Rutgers University Press, 1959.

Coch, L., and J. R. P. French, Jr., "Overcoming Resistance to Change," *Human Relations*, 1 (1948), 512-532.

Dean, D. G., "Alienation: Its Meaning and Measurement," *American Sociological Review*, 26, No. 5. (October, 1961), 753-758.

Dean, Lois, "Union Activity and Dual Loyalty," *Industrial and Labor Relations Review*, VII (1953-4), 526-536.

Dearborn, D. C., and H. A. Simon, "Selective Perception: A Note on the Departmental Identifications of Executives," *Sociometry*, 21 (1958), 140-144.

Deese, J., *The Psychology of Learning* (2nd ed.). New York: McGraw-Hill Book Company, 1958.

Eckerman, W. C., "The Relationship of Need Achievement to Production, Job Satisfaction, and Psychological Stress." Unpublished doctoral dissertation, University of Michigan, 1963.

Edwards, W., "Behavioral Decision Theory," *Annual Review of Psychology*, Vol. 12. Palo Alto: Annual Reviews, Inc., 1961.

Elmer, G. A., "An Experiment in Measurement of Identification with the Work Situation." Unpublished doctoral dissertation, Ohio State University, 1951.

Ezekiel, M., *Methods of Correlation Analysis* (2nd ed.) New York: John Wiley & Sons, Inc., 1941.

Feather, N., "Valence of Outcome and Expectation of Success in Relation to Task Difficulty and Perceived Locus of Control," *Journal of Personality and Social Psychology*, 7, No. 4 (December, 1967), 372-386.

French, Elizabeth G., "Effects of the Interaction of Motivation and Feedback on Task Performance," in *Motives in Fantasy, Action, and Society*, ed. J. W. Atkinson. Princeton, N.J.: D. Van Nostrand, Co., Inc., 1958, pp. 400-408.

French, J. R. P., Jr., R. L. Kahn, F. C. Mann, and D. Wolfe, *The Effects of the Industrial Environment on Mental Health*. Ann Arbor, Mich.: Institute for Social Research, 1959.

———, H. Morrison, and G. Levinger, "Coercive Power and Forces Affecting Conformity," *Journal of Abnormal and Social Psychology*, 61 (1960), 93-101.

———, and J. Sherwood, *Self-Actualization and Self Identity Theory*. Institute paper No. 107. Purdue University: Institute for Research in the Behavioral, Economic and Management Sciences, April, 1965.

Geismar, L., "A Scale for the Measurement of Ethnic Identification," *Jewish Social Studies*, 16 (1954), 33-60.

Gellerman, S. W., *Motivation and Productivity*. American Management Association, 1963.

Havighurst, R., *The Meaning of Work and Retirement*. Chicago: University of Chicago Press, 1954.

Hearnshaw, L. S., "Attitude to Work," *Occupational Psychology*, 28 (1954), 129-138.

Hertzberg, F., *et al., Job Attitudes: Review of Research and Opinion*. Pittsburgh: Psychological Service of Pittsburgh, 1957.

———, B. Mausner, and B. Snyderman, *The Motivation to Work* (2nd ed.). New York: John Wiley & Sons, Inc., 1959.

Hoppock, R., *Job Satisfaction*. New York: Harper and Row, Publishers, 1935.

Hughes, E. C., "Work and Self," in *Social Psychology at the Crossroads*, ed. John H. Rohrer and M. Sherif. New York: Harper & Row, Publishers, 1951.

Kagan, J., "The Concept of Identification," *Psychological Review*, 65 (1958), 296-305.

Kahn, R. L., and J. R. French, Jr., "Work, Health, and Satisfaction: A Summary of Some Tentative Conclusions," *Journal of Social Issues*, 18, 3 (1962), 122-127.

——, D. M. Wolfe, R. P. Quinn, J. D. Snoek, and R. A. Rosenthal, *Organizational Stress: Studies in Role Conflict and Ambiguity.* New York: John Wiley & Sons, Inc., 1964.

Kasl, S., "Some Effects of Occupational Status on Physical and Mental Health." Unpublished doctoral dissertation, University of Michigan, 1962.

——, "Some Evidence of Construct Validity of the Achievement Risk Preference Scale." Unpublished Manuscript, University of Michigan Research Center for Group Dynamics, 1966.

Katz, D., "Satisfactions and Deprivations in Industrial Life," in *Industrial Conflict*, ed. A. Kornhauser, R. Dubin, and A. M. Ross. New York: McGraw-Hill Book Company, 1954, pp. 86-106.

——, and H. Hyman, "Industrial Morale and Public Opinion Methods," *International Journal of Opinion and Attitude Research*, I (1947), 13-30.

——, and R. L. Kahn, "Human Organization and Worker Motivation," in *Industrial Productivity*, ed. L. R. Tripp. Madison, Wisc.: Industrial Relations Research Association, 1951, pp. 146-171.

——, and R. L. Kahn, *The Social Psychology of Organizations.* New York: John Wiley & Sons, Inc., 1966.

Kaustler, D. H., "A Study of the Relationship Between Ego-Involvement and Learning," *Journal of Psychology*, 32 (1951), 225-230.

Lansing, J. B., Eva Mueller, W. Ladd, and Nancy Barth, *The Geographical Mobility of Labor: A First Report.* Ann Arbor, Mich.: Survey Research Center, Institute for Social Research, April, 1963.

Lazerwitz, B., "Some Factors in Jewish Identification," *Jewish Social Studies*, 15 (1953), 3-24.

Lecky, P., *Self-Consistency: A Theory of Personality.* New York: Island, 1945.

Likert, R., "A Motivational Approach to a Modified Theory of Organization and Management," in *Modern Organization Theory*, ed. Mason Haire. New York: John Wiley & Sons, Inc., 1959.

——, *New Patterns of Management.* New York: McGraw-Hill Book Company, 1961.

Lipset, S. M., M. Trow, and J. S. Coleman, *Union Democracy.* New York: The Free Press, 1956.

McClelland, D. C., *The Achieving Society*. Princeton: D. Van Nostrand Co., Inc., 1961.

———, J. W. Atkinson, R. A. Clark, and E. L. Lowell, *The Achievement Motive*. New York: Appleton-Century-Crofts, 1953.

McIver, R. M., *The Ramparts We Guard*. New York: The Macmillan Company, 1950.

Manzer, C. W., "The Effect of Knowledge of Output on Muscular Work," *J. Exp. Psychol.*, 18 (1935), 80-90.

Maslow, A. H., "A Theory of Human Motivation," *Psychological Review*, 50 (1943), 370-396.

Mayo, E., and G. Lombard, "Teamwork and Labor Turnover in the Aircraft Industry of Southern California," *Business Research Studies*, No. 32. Boston: Harvard University, 1944.

Metzner, H., and F. C. Mann, "Employee Attitudes and Absences," *Personnel Psychology*, VI (1953), 467-485.

Miller, D., "The Study of Social Relationships: Situation, Identity and Social Interaction," in *Psychology: A Study of Science*, Vol. 5, ed. S. Koch. New York: McGraw-Hill Book Company, pp. 639-737.

Morse, N. C., *Satisfaction in the White Collar Job*. Ann Arbor: Institute for Social Research, 1953.

———, and R. S. Weiss, "The Function and Meaning of Work and the Job," *American Sociological Review*, XX (1955), 191-198.

Murray, H. A. and others, *Explorations in Personality*. New York: Oxford University Press, 1938.

Noland, E. W., "Attitudes and Industrial Absenteeism: A Statistical Appraisal," *American Sociological Review*, X (1945), 503-510.

O'Connor, Patricia, and J. W. Atkinson, "The Development of an Achievement Risk Preference Scale: A Preliminary Report." Unpublished manuscript, Psychology Department, University of Michigan, 1960.

Palmer, G. L., "Attitudes Toward Work in an Industrial Community," *American Journal of Sociology*, LXIII (1957), 17-26.

Patchen, M., "Absence and Employee Feelings about Fair Treatment," *Personnel Psychology*, 13, No. 3 (Autumn, 1960), 349-360.

———, "Labor-Management Consultation at TVA: Its Impact on Employees," *Administrative Science Quarterly*, 10, No. 2 (September, 1965), 149-174.

———, "Supervisory Methods and Group Performance Norms," *Administrative Science Quarterly*, 7, No. 3 (December, 1962), 275-294.

———, with the collaboration of D. Pelz and C. Allen, "Some Questionnaire Measures of Employee Motivation and Morale." Ann Arbor: Institute for Social Research Monograph 41, 1965.

Purcell, T. V., *Blue Collar Man: Patterns of Dual Allegiance in Industry*. Cambridge, Mass.: Harvard University Press, 1960.

Riegel, J. W., *Employee Interest in Company Success*. Ann Arbor: Bureau of Industrial Relations, Report No. 7, 1956.

Roethlisberger, F. J., and W. J. Dickson, *Management and the Worker*. Cambridge, Mass.: Harvard University Press, 1939.

Ross, I. C., and A. Zander, "Need Satisfaction and Employee Turnover," *Personnel Psychology*, 10 (1957), 327-338.

Roy, D., "Quota Restriction and Gold Bricking in a Machine Shop," *American Journal of Sociology*, 57 (1952), 427-442.

Sanford, N., "The Dynamics of Identification," *Psychological Review*, 62 (1955), 106-118.

Schaffer, R. H., "Job Satisfaction as Related to Need Satisfaction in Work," *Psychological Monographs*, 67 (1953), No. 14.

Seashore, S., *Group Cohesiveness in the Industrial Work Group*. Ann Arbor: University of Michigan Survey Research Center, 1954.

Seeman, M., "On the Meaning of Alienation," *American Sociological Review*, 24 (1959), 783-791.

Seidman, J. M., "Dissatisfaction in Work," *Journal of Social Psych.*, 17 (1943), 93-97.

Shepard, H. A., "Democratic Control in a Labor Union," *American Journal of Sociology*, 54 (1949), 311-316.

Sherif, M., and H. Cantril, *The Psychology of Ego Involvements, Social Attitudes and Identifications*. New York: John Wiley & Sons, Inc., 1947.

Sherwood, J. J., "Self-Identity and Self-Actualization: A Theory in Research." Unpublished doctoral dissertation, University of Michigan, 1962.

Sirota, D., "Some Effects of Promotional Frustration on Employees' Understanding of and Attitudes Toward Management," *Sociometry*, 22, No. 3 (1959), 273-278.

Slater, Carol W., "Some Factors Associated with Internalization of Motivation Towards Occupational Role Performance." Unpublished doctoral dissertation, University of Michigan, 1959.

Smith, C., and A. Tannenbaum, "Organizational Control Structure: A Comparative Analysis," *Human Relations*, 16 (Fall, 1963), 299-316.

Stagner, R., "Dual Allegiance as a Problem in Modern Society," *Personnel Psychology*, VII (1954), 41-80.

Stotland, E., "Identification as a Cognitive Process." Unpublished Manuscript, Psychology Dept., University of Washington, 1962.

————, and R. Dunn, "Identification, 'Oppositeness,' Authoritarianism, Self-Esteem, and Birth Order," *Psychological Monographs*, 76 (1962), No. 9.

————, and M. Patchen, "Identification and Changes in Prejudice and in Authoritarianism," *Journal of Abnormal and Social Psychology*, 62 (1961), 265-274.

————, A. Zander, and T. Natsoulas, "Generalization of Interpersonal Similarity," *Journal of Abnormal and Social Psychology*, 62 (1961), 250-256.

Stouffer, S., and others, *The American Soldier, Vol. 1: Adjustment During Army Life*. Princeton, N.J.: Princeton University Press, 1949.

Tannebaum, A. S., and R. L. Kahn, *Participation in Union Locals*. White Plains, N.Y.: Row-Peterson & Co., 1958.

Thomas, E. J., and A. Zander, "The Relationship of Goal Structure to Motivation Under Extreme Conditions," *Journal of Individual Psychology*, 15 (May, 1959), 121-127.

Tilgher, Adriano, *Work: What it Has Meant to Men Through the Ages*. New York: Harcourt, Brace, & Horld, Inc., 1930.

U.S. Census of Population: 1960, Lifetime and Recent Migration, Final Report PC (Z)-ZD. Washington, D.C.: U.S. Government Printing Office, 1963.

Vroom, V. H., "Ego-Involvement, Job Satisfaction, and Job Performance," *Personnel Psychology*, 15 (1962), 159-177.

————, *Some Personality Determinants of the Effects of Participation*. Englewood Cliffs, N.J.: Prentice Hall, Inc., 1960.

————, *Work and Motivation*. New York: John Wiley & Sons, Inc., 1964.

Walker, C. R., and R. Guest, *Man on the Assembly Line*. Cambridge, Mass.: Harvard University Press, 1952.

Walker, J., and R. Marriott, "A Study of Some Attitudes to Factory Work," *Occupational Psychology*, 25, No. 3 (July, 1951), 181-191.

Wertheimer, M., "The Laws of Organization of Perceptual Forms," in *A Sourcebook of Gestalt Psychology*, ed. W. D. Ellis. London: Routledge and Kegan Paul, Ltd., 1950.

White, R. W., "Motivation Reconsidered: The Concept of Competence," *Psychological Review*, 66 (1959), 287-333.

Whyte, W. F., *Money and Motivation*. New York: Harper & Row, Publishers, 1955.

Willerman, B., "Group Identification in Industry." Unpublished doctoral dissertation, Massachusetts Institute of Technology, 1949.

Zaleznik, A., C. R. Christensen and F. Roethlisberger, *The Motivation, Productivity and Satisfaction of Workers: A Prediction Study*. Boston, Mass.: Harvard Business School, 1958.

Zander, A., E. Stotland and D. Wolfe, "Unity of Group, Identification with Group, and Self-Esteem of Members," *Journal of Personality*, 28, No. 4 (December, 1960).

Zipf, Sheila, "An Experimental Study of Resistance to Influence," Unpublished doctoral dissertation, University of Michigan, 1958.

INDEX

DATE DUE